D1613973

Fenton Art Glass

Colors

and
Hand-Decorated Patterns

1939 – 1980

IDENTIFICATION & VALUE GUIDE

Margaret & Kenn Whitmyer

COLLECTOR BOOKS

A Division of Schroeder Publishing Co., Inc.

Front Cover

Top: No. 5162 Daisies on Cameo Satin Bunny $25.00 – 30.00; #1925-6"
Rose Overlay basket, $40.00 – 45.00; No. 5197 Independance Blue Hap-
piness Bird, $35.00 – 40.00; No. 7492 Scenic Decorated Burmese Fairy
Light, $50.00 – 60.00. Bottom: #189 Ivy Overlay 10" DC Vase, $120.00 –
130.00; Blue Opalescent Horizontal Rib DeVilbiss Atomizer, $65.00 –
75.00; #7202 Rose Burmese Epergne Set, $270.00 – 295.00.

Back cover

Top: No. 7329 Leaf Decorated Burmese Fairy Light, $175.00 – 225.00;
No. 5169 Blue Satin Duckling Figure, $45.00 – 55.00; No. 8476 Choco-
late Jefferson Compact, $110.00 – 130.00. Bottom: No. 9188, Orange
Candy or Tabacco Jar, $150.00 – 170.00; No. 8200, Carnival Heart-
shaped Candy Box, $75.00 – 95.00.

Cover design by Beth Summers
Book design by Heather Warren

COLLECTOR BOOKS
P.O. Box 3009
Paducah, Kentucky 42002-3009

www.collectorbooks.com

The current values in this book should be used only as a guide. They are not intended to
set prices, which vary from one section of the country to another. Auction prices as well as
dealer prices vary greatly and are affected by condition as well as demand. Neither the
author nor the publisher assumes responsibility for any losses that might be incurred as a result
of consulting this guide.

Searching For A Publisher?

We are always looking for people knowledgeable within their fields. If you feel that there is
a real need for a book on your collectible subject and have a large comprehensive collection,
contact Collector Books.

Contents

Acknowledgments

This third book in a series about Fenton Art Glass has been made possible through the efforts of many faithful collectors and dealers who have been willing to share their knowledge and information with us. We want to thank all of our readers who have sent us pictures and other information that has helped to verify the existence of the many pieces listed in this book. Due to the volume of mail, we have not been able to respond personally to all of your letters, but we have tried to answer as many as possible. We apologize if you have written to us and have not received an answer. However, we want you to know your letter has been read and the information or suggestions in it are appreciated.

It is probably hard for the casual reader to appreciate that producing a volume of this magnitude involves the energy of a virtual army of dedicated people — not just the authors. It is very difficult to give these hard workers the recognition they deserve, but without their efforts this book would not have been possible. Many of these names will be familiar to readers as serious collectors of Fenton glassware and others are close friends and associates who have helped us on previous works. We would like to thank all of them for their patience and cooperation.

Foremost on the list is Frank Fenton. Without his knowledge, assistance, and encouragement, this book would not exist. He provided us with historical information and granted us complete freedom to copy company records and catalogs. He also allowed us to photograph at will in the Fenton Art Glass Museum. He graciously assisted by answering our questions and provided anything we needed for our photography and research.

Several people again opened up their homes and allowed us to invade their privacy for our seemingly unending photography sessions. The contributions of Carrie and Gerry Domitz, Caroline and Woody Kriner, and Jackie Shirley are especially appreciated. Without the thoughtfulness and dedication of these individuals, this volume would lack many exciting pieces.

Several Fenton employees also deserve special acknowledgment. Among them are Anne Martha, Frank's secretary, who is knowledgeable enough to know all his hiding places. Jennifer Maston is the sweet girl who is mistress (and a very gracious hostess) of the Fenton Art Glass Museum. Tamara Armstrong is an information specialist who has actually performed the miracle of cataloging Fenton's archives. Also appreciated was "Muscles" Charley, who graciously removed many of the heavy covers from the cases in the museum so we could proceed with our photography.

Berry Wiggins, a noted author and researcher of early glassware, was often at the Fenton plant to offer help and lend support. We appreciate his guidance in some areas in which we had little experience. His knowledge was invaluable.

The Pacific NW Fenton Association was extremely hospitable. Their convention was a great learning experience. Members provided us with valuable information and allowed their treasures to be photographed.

We are also very grateful to the following people who either helped with pricing or supplied us with much-needed information:

Bill Harmon	Geri and Dan Tucker
Gordon and Darlene Cochran	Tom Smith
Nancy Maben	Berner's Auction
Leora and Jim Leasure	Springfield Antique Center
Sam and Becky Collings	Jeffrey's Antique Gallery
Rick and Ruth Teets	Heart of Ohio Antique Center
Lynn Welker	Lorraine and Dave Kovar
Kevin Kiley	Jackie Shirley
Fred McMorrow	

Hopefully, we have included everyone, but if someone's name has mysteriously been lost in our mountain of papers, please understand that we are not unappreciative of your cooperation. We do try to keep track of where the information is coming from, but sometimes finding names at the moment you need them is a problem.

Dedication

Berry Wiggins — dedicated researcher

You will be missed.

Introduction

Fenton Art Glass: Colors and Hand-Decorated Patterns 1939 – 1980 is an in-depth look at the regular line production of Fenton glass-ware over four decades. This is the third book of a series that examines the history of Fenton glassmaking from its beginnings in 1907 through 1979. The first book, *Fenton Art Glass 1907 – 1939* covers subjects such as early carnival glass, stretch glass, and opaque and transparent colors and patterns that were made prior to 1940. A second book, *Fenton Art Glass Patterns 1939 – 1980*, provides insight to such patterns as Coin Dot, Crests, Hobnail, and Spiral Optic. An additional chapter provides information about miscellaneous patterns that only consist of a few pieces or were only made in a few colors.

Fenton Art Glass: Colors and Hand-Decorated Patterns 1939 – 1980 examines the same years as *Fenton Art Glass Patterns 1939 – 1980*. This book is designed to complement the second book and will evaluate shapes and colors that were omitted in the previous volume.

The primary focus of this third book is to identify the colors, shapes, and decorations made for the regular Fenton line. An effort has been made to illustrate some sample items and a few of the more frequently seen pieces that Fenton made for other companies. However, comprehensive coverage of this type of production is beyond the scope of this book. In most instances, examples of sample items and private contract production will be illustrated with the appropriate color or decoration. In a few instances, these items will be discussed at the end of a chapter.

Pattern and Shape Identification

Prior to July 1952, Fenton identified patterns or shapes with a mould number. For example, the number "389" was used to represent the entire Hobnail pattern. All pieces of this pattern were identified by this number and a further description was necessary to identify an individual item. Also, in the Crest pattern and overlay colors, the mould number *711* was used to represent all items with the Beaded Melon shape.

After July 1952, Fenton switched to a ware number system. With this new system each item in regular line production was assigned a four digit number followed by a two letter code. The numerals represent the pattern and shape and the letters indicate the color or hand painted decoration. As an example, examine Ware No. 2858-AG:

The first two numbers — 28 — represent the Wild Rose and Bowknot pattern;
the second two digits — 58 — represent a 7½" vase;
the two letters — AG — represent the cased 1950s color Apple Green.

With very few exceptions, each item has a unique ware number. There have been instances where numbers and letters have been reused. Most of the time there has been a significant time gap between the two occurrences and there should not be any confusion about the description.

Identification of items by using the photographs and many of the catalog reprints in this book may be accomplished by referring to the number and description below each item. Generally, if the number is preceded by "No," the number is a mould number that was used prior to July 1952. This number will be found with the item descriptions in the accompanying price listing — for example — Bowl, #389-7" flared. If the number accompanying the item has no prefix, it is a ware number. (The abbreviation No. is, however, frequently used within the text when referring to either kind of number. The abbreviation # has been used for mould numbers only.) Ware numbers are listed in a separate column in the price listing. If a piece was made both before and after the conversion, both numbers will be provided. The mould number will be with the item description and the ware number will be listed in the "Ware No." column.

Determining Dates of Production

Columns in the price listing labeled "Introduced" and "Discontinued" provide the date each item entered the regular line and the year that item was no longer listed as available in the price listing. As an example:

Peach Crest	Ware No.	Introduced	Discontinued	Value
Basket, #1924-5" handled	7235-PC	1942	1954	$40.00 – 45.00

The Peach Crest basket in the above illustration was introduced in January 1942. It was in production through December 1953 and was no longer available in the price listing issued in January 1954. Also the ware number for this basket is No. 7335-PC and the mould shape is #1924. It is not possible to determine the exact dates for some of the items produced before 1947. For some of these earlier items and patterns we have been fortunate to have inventory records and the recollection of Frank Fenton as our guide. Accurate dates of production are only listed for items introduced and discontinued in the period from 1939 through the end of 1979. Items that entered the line prior to 1980, but which have continued in production, will be designated "1980+" in the discontinued column.

Consulting the Price Guide

The prices in this book represent average retail prices for mint condition pieces. Pieces that are chipped, cracked, or excessively worn should only bring a fraction of the listed price. Also, collectors should be aware that certain currently rare items that are now valued at a high dollar amount may prove hard to sell if a large quantity of these items is discovered. A few items that have been found listed in the company catalogs, but are not known to be available, may not be priced in the listings.

A few pieces do not come up for sale often enough to have firmly established values. A piece with a value that has not been determined has a price listing of "UND."

A price range is included to allow for some regional differences. This book is intended to be only a guide, and it is not the intention of the authors to set or establish prices.

Prices are generally for each piece unless a set is indicated in the description. Candleholders are priced each. Salt and pepper shakers were listed in the Fenton price lists as sets and are prices in the price lists in this book as sets. The prices listed are those we have seen collectors pay and prices collectors have told us they would be willing to pay.

A Note Concerning Fenton Reissues

Periodically, when Fenton has determined that market conditions are appropriate, old moulds may be reused to produce items for the regular line. The management of Fenton is well aware of the collectability of their older glassware. As a result, certain steps have been taken to ensure that newer issues will enhance the collectibility of Fenton glassware and preserve the value of the older collectibles.

Many of the older moulds that are brought out of retirement are used for special purposes, such as the Family Signature Series, the Connoisseur Collection, or the Historical Collection. These special series usually feature pieces in colors that have not been made previously.

Beginning in 1970, moulds were marked with an oval Fenton logo. This process was completed by about 1974. All items made after this date for the regular line will be marked on the bottom with the oval logo. As production has progressed through each successive decade, a small number has been added to the logo. The 1980s pieces have an *8* and the 1990s pieces bear a *9*.

Over the past several decades, Fenton has purchased numerous moulds from companies that have ceased production. In recent years, production from moulds used from this source has been marked with a script *F* encased in an oval.

Intentional Omissions

Not included in this volume are the multitude of special issues that were not a part of the regular line. Numerous items have been made in small numbers for clubs, organizations, and individuals over the years. In many cases, these are regular line items that have been produced in a special color. It would be virtually impossible to catalog all of these variations. Another source of non–regular line glassware is the Fenton Gift Shop. This is a retail outlet located at the Fenton plant. The Fenton Gift Shop is a separate corporation from the factory that orders and buys glass just like any other company. Over the years, numerous items have been sold through the Gift Shop in colors and decoration that have not been in the regular line.

Private mould work commissioned by other companies and using non-Fenton moulds has not been covered. Some examples of special-order items using Fenton moulds will be found included with specific colors. In cases where there are numerous examples, these have been included on a special page at the end of the chapter.

Hand-painted patterns on Crest, Hobnail, and Thumbprint shapes are discussed in the book *Fenton Art Glass Patterns 1939 – 1940*. Except fot a few instances where decorations are found on various backgrounds, decorations on these shapes are not repeated in this book.

Color Codes and Color Descriptions

Fenton implemented a two-letter color code that was used in combination with ware numbers to identify each item in the line. With a few exceptions, each color made by Fenton after July 1952 is identified by a unique two-letter combination. Most of the color codes used between 1952 and 1980 are identified on the following pages. The dates of manufacture are only pertinent to the scope of the time period covered by this book — 1939 through 1980. Remember, some of Fenton's colors have been in use since the early 1900s. For more information about earlier Fenton glassware, see the book *Fenton Art Glass 1907 – 1939*.

Color	Code	Years of Manufacture	Description
Amber	AR	1959 – 1980	Transparent amber was called Antique Amber prior to 1963. In 1963, this color became known as Colonial Amber (CA), and both the AR and CA designations were used as codes for transparent amber that year. After 1963, the CA code was used to signify amber.
Amber with Milk	MA	July 1952 – 1955	This color code was used for a transparent amber ivy ball attached to a milk glass foot.
Amethyst	AY		Amethyst is a deep purple transparent color.
Amethyst with Milk	MY	July 1952 – 1955	Fenton used this color designation for transparent amethyst glass in combination with milk glass for the footed ivy ball, hen on the basket, and chicken server.
Apple Blossom Crest	AB	1960 – July 1961	Twelve pieces of this pattern, milk glass trimmed with an opaque pink crest, were made in 1960.
Apple Green Overlay	AG	1961	Apple Green Overlay pieces have a light green exterior layer of glass applied over a milk glass interior. This color was only made in 1961, although examples were still illustrated in the 1962 catalogue.
Aqua Crest	AC	1940 – 1943 and 1948 – 1954	Pieces in this pattern have a milk glass body and a transparent light blue edge.
Antique Amber	AR	1959 – 1964	This transparent amber became known as Colonial Amber after 1964.
Autumn Mist		1964	This is a cased glass color with an interior layer of opal and an exterior layer of crystal. A frit of orange, brown, and silver flecks was also combined with the interior opal layer.
Autumn Orange	AO	July 1964 – 1968	This was a color used with the Vasa Murrhina pattern. It was a cased glass with an opal interior layer and a crystal exterior layer. Flecks of orange, brown, white, and silver frit were rolled in the interior layer.
Aventurine Green with Blue	GB	1964 – 1969	This was a cased color used with the Vasa Murrhina pattern. The exterior layer was crystal and the interior layer was opal with a mixture of blue, white, and green frit. Lamps were also made in this color in 1971.

Color	Code	Years of Manufacture	Description
Black	BK	1968 – 1976	Black was also called Ebony at various times. This color was used for items in many of the patterns in Fenton's line during this period.
Black and White	BW	1962 – 1978	This color code was used with the Hobnail pattern for a combination of shakers with one black and one white shaker.
Black Crest	BC	1970s	These items have a milk glass body with spun black trim. This color code was also used for Blue Crest in 1963.
Black Rose	BR	1953 – 1955	Black Rose is a cased glass with an ebony crest. The cased glass consists of a gold ruby inner layer and a milk exterior. Later, this color code was used for Burmese.
Black with Milk	MK	1953 – 1954	This color code was used with the black decorated milk glass No. 5156 fish vase.
Blue	BU	July 1952 – 1965	This is a light transparent blue color used to produce a Polka Dot decanter, Georgian tumblers, and Swirl ashtrays.
Blue Crest	BC	1963 – 1964	Blue Crest was produced by using Colonial Blue for the crest edge. This color code was also used for Black Crest during the 1970s.
Blue Favrene	BF	1974	Blue Favrene is an iridescent blue color similar to Steuben's Blue Aurene. The Jefferson comport was attempted in this color. However, production problems developed and a lighter cobalt color called Independence Blue was finally substituted.
Blue Marble	MB	1970 – 1973	This color is created by adding opal to molten light blue opaque glass. This produces interesting white swirls in the resulting product.
Blue Mist	BM	1964	Blue Mist is a cased glass incorporating two layers of crystal in which the interior layer has incorporated flecks of blue and white frit.
Blue Opalescent	BO	1940 – 1980+	Although the color code system was not designed until 1952, numerous items in patterns such as Hobnail and Coin Dot were produced in Blue Opalescent prior to that date.
Blue Opalescent with Silver Crest	BS	1949 – 1955	This color code was used for Diamond Lace pattern items made in the early 1950s in Blue Opalescent with a spun silver crest.
Blue Opaline	BN	1960	Blue Opaline is a pale blue color cased over an opal interior. Only two vases in the Jacqueline pattern were in the regular line in this color in 1960.
Blue Overlay	BV	1943 – 1954	Blue Overlay is a cased glass with a pale blue exterior layer over a milk glass interior layer.
Blue Pastel	BP	1954	This is a light blue colored opaque glassware.

Color	Code	Years of Manufacture	Description
Blue Satin	BA	1952 – 1954 1971 – 1984	Glassware from this era is a blue opalescent satin color. During the 1970s and 1980s, this color code was used for a medium blue opaque satin glassware.
Burgandy	BY	1955	Burgandy is a cased glassware that was produced by combining an interior layer of Rose Opal with an exterior layer of French Opalescent.
Burmese	BR	1970 – 1980+	This opaque custard-colored glassware with a rose blush was first issued plain. In subsequent years, this colorful background has been decorated with many patterns. During the 1950s, this color code was used for Black Rose.
Cameo Opalescent	CO	1979 – 1983	Cameo Opalescent is a translucent pinkish amber–colored glassware with silky opal edges.
Camphor	CA	1954	Fenton's octagonal three-piece ashtray set was produced in a translucent opaline color called Camphor.
Carnival	CN	1970 – 1983	An overspray of metallic salts on a deep amethyst base produced a colorful iridescence on Fenton's new line of carnival glass in 1970. These later issues of carnival glassware have the embossed Fenton logo.
Cased Lilac	LC	July 1955 – July 1956	Cased Lilac is formed by casing an inner layer of Gold Ruby with a turquoise exterior.
Chocolate	CK	1976	Chocolate is a heat sensitive opaque color that was only used in the regular line for seven shapes in the Bicentennial assortment. Several other shapes were made for Levay.
Colonial Amber	CA	1964 – 1980	Fenton's transparent amber was called Antique Amber prior to 1964.
Colonial Blue	CB	1962 – 1980	This deep transparent blue color was used with major patterns such as Hobnail, Diamond Optic, Thumbprint, and Valencia. Other accessory items were also made.
Colonial Blue Overlay	OB	1967 & 1971	A Colonial Blue exterior is cased with a milk glass interior layer. Examples include four different Roses-pattern lamps with two different styles made during each period of production.
Colonial Green	CG	1963 – 1977	This is an olive green transparent color used with the major patterns and also with numerous accessory pieces.
Colonial Pink	CP	1962 – 1969	Fenton's Colonial Pink was a transparent deep rose color.
Coral	CL	1961	Coral is a cased orange exterior color over an interior layer of milk glass.
Cranberry	CR	1936 – 1980+	Cranberry is an opalescent color produced by casing Gold Ruby with with a French Opalescent exterior.

Color	Code	Years of Manufacture	Description
Cranberry Mist	CM	1968	Cranberry Mist is a spatter color that is similar to, but slightly deeper than, Rose Mist. The color was used to produce items for the Sears Vincent Price National Treasures collection. It is a cased color that combines two layer of crystal, the inner layer containing colored frit.
Cranberry Mist Crest	CC	1968	Items in Cranberry Mist with a Silver Crest edge were made for Sears as a part of its Vincent Price National Treasures Collection.
Crystal	CY	1950 – 1980+	For many years after the 1930s, production of transparent colorless glassware was limited to necessary items such as ladles or to minor accessory items like ashtrays. However, in the early 1950s Priscilla was made in crystal, and in the late 1960s Hobnail and Valencia were in the regular line in crystal.
Crystal Satin	CS	1972 – 1975	The satinized crystal color was used with a series of small figures.
Crystal Velvet	VE	1977 – 1980+	The satin Crystal Velvet color is a soft satin crystal color that is more translucent than crystal satin. This was a popular color that had a long run into the late 1980s.
Custard	CT	1973 – 1977	This shiny version of custard has little representation (only two pieces) in the Fenton regular line. Most pieces of this color were acid treated to form Custard Satin, but a number of items in Hobnail may be found in the shiny form. Most of these items were probably sold through the Fenton Gift Shop.
Custard Hanging Heart	CI	1976	This color code was used for Fenton's Hanging Hearts design against a custard iridescent background.
Custard Satin	CU	1972 – 1980+	Fenton's opaque satin custard color entered the regular line in 1972. Lamps were a popular item in this color, and the neutral background was suitable for numerous hand-painted decorations.
Dark Green	DG	1952 – 1954	Dark Green is a deep transparent green color that approaches an ivy color. The color was used for a number of ashtrays, vases, and Georgian tumblers in the early 1950s.
Dusk	KV	1953 – 1955	Dusk is a cased colored glassware used in the Horizon pattern that was produced in two ways. Some pieces were made with an interior layer of black and an exterior layer of gray. Other pieces were made by reversing this combination.
Emerald Crest	EC	1949 – 1956	Pieces of Emerald Crest have a milk glass body with transparent green trim.

Color	Code	Years of Manufacture	Description
Flame Crest	FC	1963	Ruby glass was used to produce the crest edge in Flame Crest items. Since this ruby glass is heat sensitive, the crest color may vary.
French Opalescent	FO	1940 – 1969	Fenton's combining of crystal with opal to produce French Opalescent glassware is a process that has been used almost since the founding of the company. Major production of this color was in the Hobnail and Coin Dot patterns during the 1940s and 1950s. The color returned to the line as French Cream after 1980.
French Opalescent Satin	FA	1954 – 1955	A satin version of French Opalescent was used with the Swirled Feather pattern and for the No. 1974 Daisy and Button two-light candleholder.
French Opalescent with Aqua Crest	FB	1948 – 1955	This color combination was used with Diamond Lace items.
French Opalescent with Emerald Crest	FE	1949 – 1955	This color combination was used with Diamond Lace items.
Gold Crest	GC	1943 – 1945 and 1963 – 1965	Pieces of this pattern consist of a milk glass body with an amber edge and trim. Look for the early production milk glass to have a more translucent appearance than that of the later pieces.
Goldenrod	GD	July 1956 – 1957	Goldenrod is a cased color with a milk glass and deep yellow color combination. Vases have a yellow exterior with a white interior; bowls and candles have the reverse color.
Gold Overlay		1949	Gold Overlay is a cased glassware made by combining an exterior layer of transparent amber with an interior layer of milk glass.
Green Marble	GL	1952 – 1954	This is a swirled slag-like green and white opaque glassware used for the large pipe ashtray.
Green Overlay	GV	1949 – 1954	Green Overlay is a cased glassware with an interior layer of milk glass and an exterior layer of transparent green. This color is lighter than the dark green Ivy Overlay color.
Green Pastel	GP	1954 – 1956	This is a pale opaque green glassware.
Green Satin	GA	1952 – 1955	An opalescent green satin 10" Shell bowl was listed in the Fenton regular line during the early 1950s. This satin opalescent color was also used for Swirled Feather.
Green Snowcrest	GS	Sept. 1950 – 1954	This pattern consists of transparent dark green Spiral Optic pieces trimmed with an opal ring.
Green with Milk	MG	1952 – 1957	Pieces with this color code have a dark transparent green part combined with milk glass. The footed ivy ball, chicken server, and covered hen boxes were made in this color combination.

Color	Code	Years of Manufacture	Description
Honey Amber Overlay	HA	1961 – 1968	Honey Amber is a cased glassware that was produced by combining an exterior layer of amber with an interior layer of milk glass.
Honeysuckle Overlay		1948 – 1949	This color was used with the Coin Dot pattern. It is a cased glassware with amber on the outside and French Opalescent on the inside.
Independence Blue	IB	July 1974 – 1977	Fenton developed a special blue carnival color used with pieces designed to celebrate America's Bicentennial. The color is lighter and more vivid than the older Royal Blue.
Ivy Overlay	IV	1949 – 1954	A dark green exterior layer is cased with milk glass to produce this color. The result is a deep ivy color that is much darker than Green Overlay.
Jamestown Blue Overlay	JB	1957 – 1959	Jamestown Blue is a cased color with an inner layer of milk glass and an outer layer of dark transparent peacock blue.
Jamestown Blue Transparent	JT	1957 – 1960	Jamestown Blue is a deep blue transparent color used primarily with Fenton's Polka Dot pattern.
Jamestown Blue with Milk	JM	1957 – 1960	The transparent Jamestown Blue color was used on an ivy ball combined with a milk foot.
Lavender Satin	LN	1977 – 1979	This opaque lavender color changes colors depending upon the light source. Numerous pieces have also been found without the satin finish.
Light Green	LG	1952 – 1958	Light green was a transparent medium green used primarily for cigarette sets and Georgian tumblers.
Lilac	LC	July 1955 – July 1956	Lilac is an overlay color with Gold Ruby used as the interior layer and turquoise as the exterior layer.
Lime	LM	July 1974 – 1977	This opaque shiny lime color was only in the regular line in the forms of Hobnail candle bowls with floral arrangements and a 6¼" Hobnail vase.
Lime Opalescent	LO	1952 – 1955	This green opalescent color is produced by casing dark green inside a French Opalescent exterior.
Lime Sherbet	LS	1973 – 1979	Satin lime green opaque glassware was a mainstay of the Fenton line during the 1970s.
Milk	MI	1939 – 1980+	White opaque glassware had a conservative place in the Fenton line during the pre-1940s era. It was a base color for Silver Crest and an interior color for some overlay patterns during the 1940s. Sales of milk glass exploded when the color was used with the Hobnail pattern during the 1950s.
Milk with Amethyst	YM	1953 – 1955	This is the reverse combination of the transparent Amethyst and milk colors (MY) used on the chicken server and the covered hen boxes.

Color	Code	Years of Manufacture	Description
Milk with Black	KM	1953	The milk glass No. 5188 chicken server with a black head and the white No. 5156 fish vase with black trim used this color code.
Milk with Green	GM	1953 – 1955	Dark transparent green was used in combination with milk glass to create the colorful No. 5188 chicken server and the No. 5185 covered chick box.
Milk with Light Green	LM	1953 – 1955	The LM color code was used for the combination of transparent light green with milk glass.
Mixed Colors	MX	1952 – 1958	This color code was used to designate assorted color eight-piece sets of Georgian tumblers.
Mulberry	MG		Mulberry is a cased color formed by casing an interior layer of Gold Ruby with an exterior layer of dark blue.
Opal	OP	1969	Opal is a heat resistant translucent white glassware that was used briefly in the production of the No. 3604 Hobnail Boudoir Lamp and the No. 3608 Hobnail Fairy Light.
Opaque Blue Overlay	OB	1962 – 1972	Pieces have a Colonial blue exterior and opal interior. The name was changed to Colonial Blue Overlay in 1967 when Roses pattern lamps were made in this color.
Orange	OR	1963 – 1978	Orange is a transparent red-amber color that may run toward yellow in highlighted areas. The color was used with several tableware patterns and also was used with some of the Verly's moulds and with a number of other accessory pieces.
Orange Carnival	CO	July 1971 – 1974	Pieces of Orange Carnival bear the embossed Fenton logo. This color code was later used with Fenton's Cameo Opalescent color.
Patriot Red	PR	1975 – 1977	Patriot Red is an opaque slag-like deep red glassware similar in color to the older Mandarin Red. This color was only used for Bicentennial items.
Peach Blow	PB	1939 and 1952 – 1957	Peach Blow is an overlay consisting of a layer of milk glass over a Gold Ruby interior. The interior appears pink and the exterior is white — often with a slightly pinkish cast.
Peach Crest	PC	1940 – 1969	Peach Crest is the same type of cased glass as Peach Blow. However, pieces have the added feature of a crystal ring around the top edge.
Peach Satin	PA	1952 – 1954	Peach satin is a satin opalescent deep peach colored glass that was in the line in the early 1950s in the form of a 10" shell bowl.
Pink Opaline	PN	1960	Pink Opaline is a light pinkish lavender color resulting from an pink exterior layer cased over an opal interior layer. Production was limited to two Jacqueline pattern vases in 1960.

Color	Code	Years of Manufacture	Description
Plated Amberina	PA	1962 – 1964	Plated Amberina is a cased glass that is produced by gathering Selenium Ruby over opal. Production was limited to five different items.
Plum Opalescent	PO	1959 – 1962	This is a deep purple opalescent, heat-sensitive color that was obtained by pressing items made with the Cranberry Gold Ruby formula. Items found in this color with the Fenton logo were made in the 1980s for the Levay Distributing Company.
Powder Blue Overlay	BV	1961	The code is the same as that used for the earlier Blue Overlay. An opal interior layer of glass is combined with a light blue exterior layer.
Rosalene	RE	1976 – 1979	Rosalene is a heat-sensitive glass combining opaque pink with swirls of white to produce a soft pink slag-like glass.
Rose Crest		1946 – 1948	Rose Crest is milk glass with transparent pink used for handles and a ribbon of pink glass lining the outer edges.
Rose Mist	RM	1964 – 1966	Rose Mist incorporates two layers of crystal glass with bits of pink and white colored glass encased in the inner layer of crystal that produces a variegated spatter effect.
Rose Overlay		1943 – 1949	Rose overlay is a cased glass consisting of a layer of light pink glass over a layer of milk glass.
Rose Pastel	RP	1954 – 1957	This is a light pink opaque glass.
Rose Satin	RA	1952 – 1954	Rose Satin from this era is a cased glass with French Opalescent over Gold Ruby. This is the name for the satin version of Cranberry Opalescent. The color was used with the Diamond Optic and Rib Optic patterns.
Rose Satin	RS	1974 – 1978	Rose Satin from this later time is an opaque light pink frosted heat-sensitive glass.
Rose with Aventurine Green	RG	1964 – 1970	This Vasa Murrhina glass has bits of green and pink glass and small particles of mica encased in an opal layer. This opal layer containing the colored bits is covered with a crystal exterior layer. Notice production of this color occurred before Fenton began using its logo in the moulds.
Ruby	RU	1952 – 1980+	Ruby is a transparent heat-sensitive glass that achieves a true red color through a reheating process. Improper reheating often results in an amberina color.
Ruby Iridescent	RN	1976 – 1978	Ruby glassware spaying with hot metallic salts produces an interesting iridescent effect. Fenton made this type of glassware in the early 1900s and revisited this red carnival color in the 1970s.

Color	Code	Years of Manufacture	Description
Ruby Overlay	RO	1942 – 1975	Ruby Overlay is a cased glassware with an interior layer formed from Gold Ruby and an exterior layer of crystal.
Ruby Snowcrest	RS	Sept. 1950 – 1954	This pattern consists of transparent ruby Spiral Optic pieces trimmed with an opal ring.
Ruby with Milk	MR	1955 – 1967	This color code was used for Fenton's No. 1021 footed ivy ball that has a transparent ruby globe and a milk glass foot.
Satin Blue Overlay	SB	1976 – 1978	Satin Blue Overlay is a cased color using Colonial Blue as the exterior layer over an interior layer of milk glass. Pieces were satin finished. Only lamps were produced in this color.
Satin Honey Amber	SH	July 1976 – 1977	Satin Honey Amber is a cased color using transparent amber glass over an inner layer of milk glass. Pieces were satin finished, and production was limited to lamps.
Satin Rosalene	SR	July 1976 – 1978	This satin version of Rosalene was limited to the production of lamps.
Shelley Green Overlay	OG	1967	This cased glass is formed by combining an exterior layer of Colonial Green with an interior layer of milk glass. The color was only used for a line of lamps.
Silver Crest	SC	1943 – 1980+	Silver Crest pieces have a milk glass body and a spun crystal edge.
Silver Jamestown	SJ	1957 – 1960	Silver Jamestown is a cased glassware. Seven different shapes were made in this pattern. Five of the shapes had an interior layer of Jamestown Blue and an exterior layer of milk glass. On the other two shapes these layers were reversed. All pieces were trimmed with a spun Silver Crest edge.
Silver Rose	SR	1956 – 1958	Opaque Rose Pastel glassware was adorned with a spun silver crest to produce this pattern.
Silver Turquoise	ST	1956 – July 1959	This pattern was created by adding a spun Silver Crest edge to pieces of opaque turquoise glassware.
Smoke	SK	1954	This dusty gray color was reserved for two ashtrays and a relish produced from moulds acquired from Rubel.
Springtime Green	GT	1977 – 1979	Springtime Green is a transparent emerald green color.
Turquoise	TU	1955 – 1959	Turquoise is a light blue-green opaque glass.
Turquoise Hanging Heart	TH	1976	This color code was used on Fenton's Hanging Hearts design set against a turquoise background with an iridescent finish.

Color	Code	Years of Manufacture	Description
Valley Forge White	VW	1975 – 1977	Valley Forge White was an opaque white satin color used in the production of seven Bicetennial pieces.
White Satin	WS	1972 – 1980+	White satin is opaque white glass with a satin finish.
Wild Rose	WR	1961 – 1969	Wild Rose is cased glassware with a ruby exterior and a milk glass interior. Lamps were made in this color in 1967.
Wisteria	WT	1977 – 1979	Wisteria is a light transparent lavender color.
Yellow Opaline	YN	1960	Yellow Opaline is a bright yellow color which was limited to two vases in the Jacqueline pattern. This is a cased color created by encasing opal with a translucent yellow overlay.
Yellow Overlay		Oct 1949 – 1951	Originally, this cased color used milk glass for the interior layer and yellow as the exterior layer. However, problems with cracking resulted and these were resolved by reversing the color combination. Therefore most pieces of this color will have a white exterior. Some early examples may also be found with a yellow exterior.

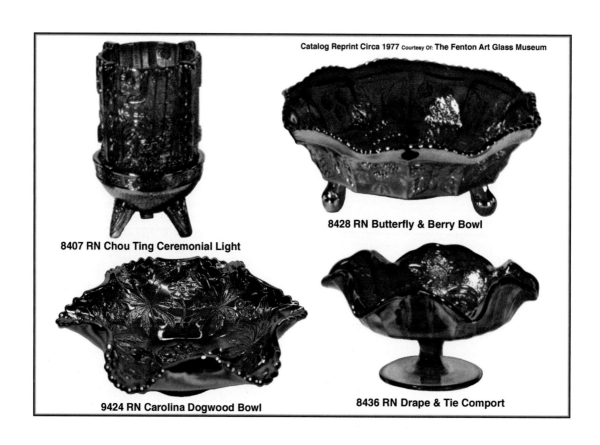

Catalog Reprint Circa 1977 Courtesy Of: **The Fenton Art Glass Museum**

8407 RN Chou Ting Ceremonial Light

8428 RN Butterfly & Berry Bowl

9424 RN Carolina Dogwood Bowl

8436 RN Drape & Tie Comport

Fenton's Carnival Glass Colors

The Fenton Art Glass Company was one of the pioneers in the development of carnival glass in the early 1900s. Between 1908 and the mid-1920s, Fenton was among the leaders in producing colorful carnival glass. In the latter part of the 1920s, interest in carnival glass began to fade, and the glass companies turned their attention to other products. After staying in seclusion for almost half a century, carnival glass in various colors was being revived by such companies as Westmoreland and Imperial in the late 1960s. Perhaps the successes of these companies with Carnival Glass caused Fenton to consider the possibility of proceeding with such a line.

Fenton ventured into the 1970s with a brightly iridized new line of wares. This reintroduction of carnival glass was the first small step in the development of a major new line of glassware. These new pieces were marked with an embossed Fenton logo, and all came complete with a descriptive tag attached. The deep amethyst base color of the carnival glass was enhanced by a sprayed-on mixture of metallic salts. These hot salts added a rich blue-green iridescence to the base color. The early success of the new line of carnival glass led to the introduction of new pieces. In the following years, old Fenton moulds and moulds purchased from closed glass companies were often altered to adapt them to the needs of the Fenton glass makers. Fenton has continued with an almost continuous production of carnival glass. Over the years, new shapes and patterns have been added, and many of the older pieces have been discontinued. Also, new colors have been developed and some of the original colors have been retired.

In 1970, a new line of collectibles in the form of plates was initiated. The Collector's Series and Christmas Series were both initiated that first year. The Mother's Day Series of plates began in 1971. For a listing of these plates, see page 33.

Orange Carnival, a color commonly referred to by collectors as marigold, was revealed in July 1971. A total of fourteen different shapes were made before the color was retired at the end of 1973.

Fenton introduced a new carnival color and designed new patriotic items to help celebrate the 200th anniversary of the United States. Independence Blue was introduced in July 1974. Three pieces — a Patriot's bell, a Jefferson comport, and an Eagle plate — were made. This color and the new items were well received. In July 1975, another series of three special items was offered for the Bicentennial celebration. The color was so popular that Fenton included it in the regular line for 1976. An assortment of twelve different items was made for one year. Independence Blue was retired at the end of 1976.

In 1976, Fenton commemorated the past by reviving its historical Red Carnival. This new version of the color was called Ruby Iridescent. Ten shapes were introduced in this color in the first year. In 1977, five more shapes were added to the line. The color was discontinued at the end of 1977. After careful consideration, it was deemed necessary to rejuvenate the product base in 1982. As a result, the entire segment of carnival glass production was discontinued at the end of 1982. When the new line of carnival glass items appeared in 1983, Fenton switched to a new annual policy. New Carnival pieces were introduced each year and all the old items were discontinued. In the years beyond 1980, Fenton introduced numerous new carnival colors — some were used in the regular line and others were for special limited editions or for special-order customers like Levay or QVC. Fenton's production of carnival glass from 1970 until 1980 is discussed on pages 26 – 37, but the following outlines much of Fenton's contribution beyond 1980:

1980 A nine-piece assortment was offered in the January supplement. The assortment included seven Carnival Hobnail pieces along with the cat and owl figures.

Levay entered the picture with several different carnival assortments. Aqua Opal Carnival (IO, Blue Opalescent iridized with marigold) and Electric Blue Carnival (BN) were the primary colors. A Hobnail pitcher and bowl were also made in IQ (Blue Opalescent with a light mother-of-pearl iridescence).

1981 Peach Opalescent Atlantis pattern pieces were made for MLT Glass. The final plate in the Craftsman series was produced.

A 500 set limited-edition God and Home pattern seven-piece miniature water set was made for Dorothy Taylor in Red Bermuda Carnival (RN).

1982 Selected items from Fenton's Cactus pattern were produced in a color called Red Sunset Carnival (RN) for Levay Distributing. A Red Carnival Kittens basket was made for Dorothy Taylor.

Catalog Reprint Composite Courtesy Of: The Fenton Art Glass Museum

8229 CN Hearts & Flowers
Cupped Bowl

8238 CN
Persian Medallion Basket

8233 CN Orange Tree & Cherry
Crimped Bowl

8240 CN
Butterfly & Berry
Tumbler

8228 CN Hearts & Flowers
Flared Bowl

1966 CN
Daisy & Button Bell

5172 CN Swan
Candleholder

9222 CN Rose Comport

8257 CN
Peacock Vase

8200 CN Heart-Shaped
Candy Box

8225 CN Grape Nappy

8230 CN Butterfly
Handled Bonbon

8236 CN Daisy Pinwheel & Cable Bowl

8231 CN
2-Handled Fruit Comport

8232 CN Orange Tree & Cherry Cupped Bowl

8226 CN Hexagonal Bowl

8237 CN 8 1/2" Heart & Vine Bowl

8220 CN Holly Bowl

8255 CN Swung Vase

Grist Mill, the first of a series of four Currier & Ives carnival limited-edition plates was introduced. Plates in this series were limited to 3500 pieces.

At the end of 1982, the old shapes in carnival were discontinued. New Carnival shapes in the January Supplement included:

Basket, Butterfly & Berry	9134-CN	Fairy light, Faberge	9404-CN
Basket, oval Daisy & Button	1939-CN	Napkin holder, miniature	8259-CN
Basket, 7" Strawberry	9433-CN	Rose bowl, miniature	8250-CN
Bell, Sable Arch	8266-CN	Vase, cuspidor	9243-CN
Candy box, Daisy & Button	1980-CN	Vase, Faberge bud	9453-CN
Comport, Strawberry	9428-CN		

1983 New shapes in carnival glass found their way into the 1983/84 catalog.

This began a tradition of introducing new items in carnival, retiring them at the end of each year, and coming out with a new grouping the following year. New items for this year consisted of the following:

Basket, 7" Sunburst	8636-CN	Toothpick, Aztec	8695-CN
Bell, Whitton	9066-CN	Vase, 4½" Sunburst	8653-CN
Candy and cover, Sunburst	8686-CN	Vase, Fine Cut & Block bud	9150-CN
Comport, 6½" ftd. Puritan	8625-CN	Vase, 10" Lucille bud	8650-CN
Fawn figure	5160-CN		

In addition, sales of the second in a series of four carnival Currier & Ives plates resumed. The second plate in this limited edition of 3500 was titled Harvest. A Blue Carnival Kittens basket was also made for Dorothy Taylor.

The Craftsman stein and bell were issued in White Satin Carnival. The bell — 9660-WI — was limited to 3500 pieces, and the stein — 9640-WI — was limited to 1500 pieces.

1984 The January 1984 Supplement introduced a new Fenton carnival color — Cobalt Marigold Carnival (NK). The Marigold spray produced exciting gold patina effects on Fenton's newly introduced cobalt color glass. The following items were in the initial offering:

Basket, 7" oval	9633-NK	Candleholder, 6" Orange Tree	8472-NK
Bear cub figure	5151-NK	Candy and cover, Butterfly	9280-NK
Bell, Faberge	8464-NK	Comport, Persian Medallion	9623-NK
Bell, Miniature Lovebird	8268-NK	Elephant figure	5158-NK
Bowl, 6" handled nut	8629-NK	Nut dish, 3-toed	8442-NK
Bowl, Orange Tree & Cherry	8233-NK	Vase, 7½"	8654-NK

Special offerings included the third plate of a series of four limited edition Currier & Ives plates. This plate was titled Winter in the Country. The Connoisseur Collection featured a Ruby Carnival Famous Woman bell.

In the fall of 1984, Fenton produced a few different pieces in Iridized Plum Opalescent (IP) for Levay. Among the items made were a 9436-8½" basket, 9435-8½" ribbon candy–edge basket, 9425-8" ribbon candy–edge bowl, 8454-5" rose bowl, and 9456-12" swung vase. All these pieces will have an embossed Fenton logo.

1985 The 1985 catalog continued to promote the successful Cobalt Marigold Carnival treatment with the introduction of a line with all new shapes. Included in the listing were the following pieces:

Basket, 8¼" Sunburst	8633-NK	Mallard	5147-NK
Basket, Leaf w/Butterfly	9637-NK	Pitcher, 8½" Sunburst	8667-NK
Bell, 6½" Beauty	9665-NK	Plate, 8" Garden of Eden	9614-NK
Bell, 6¾" Garden of Eden	9663-NK	Snail	5134-NK
Clown figure	5111-NK	Spaniels	5159-NK

Winter Pastime was the theme of the Cobalt Marigold fourth plate in the Currier & Ives series. In the early spring, Fenton made a limited run of 250 Rose Pink Carnival Alley Cats for Levay.

1986 The new assortment featured in the 1986 general catalog included the following items in Fenton's Cobalt Marigold color:

Basket, Butterfly & Berry	9234-NK	Kitten	5119-NK
Bell, Barred Oval	8361-NK	Mouse	5148-NK
Bell, Syndenham	9063-NK	Pitcher, Quintec	9269-NK
Bowl, Orange Tree & Cherry	8289-NK	Rose bowl, Faberge	9653-NK
Comport, 7" Marquette	9279-NK	Toothpick/votive	9292-NK
Comport, ftd. Innovation	9276-NK	Vase, 8" Dogwood	9658-NK

The Christmas 1986 catalog displayed the True Blue Friends collection of animal figurines in an iridized light blue color. The collection consisted of the following eight animals:

Bear cub	5151-IK	Kitten	5139-IK
Bird, small	5163-IK	Mallard	5147-IK
Cat	5165-IK	Mouse	5148-IK
Fawn	5160-IK	Pig	5220-IK

1987 Cobalt Marigold Carnival continued to be a feature in the regular line. New items for this year included:

Basket, Open Edge	8335-NK	Fox figure	5226-NK
Basket, 9½" Acanthus	9738-NK	Pig figure	5220-NK
Bell, Famous Women	9163-NK	Pitcher, 32 oz. Plytec	9461-NK
Bell, Wave Hobnail	3067-NK	Puppy figure	5225-NK
Bowl, 8½" Acanthus	9728-NK	Rose bowl, Wave Hobnail	3022-NK
Candy, ftd. Rose	9284-NK		

1988 New items produced for QVC were the No. C3522-TC Spanish Lace comport in White Carnival with a teal crest, the No. C3538-TC Spanish Lace basket in White Carnival with a teal crest, and the No. C9134-OM Butterfly and Berry basket with a milk glass crest and handle.

1989 The Carnival Glass feature of the January, 1989 supplement was the marigold iridized teal color Fenton called Teal Marigold (OI). This supplement provided collectors with the following shapes:

Basket, Fine Cut & Block	9137-OI	Epergne set, 4-pc. Diamond	
Bear cub figure, reclining	5233-OI	Lace	4801-OI
Bell, 6¾" Open Edge	8632-OI	Fairy light, 7" Heart	8406-OI
Boot, 4" Daisy & Button	1990-OI	Pitcher, 36 oz. Water Lily	8464-OI
Bowl, 10" Orange Tree & Cherry	8283-OI	Swan, open	5127-OI
Cat figure, 3¾"	5163-OI	Vase, 9½" Mandarin	8251-OI
Comport, 5" Pinwheel	8227-OI		

A 16-piece assortment of iridized opal novelty items from the Pearly Sentiments collection rounded out the iridescent section of the catalog.

Fenton also made the following iridized items for QVC:

Basket, Lilac Carnival Corn Shock	C5838-LU	Bowl, Hobnail	C3938-DO
Basket, Dusty Rose Carnival Butterfly and Berry with milk glass crest and handle	C9134-DN	Pitcher, Dusty Rose Carnival Hobnail with teal Crest	C3360-DO
Bowl, Black Carnival Butterfly & Berry	C8428-XB		

1990 The following were among the iridized items Fenton made for QVC:

Basket, Black Carnival Basket Weave	C8335-XB	Vase, Holiday Green Carnival Pinwheel	C8654-GZ
Bell, Holiday Green Carnival Temple Bells	C9560-GZ	Water Set, Black Carnival Hobnail	C3008-XB
Comport, Black Carnival Puritan	C8625-XB		

1990 Red Carnival (RN) resumed in the Fenton line with the following 12-piece assortment:

Basket, 6" Rose	9240-RN	Comport, 6½" Puritan	8625-RN
Basket, 9½" Grape & Cable	9074-RN	Lion, 3" x 5"	5241-RN
Bear, 4"	5233-RN	Pitcher, 5" Sandwich	9666-RN
Bell, 6¾" Templebells	9560-RN	Slipper, 6" Rose	9295-RN
Bowl, 10½" Grape & Cable	9059-RN	Trinket box, 4" Floral	9384-RN
Clock, 4½" alarm	8691-RN	Vase, 7¾" Daffodil	9752-RN

1991 Light Amethyst Carnival (DT) was produced as a limited edition Historic Collection issue. This lighter color of Amethyst Carnival Glass had not been made by Fenton since the early years of production. Historic Collection items included:

Basket, Innovation	4646-DT	Lamp. 15" Innovation	4603-DT
Basket, 3-toed Innovation	4637-DT	Owl figure, 5½"	5254-DT
Bell, 6" Sables Arch	9065-DT	Plate, 12" Paneled Grape/Good	
Bowl, Good Luck	4619-DT	Luck	4611-DT
Bowl, 10" oval	4618-DT	Punch bowl set, Paneled Grape	4601-DT
Butter and cover, Regency	8680-DT	Punch cup, Paneled Grape	4642-DT
Covered box, Eagle	4679-DT	Toothpick, Diamond & Panel	4644-DT
Cuspidor, 3-toed Innovation	4643-DT	Tumbler, 6 oz. Fruit	4645-DT
Fenton logo	9799-DT	Water set, 5-pc. Fruit	4609-DT

A Baroque candy box C9388-RN was also made in Ruby Carnival for QVC.

1992 A featured attraction of the Sentiments Collection for 1992 was an assortment of colorful cats and kittens in pink, blue, and green carnival. The 13-piece assortment included two cats of two styles in three colors, plus one free cat. The Sentiments Collection also included two other iridized assortments. The first, a 20-piece Pearly Sentiments Assortment, combined opal iridescent novelty figures with sculpted porcelain roses. The second was an 18-piece Pink Pearl assortment that showcased small gift items in iridescent pink.

It appears that 1992 was a banner year for the production of iridescent glassware. Persian Pearl was a limited edition offering as part of the Historic Collection. Fenton's new version of the Persian Pearl color was an iridescent spray over green opalescent glass. (Persian Pearl from the 1920s was an iridized crystal glass.) A 14-piece assortment was offered to collectors. It included four pieces of Hobnail, the Paneled Grape punch set, a Fern water set, a miniature water set, three baskets, two vases, and a 21" Fern lamp with prisms. The complete list includes:

Basket, 4" Button & Arch	2728-XV	Lamp, 21" student Fern	1801-XV
Basket, 7" Button & Arch	9435-XV	Pitcher, 8½" Fern	1875-XV
Basket, 11" Spiral	3077-XV	Punch cup, Paneled Grape	4642-XV
Bell, 6" Spanish Lace	3567-XV	Punch set, 14-pc. Paneled Grape	4601-XV
Bowl, 12" Hobnail	3938-XV	Tumbler, Fern	1876-XV
Candlestick, 6" Hobnail	3674-XV	Tumbler, 2" mini	2727-XV
Candy box, ftd. Hobnail	3784-XV	Vase, 5" Curtain	2056-XV
Creamer, 4" Button & Arch	2726-XV	Vase, 6½" tulip	3183-XV
Epergne set, 4-pc. Hobnail	3701-XV	Water set, 5-pc. miniature	2730-XV
Fenton logo, 2¼" x 5"	9709-XV	Water set, 5-pc. Fern	1870-XV

Another iridized color from the 1992 Historic Collection was an iridescent topaz opalescent color called Gold Pearl. Six items in the Hobnail pattern were featured in this collection. Others items included the Swan covered box, a Diamond Lace four-piece epergne set, and an owl figure. Seven hand-painted pieces with a Starflower design were also included as part of this collection.

Five pieces of iridized crackle glass in pink, Twilight Blue, and Sea Mist Green were introduced in the January catalog. Six additional items in each color were added in the June supplement.

1993 Iridescent glass continued to be a principal factor in the regular line. Production of iridized pink, green, and blue crackle glass assortments continued, and the iridescent opal Pearly Sentiments line of novelty items was expanded. Pieces of the best-selling Dusty Rose color were iridized to produce a 17-piece assortment called Rose Pearl (DW). Rose Pearl was no longer listed in the 1994 catalog.

The Red Carnival 2752-RN-9" Alpine Thistle vase made as part of the Fenton Family Signature Series was signed by Frank M. Fenton. The Red Carnival offered in the regular catalog consisted of the following 13 pieces:

Basket, 7" Button & Arch	2734-RN	Pitcher, Button & Arch	2776-RN
Basket, 7½" Vintage	2733-RN	Raccoon, 3½"	5142-RN
Bell, 7" Fenton trademark	9660-RN	Unicorn, 5"	5253-RN
Candy, Lily of the Valley	8489-RN	Vase, 8" Elite	6564-RN
Lamp, 20" Paisley w/prisms	6703-RN	Vase, 8" Hobnail tulip	3356-RN
Perfume w/stopper	1940-RN		

Green iridescent Persian Pearl was the color of choice for the limited edition Historic Collection with sales limited through May 30, 1993. Notice some of the pieces are the same as those listed in the 1992 Historical Collection offering. Items included:

Basket, 4" Button & Arch	2728-XV	Fenton logo, 2¼" x 5"	9709-XV
Basket, 7" Button & Arch	9435-XV	Lamp, 21" student Fern	1801-XV
Basket, Drapery	9435-XV	Lamp, 24" Poppy GWTW	9101-XV
Basket, 11" Spiral	3077-XV	Pitcher, 8½" Fern	1875-XV
Bell, 6" Spanish Lace	3567-XV	Swan, open	5127-XV
Bowl, Drapery	8454-XV	Tumbler, Fern	1876-XV
Bowl, Swan	2754-XV	Tumbler, 2" mini	2727-XV
Candlestick, Swan	5172-XV	Vase, 5" Curtain	2056-XV
Creamer, 4" Button & Arch	2726-XV	Water set, 5-pc. miniature	2730-XV
Epergne set, 4-pc. Hobnail	3701-XV	Water set, 5-pc. Fern	1870-XV
Epergne set, mini Hobnail	3801-XV		

The year's Easter assortments featured numerous items in Pink Pearl, Jade Pearl, and the hand-painted decoration Violets on Iridized Opal Pearl.

1994 Red Carnival continued to be offered in the regular line in a varied assortment. The special Family Signature Series piece, signed by Tom Fenton, was the No. 2779 Lion/Leaf 8½" basket. Items in the regular line included:

Angel, 3½"	5533-RN	Fox, 6"	5226-RN
Basket, 10½" Hearts & Flowers	5488-RN	Lamp. 20" student	2792-RN
Bell, 6" Whitton	9066-RN	Pitcher, 12 oz. Hobnail	3762-RN
Candy & cover	9280-RN	Rose bowl, 3" Water Lily	8429-RN
Comport, 7" Persian Medallion	9422-RN	Vase, 7" Vessel of Gems	8253-RN
Fairy light, 3-pc. Hobnail	1167-RN	Vase, 11"	3161-RN

1995 Fifteen different pieces were in the regular line in Red Carnival. Some of the pieces were hand decorated with the Buttercups and Berries pattern. These pieces use the pattern code (RI). The Red Carnival covered candy No. 2790-RN was a Fenton Family Signature piece, inscribed with the signature of Mike Fenton. More specifically, items included:

Basket, 8" Daisy & Button	1936-RN	Pitcher, 8¾" Apple Tree	6575-RN
Basket, 8½" Holly	2980-RN	Polar bear. 4½"	5109-RI
Bell, 7" Paisley	6761-RI	Rose bowl, 6" Wild Rose	2927-RN
Fairy light, 5¾"	8405-RI	Slipper, 5"	2931-RN
Fenton logo, 5" oval	9499-RN	Tumbler, 4" Apple Tree	6576-RN
Lamp, 20" Basket Weave	4605-RI	Vase, 7¼" Wild Rose	2857-RN
Nut dish, 4½"	2926-RN	Water set, 5-pc. Apple Tree	6555-RN
Pear box, 4¼"	2980-RN		

1996 Red Carnival (RN) continued and select pieces were also offered in the hand-painted Damask Rose pattern on Red Carnival (RC). The 12-piece assortment included three baskets, two animals, a 20" student lamp, the Grape and Cable tobacco jar, the Butterfly bell and a boot, a Verly's bowl, and one vase. Production of the following was limited to one year:

Basket, 7½" Spanish Lace	1231-RN	Bowl, 9" Verly's	9529-RN
Basket, 8"	2936-RC	Lamp, 20" student	9307-RC
Basket, 8½" Ribbon Tie	7538-RN	Owl, 6"	5258-RN
Bell, 7" Butterfly	9265-RN	Pig figure, 3"	5220-RC
Boot, 2½"	9590-RC	Tobacco Jar, 7" Grape & Cable	9188-RN
Hen on Nest, 6½"	5182-RN	Vase, 8" Melon	5351-RC

1997 Red Carnival which had enjoyed a lengthy run in the Fenton line was replaced by Plum Carnival. Fenton's Plum color was iridized, combined with new moulds and attractive hand painting to add appeal. A four-piece hand-painted clown set with matching numbers in this color was limited to 970 sets. Other key pieces included bells, baskets, vases and a 20" lamp with prisms. Items and numbers are as follows:

Basket, 7½" Hummingbird	5731-PX	Clowns, 4-pc. set	5205-P2
Basket, 9½" Diamond Panel	1535-PX	Lamp, 20" Paisley	6705-PX
Bell, 6½" Templebells	9560-PX	Perfume and stopper, 5"	5305-PX
Bird, 4"	5163-P2	Pitcher, 9½"	6869-PX
Candy and cover, 7"	6780-PX	Vase, 8" Swan	9458-PX
Cat figure, 3¾"	5165-P2	Vase, 10" Thistle	8769-PX

1998 Plum remained in the line for another year featuring an all new selection of carnival items. Hand-painted Carnival pieces included a 20" student lamp, the Medallion bell, two sizes of vases and a limited edition three-piece bear set. The bear sets were numbered and limited to a total of 1250 matched sets. Pieces and numbers included:

Basket, 6" Ruffles	2035-PX	Candleholders, 5½" Viking	7676-PX
Basket, 8" 3-toed	6838-PX	Jug, 6½" Aztec	9014-PX
Bear set, 3-pc.	5207-AX	Lamp, 18" student	8999-AX
Bell, 7" Medallion	6866-AX	Rooster figure, 5½"	5292-PX
Bowl, 13½" Viking	7677-PX	Vase, 4½"	9357-AX
Box and cover, 8½"	2970-PX	Vase, 6½" Rose	9252-AX
Box, 5½" square	7640-PX	Vase, 7½" Daffodil	7653-PX

1999 Violet Satin and Spruce Carnival were two new iridescent colors offered for the first time. The Violet Satin color was limited to a one year production period. Hand-painted items in this color included a bear figure, a cat figure, a fairy light, a covered 5" box, a 24" Gone with the Wind lamp and an 11" tulip-shape vase. The covered box was part of the Family Signature Series and was inscribed with the signature of George Fenton. Spruce Carnival is a green iridescent color. Hand-painted pieces included a Whitton-style bell, a three-piece limited edition and numbered cat set, a 20" student lamp, an 8" basket, and a 6" Melon vase. The student lamp was sold with and without prisms. A special Marigold iridescent and floral hand-painted oval-shaped 7" bell was included as part of the Designer Bell Series. This #7566-HT bell was designed by Martha Reynolds. Violet Satin items included the following:

Basket, 7"	2777-XP	Perfume and stopper, 7½"	5320-XK
Bear figure, 3½"	5151-XP	Slipper, 6" cat	5290-XK
Bell, 6½" Templebells	9560-XK	Vase, 7" Jack-in-the Pulpit	2963-XK
Box and cover, 5"	7484-XP	Vase, 8" Lance	4559-XK
Cat figure, 5"	5065-XP	Vase, 11" tulip	7255-XP
Fairy light, 5"	5405-XP	Water set, 5-piece	4650-XK
Lamp, 24" GWTW	1602-XP	Water tumbler, 5½"	4658-XK
Logo, 5" oval "Fenton"	9499-XK		

Spruce Carnival items included the following:

Alley Cat figure, 11"	5177-SI	Dog, 3" Scottie	5214-SI
Basket, 7"	5930-SI	Lamp, 20" student	9307-US
Basket, 8"	5969-US	Pitcher, 8½"	6869-SI
Basket, 8½" Lion	2779-SI	Tobacco jar, 7¼"	9188-SI
Bell, 6¼" Whitton	9066-US	Vase, 3½" hand	5153-SI
Cat set, 3-pc.	5000-US	Vase, 6" Melon	7693-US

2000 Production of Spruce Green Carnival continued with an all-new assortment of 15 items. Hand-painted pieces included a 5" cat figure, a 7" doll figure, a 3½" puppy, a 6" Beaded fairy light, an 8" melon vase and a limited edition set that consisted of a covered Butterfly box and bell. New items included:

Basket, 7" tumbler	6589-SI	Fairy light, 6" Beaded	8405-S8
Basket, 10" Leaf	6836-SI	Lamp, 30" Spanish Lace	3500-SI
Box, 4½" Duck	6848-SI	Pitcher, 6" Drapery Bead	7685-SI
Butterfly set		Puppy figure, 3½"	5225-S8
(covered box & bell)	9966-S8	Vase, 6" Rose	5729-SI
Cat figure, 5"	5065-S8	Vase, 8" Mellon	5351-S8
Doll figure, 7"	5228-S8	Water set, 5-pc. Iris	6814-SI

2001 Red Carnival returned to the regular Fenton line with the addition of 16 new items. Hand-painted items consisted of a 9½" Ribbed Basket, a 6½" Imperial slipper, a 5½" fan vase, a 4½" Basket Weave vase and a limited edition three-piece numbered cat set. The items included:

Basket, 8½" Tulip	7132-RN	Pitcher, 4½" Panelled Daisy	7207-RN
Basket, 9½" Ribbed	5933-RM	Pitcher, 8½" Drape	6491-RN
Box and cover, 5" Rose	5740-RN	Slipper, 6½" Imperial	8595-RM
Cat set, 3-pc.	5052-RM	Vase, 4½" Basket Weave	9335-RM
Fairy light, 5" Atlantis	5204-RN	Vase, 5½" fan	1136-RM
Lamp, 30" Beauty, Pillar	7102-RN	Vase, 5½" Daffodil	7793-RN
Perfume and stopper, 6½"	5301-RN	Vase, 9-11" swung	2851-RN

Two additional carnival items were hand-painted in Fenton's blue Favrene color as a part of the Honor Collection. These limited edition pieces were the 5" 5065-FW cat figure and the 4½" 7480-FW covered box.

2002 Fifteen items in Amethyst Carnival were introduced into the line. The Family Signature Series included a 6" Wildflower covered comport signed by Frank M. Fenton. Hand-painted pieces included a frog figure, a bell, an 8" basket, a small rose bowl, and a 23" Embossed Rose student lamp. The Amethyst Carnival assortment included:

Basket, 8"	2936-CQ	Rose bowl, 4½"	7424-CQ
Bell, 5¼" Mirror & Rose	5762-CQ	Toothpick, 2½" Thistle	5520-CN
Comport, 6" covered Wildflower	2808-CN	Tumbler, 4¼" Hobstar	9047-CN
Decanter and stopper, 12"	5908-CN	Turtle figure, 4"	5266-CN
Frog figure, 2½"	5274-CQ	Vase, 6½" Embossed Leaf	5752-CN
Goldfish figure, 5"	5276-CN	Vase, 8½" Panelled Grape	5455-CN
Lamp, 23" Embossed Rose	5701-CQ	Water set, 5-pc. Hobstar	8909-CN
Pitcher, 5" Thistle	1964-CN		

2003 Fenton's carnival glass color used for the regular line was again Amethyst. Eleven new pieces were featured in this ever-popular color. Three of these items were hand painted with Robin Spindler's attractive White Blossoms decoration. Hand-painted pieces included the No. 6808-CQ 4" trinket box, the No. 5293-CQ 3½" bunny and the No. 6861-CQ 6" Beaded Melon vase.
Other Amethyst Carnival pieces included:

Basket, 6"	6331-CN	Epergne, 12" Diamond Lace	4802-CN
Butter/Cheese	4667-CN	Punch bowl w/base and 8 cups	9750-CN
Bowl, 8½" Swan	7771-CN	Punch cup	9048-CN
Comport, 9½" Daisy & Button	1985-CN	Vase, 8-10" swung	8450-CN

The punch bowl was sold as a set with a metal base, eight cups, and a crystal glass ladle. Additional punch cups could also be ordered individually.

2004 Thirteen new pieces of Amethyst Carnival entered the line. A few of the new pieces were produced from recently acquired Fostoria, Indiana, and Imperial moulds. A new hand-painted decoration, Golden Daisy, designed by Frances Burton, graced four of these pieces. Hand-painted pieces included the No. 4634-UN 8" Peacock basket, the No. 4764-UN Threaded bell, the No. 6063-UN 7½" pitcher, and the No. 5085-UN 4" puppy figure.

Additional Amethyst Carnival items in the regular line included:

Basket, 9"	4534-CN	Vase, 6" Grape	5954-CN
Candy box, 6½"	4108-CN	Vase, 7" Feather cornucopia	8395-CN
Hummingbird figure, 4½"	5066-CN	Vase, 8½" Tulip	2856-C4
Pie wagon, 5½"	4204-CN	Water set, 5-pc. Apple Tree	6555-C4
Tumbler, 4" Apple Tree	6576-C4		

The water set included an Apple Tree 8¾" pitcher and four tumblers. The pie wagon was a limiited edition piece with a maximum number of 990 produced.

Other Carnival Glass Production

In addition to making carnival glass items for the regular line, special pieces were produced for the Fenton Gift Shop and for QVC. Fenton Art Glass has also produced a number of limited edition special items for various carnival glass collectors' clubs around the country. Items are usually made in special colors in very limited runs, specifically for the benefit of the members of these clubs.

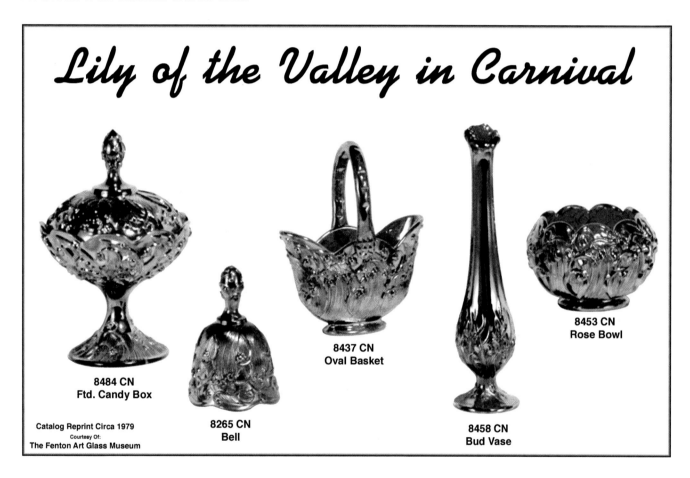

Lily of the Valley in Carnival

8484 CN
Ftd. Candy Box

Catalog Reprint Circa 1979
Courtesy Of:
The Fenton Art Glass Museum

8265 CN
Bell

8437 CN
Oval Basket

8458 CN
Bud Vase

8453 CN
Rose Bowl

Carnival

Fenton's big news in the January 1970 supplement was the reintroduction of a line of carnival glass. The same company that was once famous for producing a wide array of iridized glass was using original-formula colors to honor its past achievements. All the new pieces were marked with an embossed Fenton logo and all came complete with a descriptive tag attached. The base color of the new carnival glass was a deep Amethyst. Sprayed-on mixtures of metallic salts added a rich blue-green iridescence to this base color. Original Fenton moulds and moulds purchased from closed glass companies were often altered to meet the needs of the Fenton glass makers. A new line of collectibles in the form of plates was initiated. Several new series of plates in Carnival were offered to collectors. For a listing of these plates, see pages 34 and 35.

New items were added, and a portion of the old pieces were discontinued yearly until this entire segment of carnival glass production was discontinued at the end of 1982. When the new line of carnival glass items appeared in 1983, Fenton switched to a new annual policy. New carnival pieces were introduced each year and all the old items were discontinued.

Carnival	Ware No.	Introduced	Discontinued	Value
Alley Cat	5177-CN	July 1970	1974	$80.00 – 90.00
Basket, Persian Medallion	8238-CN	1972	1975	$75.00 – 85.00
Basket, 7" Threaded	8435-CN	1977	1979	$67.00 – 74.00
Basket, Lily of the Valley	8437-CN	1979	1980	$25.00 – 30.00
Bell, Daisy & Button	1966-CN	1971	1973	$27.00 – 35.00
Bell, Faberge	8466-CN	1977	1979	$30.00 – 35.00
Bell, Lily of the Valley	8265-CN	1979	1980	$28.00 – 32.00
Bell, Madonna	9467-CN	1975	1977	$25.00 – 27.00
Bird figure, Happiness	5197-CN	1977	1979	$28.00 – 32.00
Bird, small	5163-CN	1978	1979	$20.00 – 25.00
Bonbon, handled Butterfly	8230-CN	1973	1975	$18.00 – 22.00
Boot, Daisy & Button	1990-CN	1970	1975	$20.00 – 22.00
Bowl, Butterfly and Berry	8428-CN	1974	1977	$35.00 – 45.00
Bowl, Carolina Dogwood	9424-CN	1977	1979	$40.00 – 45.00
Bowl, Curtain	8454-CN	1978	1979	$28.00 – 30.00
Bowl, flared Hearts and Flowers	8228-CN	1971	1974	$50.00 – 60.00
Bowl, cupped Hearts and Flowers	8229-CN	1971	1974	$50.00 – 60.00
Bowl, Heart and Vine	8237-CN	1973	1974	$37.00 – 42.00
Bowl, Daisy Pinwheel and Cable	8236-CN	1972	1974	$32.00 – 37.00
Bowl, Open Edge Basket Weave	8222-CN	July 1970	1974	$18.00 – 20.00
Bowl, 3-toed Leaf & Orange Tree	8223-CN	July 1970	1976	$20.00 – 25.00
Bowl, crimped Orange Tree & Cherry	8233-CN	1972	1977	$45.00 – 55.00
Bowl, cupped Orange Tree & Cherry	8232-CN	1972	1975	$35.00 – 40.00
Bowl, 8" Persian Medallion	8224-CN	July 1970	1975	$30.00 – 35.00
Bowl, 8" Holly	8220-CN	1971	1975	$30.00 – 35.00
Boy and girl, praying	5100-CN	1977	1979	$35.00 – 40.00
Bunny	5162-CN	1978	1979	$25.00 – 30.00
Butterfly	5170-CN	1970	1973	$25.00 – 30.00

January 1970 Supplement

9088 CN Covered Candy Box

1990 CN Boot

5186 CN Small Hen on Nest

9125 CN Oval Dish

5193 CN Fish Paperweight

9185 CN Paneled Daisy Candy Box

5170 CN Butterfly

5182 CN Hen on Nest

July 1970 Supplement

Catalog Reprint Composition   Courtesy Of: The Fenton Art Glass Museum

8254 CN Mermaid Vase

8223 CN Leaf and Orange Tree Three-Toed Bowl

8227 CN Pinwheel 5" Comport

8255 CN Swung Vase

8224 CN Persian Medallion 8" Bowl

8222 CN Open Edge Basket Weave Bowl

5177 CN 10½" Alley Cat

8428 CN Butterfly and Berry Large Berry Bowl

8258 CN Love Bird Vase

8472 CN Orange Tree Candleholder

8402 CN Millersburg Cream and Sugar

1974 Catalog

8427 CN Oval Pinwheel Comport

Carnival	Ware No.	Introduced	Discontinued	Value
Candle bowl, Orange Tree	9173-CN	1973	1974	$28.00 – 32.00
Candleholder, 6" Orange Tree	8472-CN	1974	1976	$15.00 – 18.00
Candleholder, Swan	5172-CN	1971	1974	$27.00 – 32.00
Candy box, Baroque	9388-CN	1978	1979	$35.00 – 40.00
Candy box, heart shaped	8200-CN	1972	1974	$75.00 – 95.00
Candy, ftd. Lily of the Valley	8484-CN	1979	1980	$35.00 – 40.00
Candy box, Madonna	9484-CN	1977	1978	$37.00 – 40.00
Candy box, Pagoda	8201-CN	1975	1977	$75.00 – 85.00
Candy box, Paneled Daisy	9185-CN	1970	1976	$25.00 – 32.00
Candy jar, ftd. W. Strawberry	9088-CN	1970	1976	$45.00 – 50.00
Chalice, Persian Medallion	8241-CN	1972	1974	$30.00 – 35.00
Comport, Drape and Tie	8436-CN	1977	1978	$35.00 – 45.00
Comport, handled fruit	8231-CN	1973	1975	$25.00 – 29.00
Comport, Persian Medallion	8234-CN	1972	1977	$25.00 – 28.00
Comport. oval Pinwheel	8427-CN	1974	1976	$22.00 – 27.00
Comport. Pinwheel	8227-CN	July 1970	1976	$25.00 – 28.00
Comport, Rose	9222-CN	July 1973	1976	$22.00 – 25.00
Creamer and sugar	8402-CN	1974	1975	$35.00 – 40.00
Dish, oval	9125-CN	1970	1975	$25.00 – 27.00
Fairy lamp, beaded	8405-CN	1978	1979	$25.00 – 35.00
Hen on nest, large	5182-CN	1970	1974	$65.00 – 75.00
Hen on nest, small	5186-CN	1970	1974	$30.00 – 35.00
Nappy, Grape	8225-CN	1971	1974	$15.00 – 18.00
Nut dish, 3-toed Leaf	8235-CN	1971	1974	$20.00 – 25.00
Nut dish, ftd. Scroll & Eye	8248-CN	1975	1977	$20.00 – 22.00
Owl	5178-CN	1971	1973	$30.00 – 35.00
Paperweight, fish	5193-CN	1970	1973	$27.00 – 32.00
Planter bowl, Verly's hexagonal	8226-CN	1971	1974	$45.00 – 55.00
Plate, Persian Medallion	8219-CN	1971	1973	$35.00 – 40.00
Rabbit	5174-CN	1971	1973	$30.00 – 35.00
Ring tree, turtle	9199-CN	1973	1974	$32.00 – 35.00
Rose bowl, Lily of the Valley	8453-CN	1979	1980	$18.00 – 22.00
Swan	5161-CN	1978	1979	$30.00 – 35.00
Toothpick, Paneled Daisy	8294-CN	1973	1975	$20.00 – 25.00
Toothpick, Strawberry	8295-CN	1971	1976	$20.00 – 25.00
Tumbler, Butterfly & Berry	8240-CN	1972	1974	$20.00 – 25.00
Vase, 3-toed Grape	8457-CN	1978	1979	$20.00 – 25.00
Vase, bud	9056-CN	1977	1979	$18.00 – 20.00
Vase, Lily of the Valley bud	8458-CN	1979	1980	$18.00 – 22.00
Vase, Atlantis	5150-CN	1971	1973	$30.00 – 35.00
Vase, Love Bird	8258-CN	1974	1975	$35.00 – 40.00
Vase, Mermaid	8254-CN	July 1970	1973	$85.00 – 95.00
Vase, 8"	9155-CN	1974	1977	$25.00 – 30.00
Vase, 8" Peacock	8257-CN	1971	1974	$40.00 – 45.00
Vase, swung	8255-CN	July 1970	1975	$27.00 – 32.00
Vase, swung	8256-CN	1971	1974	$28.00 – 34.00

Catalog Reprint Composite

Courtesy Of:

The Fenton Art Glass Museum

9484 CN Madonna Candy Box

8436 CN Drape & Tie Comport

8435 CN 7"
Threaded Diamond Optic
Basket

5100 CN Praying Boy & Girl

9424 CN Carolina Dogwood Bowl

5197 CN Happiness Bird

8454 CN Curtain Bowl

8466 CN Faberge Bell

8405 CN Beaded Fairy Light

5163 CN Small Bird

*Carnival Glass
1977 & 1978*

5161 CN Swan

5162 CN Bunny

9388 CN Baroque Candy Box

Carnival Christmas Series Collector Plates

The Christmas in America series of plates was introduced in Fenton's July 1970 catalog supplement. Sales were accepted from July through December in each of the twelve years the plates were made. Moulds for the individual plates were destroyed on December 31 of each year. Each plate commemorates a building of religious significance in America. Beginning in 1971, plates in this series were also made in blue satin and white satin. The final plate in the series was also produced in a special hand-decorated Florentine finish. Each plate was sold with a hand-finished wooden holder.

Christmas Plate	Ware No.	Subject	Value
1970 Plate	8270-CN	"The Little Brown Church in the Vale," Bradford, Iowa	$12.00 – 14.00
1971 Plate	8271-CN	"The Old Brick Church," Isle of Wright County, Virginia	$12.00 – 14.00
1972 Plate	8272-CN	"The Two Horned Church," Marietta, Ohio	$12.00 – 14.00
1973 Plate	8273-CN	"St. Mary's in the Mountains," Virginia City, Nevada	$12.00 – 14.00
1974 Plate	8274-CN	"The Nation's Church," Philadelphia, Pa.	$12.00 – 14.00
1975 Plate	8275-CN	"Birthplace of Liberty," Richmond, Virginia	$12.00 – 14.00
1976 Plate	8276-CN	"The Old North Church," Boston, Mass.	$12.00 – 14.00
1977 Plate	8277-CN	"San Carlos Borromeo De Carmelo," Carmel, Calif.	$12.00 – 14.00
1978 Plate	8278-CN	"The Church of the Holy Trinity," Philadelphia, Pa.	$12.00 – 14.00
1979 Plate	8279-CN	"San Jose y Miguel De Aguayo," San Antonio, Texas	$12.00 – 14.00
1980 Plate	8280-CN	"Christ Church," Alexandria, Virginia	$12.00 – 14.00
1981 Plate	8281-CN	"Mission of San Xavier Del Bac," Tucson, Arizona	$15.00 – 18.00

8270 CN 1970 Plate   8271 CN 1971 Plate   8272 CN 1972 Plate

8275 CN 1975 Plate   8276 CN 1976 Plate   8277 CN 1977 Plate

CHRISTMAS IN AMERICA 1970

The theme of the first Collector's Plate in the newly introduced series of Fenton Christmas Plates is "The Little Brown Church in the Vale." We chose this famous little church because we felt it to be particularly appropriate in depicting the feeling of "Christmas in America."

The Plate will be produced in limited quantity only, from July 1 through December 30, 1970. Included with each Plate is a hand finished wooden plate holder. The back of the Plate is inscribed with "Christmas in America, No. 1." and the first verse of The Little Brown Church in the Vale.

Christmas 1970

The Little Brown Church in the Vale

8270CN Christmas Plate w/stand
C8270 CN Christmas Plate w/stand
Packed in Remailer Carton

Fenton

CATALOG SUPPLEMENT
JULY, 1970

THE FENTON ART GLASS COMPANY, WILLIAMSTOWN, WEST VIRGINIA 26187

Carnival Craftsman Series Collector Plates

In addition to the Christmas in America series, a second series of carnival glass collector's plates was introduced in 1970. This series, which became known as the Craftsman Series, featured a skilled worker engaged in an aspect of his trade. A plate was issued annually for twelve years. Each plate was available in January and was retired at the end of the year; the moulds were destroyed. The next year, a new plate with a different craftsman was offered. A hand-rubbed walnut stand was included with each plate. In 1979, a stein and bell were offered to complement the plate. According to the catalog description, the stein provided a "panoramic view of early 1700s American glass making" and the bell "featured a bas-relief of the glass Finisher." The Craftsman series of plates was also made in blue satin.

The stein was made in 1982, in Chocolate, for the Levay Distributing Company. The stein and bell returned in July 1983 in a new color called White Satin Carnival. This color was similar in appearance to Mother-of-Pearl. The stein was made in a limited edition of 1500 pieces and production of the bell was limited to 3500 pieces.

Craftman Plate	Ware No.	Subject	Value
1970 Plate	9115-CN	"The Glassworker"	$18.00 – 22.00
1971 Plate	9116-CN	"The Printer"	$16.00 – 18.00
1972 Plate	9117-CN	"The Blacksmith"	$12.00 – 15.00
1973 Plate	9118-CN	"The Shoemaker"	$12.00 – 15.00
1974 Plate	9119-CN	"The Cooper"	$12.00 – 15.00
1975 Plate	9175-CN	"The Silversmith"	$12.00 – 15.00
1976 Plate	9176-CN	"The Gunsmith"	$12.00 – 15.00
1977 Plate	9177-CN	"The Potter"	$12.00 – 15.00
1978 Plate	9178-CN	"The Wheelwright"	$12.00 – 15.00
1979 Plate	9179-CN	"The Cabinetmaker"	$12.00 – 15.00
1980 Plate	9680-CN	"The Tanner"	$11.00 – 14.00
1981 Plate	9681-CN	"The Housewright"	$11.00 – 14.00
Bell	9660-CN		$22.00 – 24.00
Stein	9640-CN		$27.00 – 32.00

9115 CN 1970 Plate   9117 CN 1972 Plate   9119 CN 1974 Plate

9177 CN 1977 Plate   9178 CN 1978 Plate   9680 CN 1980 Plate

Catalog Reprint Composite   Courtesy Of: **The Fenton Art Glass Museum**

Carnival Mother's Day Series Collector Plates

Beginning in 1971, Fenton honored Mother's Day each year with a special plate. The Carnival series was sometimes advertised as a series of ten plates. However, only nine plates were actually produced. See the listing below for the titles. Moulds for the plates were destroyed on June 30th of each year. This series of plates was also made in blue satin and white satin. A special limited edition of 5000 Mother's Day plates was produced in Ruby Iridescent in 1979. This lovely plate retailed for $35.00 and was signed by a member of the Fenton family.

Mother's Day Plate	Ware No.	Subject	Value
1971 Plate	9316-CN	Madonna with the Sleeping Child	$12.00 – 15.00
1972 Plate	9317-CN	Madonna of the Goldfinch	$12.00 – 15.00
1973 Plate	9318-CN	The Small Cowpen Madonna	$12.00 – 15.00
1974 Plate	9319-CN	Madonna of the Grotto	$12.00 – 15.00
1975 Plate	9375-CN	Taddei Madonna	$12.00 – 15.00
1976 Plate	9376-CN	The Holy Night	$12.00 – 15.00
1977 Plate	9377-CN	Madonna and Child with Pomegranate	$12.00 – 15.00
1978 Plate	9378-CN	The Madonnina	$11.00 – 13.00
1979 Plate	9379-CN	Madonna of the Rose Hedge	$11.00 – 13.00
1979 Plate	9379-RN	Madonna of the Rose Hedge	$30.00 – 35.00

Mother's Day 1979

Catalog Reprint Courtesy of: The Fenton art Glass Museum

LIMITED EDITION OF 5000—NUMBERED AND SIGNED . . . . .
By A Member of The Fenton Family

9379 RN
MOTHER'S DAY PLATE
WITH WOODEN STAND

handcrafted in Ruby Iridescent...

9378 CN 1978 Plate

9319 CN 1974 Plate

9377 CN 1977 Plate

Independence Blue Carnival

Fenton introduced a new carnival color and designed new patriotic items to help customers celebrate the 200th anniversary of the United States. Independence Blue was introduced In July 1974, in a three-piece offering — a Patriot's bell, a Jefferson comport, and an Eagle plate. Fenton placed a limit on the number of Jefferson comports its dealers could order. The comports in Independence Blue were a limited edition of 7600, and resellers were limited to two per store for orders received by August 15th, 1974. The Patriot's bell featured cameos of Washington, Jefferson, Franklin, and Adams. The Eagle plate was inscribed on the reverse side with a quotation from Daniel Webster's eulogy of Adams and Jefferson.

This color and the new items were well received. In July 1975, another series of three special items was offered for the Bicentennial celebration. The color was so popular that Fenton included it in the regular line for 1976. An assortment of twelve different items was made for one year. Independence Blue was retired at the end of 1976.

Independence Blue	Ware No.	Introduced	Discontinued	Value
Basket, Persian Medallion	8238-IB	1976	1977	$65.00 – 75.00
Bell, Patriot's	8467-IB	July 1974	1975	$25.00 – 30.00
Bell, Madonna	9467-IB	1976	1977	$27.00 – 32.00
Bird, Happiness	5197-IB	1976	1977	$35.00 – 40.00
Bowl, Basket Weave	8222-IB	1976	1977	$20.00 – 25.00
Bowl, Butterfly and Berry	8428-IB	1976	1977	$50.00 – 65.00
Bowl, Leaf and Orange Tree	8223-IB	1976	1977	$22.00 – 25.00
Candy box, Pagoda	8201-IB	1976	1977	$75.00 – 85.00
Comport, Jefferson	8476-IB	July 1974	1975	$160.00 – 175.00
Comport, Persian Medallion	8234-IB	1976	1977	$25.00 – 30.00
Comport, Pinwheel	8227-IB	1976	1977	$27.00 – 32.00
Plate, Eagle	9418-IB	July 1974	1975	$18.00 – 22.00
Plate, Lafayette	9419-IB	July 1975	1977	$18.00 – 22.00
Paperweight, Eagle	8470-IB	July 1975	1977	$25.00 – 27.00
Paperweight, Love Bird	8477-IB	1976	1977	$25.00 – 30.00
Planter, Patriot's	8499-IB	1976	1977	$32.00 – 37.00
Stein, Bicentennial	8446-IB	July 1975	1977	$28.00 – 32.00
Vase, 8"	9155-IB	1976	1977	$32.00 – 37.00

9419 IB Washington & Lafayette Plate

8470 IB Eagle Paperweight

8476 IB Jefferson Comport

8467 IB Patriot's Bell

8499 IB Patriot's Planter

8446 IB Bicentennial Stein

9155 IB Vase

8234 IB
Persian Medallion
Comport

8238 IB Persian Medallion Basket

5197 IB Happiness Bird

8477 IB Love Bird Paperweight

8201 IB Pagoda Candy

8428 IB Butterfly & Berry Bowl

9467 IB Madonna Bell

8227 IB Pinwheel Comport

8223 IB Leaf & Orange Tree Bowl

8222 IB Basket Weave Bowl

Orange Carnival

Orange Carnival, a color commonly referred to by collectors as marigold, was unveiled in July 1971. A total of fourteen different shapes were made before the color was retired at the end of 1973. All the pieces that were placed into the line in July 1971 continued in production until the color was discontinued. Some of the items were reproductions from old moulds. Collectors will be happy to note that the Fenton logo is embossed into the base of all the items from this era of production.

The *CO* color code used with this color was later used to mean Cameo Opalescent.

Orange Carnival	Ware No.	Introduced	Discontinued	Value
Bell, Daisy & Button	1966-CO	July 1971	1974	$30.00 – 35.00
Bonbon, handled Butterfly	8230-CO	1973	1974	$22.00 – 25.00
Boot, Daisy & Button	1990-C0	1972	1974	$25.00 – 28.00
Bowl, 3-toed Leaf and Orange Tree	8223-CO	July 1971	1974	$22.00 – 27.00
Bowl, cupped Hearts and Flowers	8229-CO	July 1971	1974	$45.00 – 55.00
Bowl, flared Orange Tree	8239-CO	1973	1974	$37.00 – 42.00
Bowl, 8" Persian Medallion	8224-CO	July 1971	1974	$37.00 – 42.00
Candy box, Paneled Daisy	9185-CO	July 1971	1974	$30.00 – 35.00
Candy jar, ftd. W. Strawberry	9088-CO	1972	1974	$45.00 – 55.00
Chalice, Persian Medallion	8241-CO	1972	1973	$35.00 – 40.00
Comport, handled fruit	8231-CO	1973	1974	$27.00 – 30.00
Comport, Persian Medallion	8234-CO	1972	1974	$27.00 – 30.00
Comport. Pinwheel	8227-CO	1972	1974	$27.00 – 30.00
Nappy, Grape	8225-CO	July 1971	1974	$18.00 – 20.00
Toothpick, Strawberry	8295-CO	July 1971	1974	$22.00 – 25.00

Catalog Reprint Composite
Courtesy Of:
The Fenton Art Glass Museum

1966 CO Bell

8224 CO
Persian Medallion 8" Bowl

8223 CO Leaf & Orange Tree
3-Toed Bowl

8241 CO Persian Medallion Chalice

8225 CO Grape Cluster Nappy

9185 CO Paneled Daisy Candy

8295 CO
Strawberry Toothpick

8229 CO Hearts & Flowers Bowl

Ruby Iridescent

In 1976, Fenton commemorated the past by reviving its historic red carnival color. This new version of the color was called Ruby Iridescent. Eleven shapes were introduced in this color during the first year. In 1977, five more shapes were added to the line. The color was discontinued at the end of 1977.

Ruby Carnival reappeared in the 1990s, with a multitude of pieces being made. A number of significant pieces appeared in the regular line, and special items were made for the Historical Collection and the Family Signature Series. For more information on these later pieces, see the introduction to this section.

Ruby Iridescent	Ware No.	Introduced	Discontinued	Value
Basket, Persian Medallion	8238-RN	1976	1978	$120.00 – 135.00
Bell, Madonna	9467-RN	1976	1978	$30.00 – 35.00
Bird, Happiness	5197-RN	1976	1978	$40.00 – 45.00
Bowl, Basket Weave	8222-RN	1976	1978	$28.00 – 32.00
Bowl, Butterfly and Berry	8428-RN	1976	1978	$60.00 – 70.00
Bowl, Carolina Dogwood	9424-RN	1977	1978	$50.00 – 60.00
Bowl, Leaf and Orange Tree	8223-RN	1976	1978	$30.00 – 35.00
Candy box, Pagoda	8201-RN	1976	1978	$80.00 – 90.00
Comport, Drape and Tie	8436-RN	1977	1978	$40.00 – 45.00
Comport, Persian Medallion	8234-RN	1976	1978	$32.00 – 37.00
Comport, Pinwheel	8227-RN	1976	1978	$30.00 – 35.00
Lamp, 20" Poppy student	9107-RN	1977	1978	$225.00 – 250.00
Lamp, 24" Poppy GWTW	9101-RN	1977	1978	$285.00 – 325.00
Light, Chou Ting ceremonial	8407-RN	1977	1978	$125.00 – 150.00
Paperweight, Love Bird	8477-RN	1976	1977	$27.00 – 32.00
Vase, 8"	9155-RN	1976	1978	$38.00 – 42.00

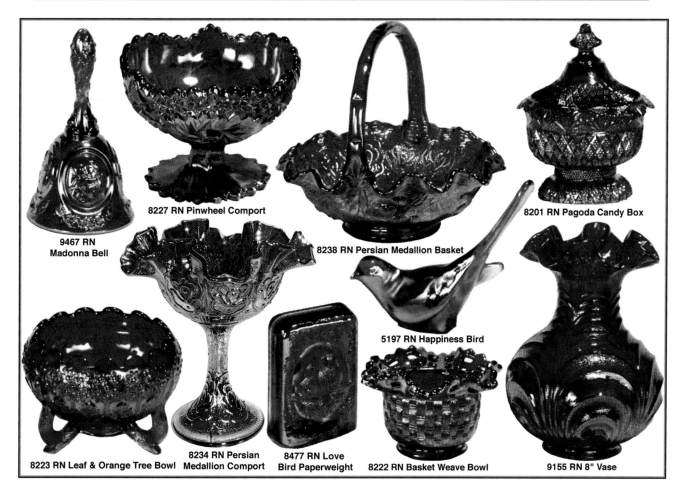

9467 RN
Madonna Bell

8227 RN Pinwheel Comport

8238 RN Persian Medallion Basket

8201 RN Pagoda Candy Box

5197 RN Happiness Bird

8223 RN Leaf & Orange Tree Bowl

8234 RN Persian Medallion Comport

8477 RN Love Bird Paperweight

8222 RN Basket Weave Bowl

9155 RN 8" Vase

Fenton's Opalescent Colors

Production of opalescent glassware began during the first decade of Fenton's glassmaking. Early examples of opalescent glassware include Dot Optic water sets in blue, green, and French Opalescent. Some pieces of early pattern glass made before 1920 in the Basket Weave with Open Edge, Beaded Stars, Drapery, Honeycomb and Clover, Stag and Holly, and Waterlily and Cattails patterns may also be found in opalescent colors. Colors that are normally found include Blue, Green, French, and Amethyst opalescent. For more information on this early opalescent glassware, see our book on early Fenton art glass — *Fenton Art Glass 1907 – 1939*.

Inventory records indicate that in the 1920s, Fenton made night sets and handled guest sets to be used at the bedside. These opalescent colored sets were made in the Rib Optic and Curtain Optic patterns. Opalescent colors made during that era were Victoria Blue, Victoria Green, and Cameo Opalescent. Some of the Rib Optic and Curtain Optic guest sets will also be found adorned with Royal Blue handles. Several styles of water sets may also be found in these two patterns in the Victoria Blue and Victoria Green colors.

Major lines with opalescent items made during the 1930s included Lincoln Inn, made in Green Opalescent, and Plymouth, made in French Opalescent. Numerous Dancing Lady pieces and Dolphin-decorated bowls and vases were made in opalescent colors.

Production of opalescent glassware began to dominate the line in about 1939. The Spiral Optic pattern was produced in Cranberry, blue, French, and green opalescent colors. Hobnail production was introduced in 1940 using these same colors. Topaz opalescent replaced green opalescent about mid-1941.

Fenton miniatures are among the more interesting opalescent items made during the early 1940s. These were introduced into the Fenton line in 1942. Miniature #37 vases and handled baskets were made in topaz, blue, and French opalescent colors. Crimped shapes of the vases were flared, tulip, square, fan, oval, and triangle. The baskets were made in flared, fan, square, and oval shapes. Additional examples of these two miniature shapes may be found in the Aqua Crest, Crystal Crest, Gold Crest, and Silver Crest patterns. The #37 handled jug was also introduced in 1942. It was made in the above three opalescent colors and in the Aqua Crest and Crystal Crest patterns. Two different mould shapes of the #38 miniature hand vase were made. One version is about ¼" taller than the other. The shorter style has a smooth round foot and a heavy ridge near the edge of the base. The taller version has a slightly scalloped foot and lacks this ridge on the base. Examples of both styles are pictured in the photo below. These miniature moulds were revived beginning in 1981 for limited edition and special order production. Items in new colors were made for Levay, Zeta Todd, Franklin Heirloom Glass, QVC, and the National Fenton Glass Society.

Opalescent glassware production during the 1940s and 1950s also consisted of many lamp parts produced for various independent lamp manufacturers. Opalescent atomizer parts were made during the 1940s and early 1950s for DeVilbiss of Toledo, Ohio.

9078-FO Ash Tray

#38 Miniature Hand Vase

9178-TO 9" Ogee Ash Tray

#38 Miniature Hand Vase

Blue Opalescent

Fenton's combination of a medium transparent blue with opal to produce Blue Opalescent originated almost at the inception of the company. In the early years, pattern glass pieces were made in this color. In the mid-1920s the color was used with a guest set, and in the 1930s a few dolphin items and some pieces of Lincoln Inn were made. In the late 1930s, the color became known as Stiegel Blue Opalescent,

During the early 1940s, Fenton expanded the use of Blue Opalescent greatly with the introduction of Hobnail in this color. At the same time, Leaf pattern plates and miniature vases and miniature baskets were made. These are detailed in the listing below. Coin Dot was introduced in 1947, and items in the Diamond Lace pattern were added a year later. For more information on Coin Dot, Hobnail, and Diamond Lace in this color, see the sections on these patterns in our previous book, titled *Fenton Art Glass Patterns 1939 – 1980.*

With the exception of pieces in the Coin Dot, Hobnail, and Diamond Lace patterns, very few other items were produced for the regular Fenton line in Blue Opalescent during the 1950s and 1960s. In the early 1950s Fenton made the No. 9078 square ashtray. Two blue opalescent ashtrays were packaged with two French Opalescent ashtrays in an attractive gift box. These were sold as the No. 9008 ashtray set. Another ashtray — the 9" Ogee — was made in the early 1960s. During this time, Fenton was also busy making a multitude of items for L. G. Wright in Blue Opalescent.

After a long and successful run, Blue Opalescent was absent from the Fenton line from January 1965 until July 1978, when the color was revived with the introduction of selected Hobnail items and special pattern glass creations. An assortment of five bells in opalescent colors was introduced into the line in January, 1980. Each of the bells was made in Blue Opalescent. For more information on this series of "Collectibells," see page 48. The color was finally retired from the Fenton regular line at the end of 1981. However, Fenton produced various items in Blue Opalescent Hobnail for Levay in 1982. Later, Fenton introduced other shades of Blue Opalescent into the regular line.

Beginning in the latter part of the 1980s, regular line items were made in a new blue opalescent color — Provincial Blue Opalescent — and Collector's Extravaganza items were produced in Persian Blue Opalescent in 1989, and in Sapphire Blue Opalescent in 1990.

Stiegel Blue Opalescent reappeared as part of a special Collector's Extravaganza offering in 1991. The 14-piece collection was made up of numerous items from old Fenton, McKee, and Westmoreland moulds. Items in the assortment included:

Basket, 6" Paneled Grape No. 4633-BO; Bell, 6¾" Templebells No. 9560-BO; Bowl, 10¼" Open Edge Ring & Petal No. 4627-BO; Cake plate, 11¼" Open Edge No. 4671-BO; Candlesticks, 3½" Open Edge No. 4672-BO; Comport, 6½" ftd. Colonial No. 4693-BO; Lamp, 15" Innovation No. 4603-BO; Lamp, 20" Basket Weave with hand painted grapes No. 4605-JU; Punch cup, Paneled Grape No. 4642-BO; Punch set, 14-piece Paneled Grape No. 4601-BO; Urn and cover, 12½" Diamond with hand-painted grapes No. 4602-JU; Vase, 10" Colonial bud with hand-painted grapes No. 4651-JU; and Vase, Paneled Grape tulip No. 4653-BO.

Other items also available in Stiegel Blue Opalescent in the Spring of 1991 included:

Basket, single crimp	4613-BO	Cream and sugar, Peacock	4673-BO
Basket, 7" Wildflower	4632-BO	Tumbler, mini	4616-BO
Butter and cover, Paneled Grape	4667-BO	Tumbler, Paneled Grape	4650-BO
Comport and cover, Saw Tooth	4612-BO	Water set, mini	4614-BO

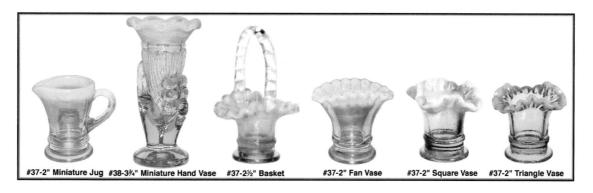

#37-2" Miniature Jug   #38-3¾" Miniature Hand Vase   #37-2½" Basket   #37-2" Fan Vase   #37-2" Square Vase   #37-2" Triangle Vase

Blue Opalescent	Ware No.	Introduced	Discontinued	Value
Ashtray, 9" Ogee	9178-BO	1960	1961	$75.00 – 85.00
Ashtray, #1728 square	9078-BO	1952	1954	$25.00 – 30.00
Basket, Lily of the Valley	8437-BO	July 1978	1980+	$37.00 – 40.00
Basket, Spiral Optic	3137-BO	1979	July 1980	$50.00 – 60.00
Basket, #37-2½" flared, fan, oval, square		1942	1944	UND $125.00 – 140.00
Bell, Lily of the Valley	8265-BO	July 1978	1980+	$32.00 – 37.00
Bowl, "Curtain"	8454-BO	July 1978	1980+	$35.00 – 40.00
Bowl, 10" Shell	9020-BO			$140.00 – 160.00
Bowl, #1942 Butterfly Net finger		1942	1943	UND
Candle, Lily of the Valley	8475-BO	1980	1980+	$20.00 – 22.50
Candy, ftd. Lily of the Valley	8484-BO	1979	1980+	$60.00 – 70.00
Candy box, Lily of the Valley	8489-BO	1979	1980+	$35.00 – 40.00
Candy box, Paneled Daisy	9185-BO	July 1978	1980	$55.00 – 65.00
Candy box, Spiral Optic	3180-BO	1979	1980	$110.00 – 125.00
Comport, Water Lily	8431-BO	July 1978	1980+	$25.00 – 27.00
Cup plate, #1942-4" Butterfly Net		1942	1943	UND
Fairy light, Lily of the Valley	8404-BO	1979	1980+	$50.00 – 60.00
Fairy light, Spiral Optic	3100-BO	1979	1980+	$47.00 – 52.00
Goblet, #1942 Butterfly Net water		1942	1943	UND
Jug, #37-2" miniature handled		1942	1944	$115.00 – 130.00
Nappy, "Grape"	8225-BO	July 1978	1980+	$17.00 – 19.00
Nut dish, Scroll and Eye	8248-BO	July 1978	1980+	$18.00 – 20.00
Pitcher, 10 oz. Spiral Optic	3166-BO	1979	1980	$35.00 – 40.00
Pitcher, 44 oz. Spiral Optic	3164-BO	1979	1980+	$110.00 – 130.00
Plate, #175-8" Leaf		1941	1944	$35.00 – 40.00
Plate, #175-11" Leaf		1941	1944	$55.00 – 60.00
Plate, #1942-6" Butterfly Net		1942	1943	UND
Plate, #1942-8" Butterfly Net		1942	1943	UND
Rose bowl, Lily of the Valley	8453-BO	1979	1980+	$22.00 – 25.00
Sherbet, #1942 Butterfly Net		1942	1943	UND
Toothpick, Paneled Daisy	8294-BO	July 1978	1980+	$18.00 – 20.00
Tumbler, #1942-12 oz. Butterfly Net		1942	1943	UND
Vase, Lily of the Valley	8450-BO	1980	1980+	$20.00 – 25.00
Vase, Lily of the Valley bud	8458-BO	1979	1980+	$18.00 – 22.00
Vase, 6½" Spiral Optic	3157-BO	1979	1980+	$35.00 – 40.00
Vase, #37-2" miniature flared, oval, square, triangle, tulip		1942	1944	$90.00 – 110.00
Vase, #38 miniature hand		1942	1944	$35.00 – 45.00

8454 BO "Curtain" Bowl　　**9078 BO Square Ashtray**　　**8294 BO "Paneled Daisy" Toothpick**　　**8225 BO "Grape" Nappy**

8248 BO Scroll & Eye Nut Dish

3100 BO Spiral Optic Fairy Lamp

8437 BO Lily of the Valley Basket

8431 BO Water Lily Comport

8404 BO Lily of the Valley
Fairy Lamp

9185 BO Paneled Daisy Candy Box

#1942 Sherbet

#1942 Water Goblet

8450 BO Lily of the Valley
Handkerchief Vase

3157 BO Spiral Optic Vase

#175-11" Leaf Plate

9020 BO 10" Shell Bowl

3166 BO 10 Oz. Spiral Optic Pitcher

8265 BO Lily of the Valley Bell

Cameo Opalescent

Cameo Opalescent (CO) is an amber opalescent color that returned to the Fenton line in 1979 after an absence of around fifty years. The last time this color had been in the line was the late 1920s. The early version of Cameo Opalescent was a pinkish opal interwoven with transparent golden hues. The new Cameo color was much darker, and in some pieces could almost be considered a brown opalescent.

Notice the prominent appearance of the new Lily of the Valley pattern in this color. In addition to the twenty pieces listed below, the initial offering included eight items in the Hobnail pattern. Cameo Opalescent shares the same color code — (CO) — with Orange Carnival.

Also, in January 1979, six items in the Spiral Optic pattern were produced in this color. All the items made in this issue will have the Fenton logo on the base. Fenton discontinued Cameo Opalescent at the end of 1982.

The Spiral pieces include:

Basket, 7"	3137-CO	Pitcher, 10 oz.	3166-CO
Candy box	3180-CO	Pitcher, 44 oz.	3164-CO
Fairy light	3100-CO	Vase, 6½"	3157-CO

Other items in Cameo Opalescent were also added to the line in the early 1980s. The January 1980 catalog includes the No. 8475 candles and the No. 8450 handkerchief vase. However, the number of pieces made in this color quickly began to diminish, and by 1981 almost half of the original items had been discontinued.

A Cameo Opalescent Hobnail lamp base was produced for E. P. Paul & Company during the 1940s. The assembled lamp was sold under the Paulix label.

An amber opalescent color with a new name — Autumn Gold Opalescent — appeared in the 1994 catalog. The color only remained in the line for one year, and the following pieces were produced:

Basket, 8"	1531-AO	Vase, 7"	1549-AO
Basket, 11"	1217-AO	Vase, 8"	1558-AO
Lamp, 21" student	1520-AO	Vase, 9½"	1559-AO
Pitcher, 32 oz.	1569-AO	Vase, 9½" "Feather"	1218-AO
Vase, 5"	1599-AO		

Cameo Opalescent	Ware No.	Introduced	Discontinued	Value
Basket, Spiral Optic	3137-CO	1979	July 1980	$45.00 – 50.00
Basket, Lily of the Valley	8437-CO	1979	1980+	$34.00 – 37.00
Bell, Lily of the Valley	8265-CO	1979	1980+	$27.00 – 32.00
Bowl, Curtain	8454-CO	1979	1980+	$32.00 – 37.00
Bowl, ftd. Lily of the Valley	8451-CO	1979	1980+	$65.00 – 75.00
Cake plate, Lily of the Valley	8411-CO	1979	1980+	$70.00 – 80.00
Candle, Lily of the Valley	8475-CO	1980	1980+	$18.00 – 22.00
Candy, Lily of the Valley	8489-CO	1979	1980+	$30.00 – 35.00
Candy, ftd. Lily of the Valley	8484-CO	1979	1980+	$60.00 – 65.00
Candy box, Spiral Optic	3180-CO	1979	1980	$90.00 – 100.00
Comport, Water Lily	8431-CO	1979	1980+	$22.00 – 25.00
Fairy light, Lily of the Valley	8404-CO	1979	1980+	$40.00 – 45.00
Fairy light, Spiral Optic	3100-CO	1979	July 1980	$37.00 – 42.00
Nappy, "Grape"	8225-CO	1979	1980+	$15.00 – 18.00
Nut dish, Scroll and Eye	8248-CO	1979	1980+	$17.00 – 19.00
Pitcher, 10 oz., Spiral Optic	3166-CO	1979	1980	$30.00 – 35.00
Pitcher, 44 oz., Spiral Optic	3164-CO	1979	1980	$90.00 – 110.00
Rose bowl, Lily of the Valley	8453-CO	1979	1980+	$20.00 – 22.00
Toothpick, Paneled Daisy	8294-CO	1979	1980+	$17.00 – 20.00
Vase, Lily of the Valley	8450-CO	1980	1980+	$20.00 – 25.00
Vase, Lily of the Valley bud	8458-CO	1979	1980+	$18.00 – 20.00
Vase, 6½" Spiral Optic	3157-CO	1979	July 1980	$30.00 – 35.00

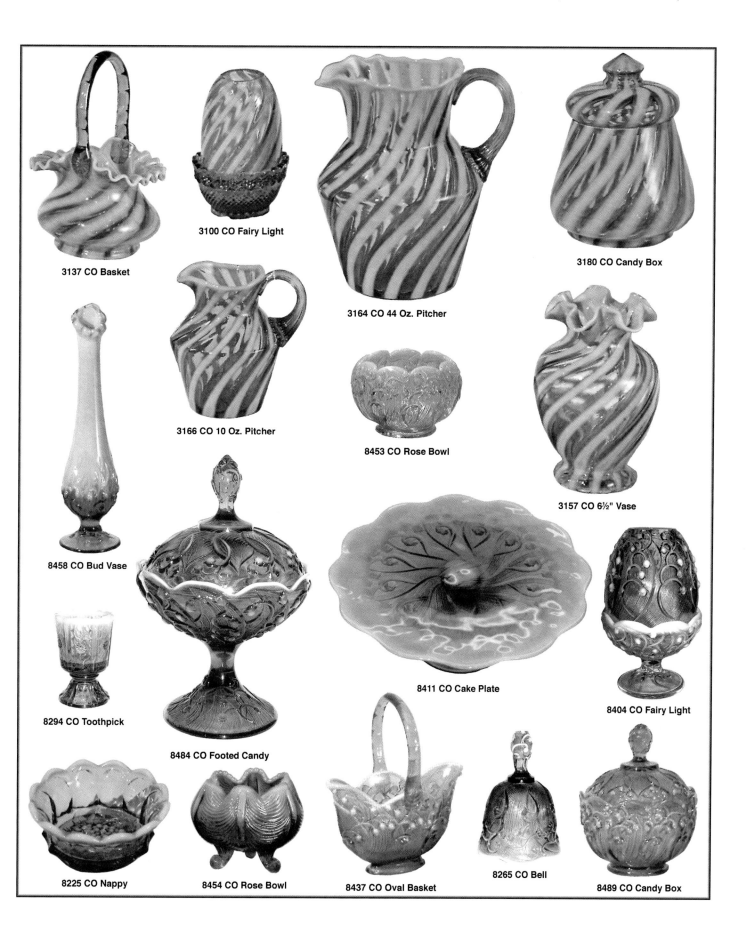

3137 CO Basket

3100 CO Fairy Light

3164 CO 44 Oz. Pitcher

3180 CO Candy Box

3166 CO 10 Oz. Pitcher

8453 CO Rose Bowl

3157 CO 6½" Vase

8458 CO Bud Vase

8411 CO Cake Plate

8404 CO Fairy Light

8294 CO Toothpick

8484 CO Footed Candy

8225 CO Nappy

8454 CO Rose Bowl

8437 CO Oval Basket

8265 CO Bell

8489 CO Candy Box

French Opalescent

French Opalescent glassware consists of crystal glass mixed with opal. Fenton used this color primarily with the Coin Dot, Diamond Lace, and Hobnail patterns from the 1940s through the 1960s. The Leaf plates and miniature vases were made in French Opalescent in the early 1940s. Two different moulds were used to make the miniature hand vase. Both styles of hand vases are shown in the photo to the right. A No. 192-6" melon rib jug is listed in the company inventory records for 1946. In 1952, the #1728 square ashtray appeared in the line. This item became the No. 9078-FO ashtray after the conversion to ware numbers in July 1952. Two French Opalescent ashtrays were boxed with two Blue Opalescent ashtrays and were marketed as the 9008 ashtray set. Two items from the Verly's moulds — the Empress and Mandarin vases — entered the line in 1968.

During the 1980s, a hand-decorated Strawberries pattern was in the line on French Opalescent. A Fenton rectangular logo sign was made in the mid-1980s. Also made during the same period were several shapes of votives.

Later, this color was sometimes given the trendy title French Cream. A 1993 supplement shows several Hobnail baskets in French Opalescent with colored crests and handles. More sizes of baskets and new colors of trim were added as part of the 1995 Easter collection.

The 1996 and 1997 catalogs sport the patterns hand-painted Trellis and Meadow Beauty. Hand-painted Trellis has pink hand-painted flowers on a French Opalescent lattice background with a spun Dusty Rose crest. Meadow Beauty features hand-painted rose-colored flowers on a French Opalescent ribbed background with an emerald crest. The animals made in both patterns are simply hand-decorated French Opalescent.

The French Opalescent Spiral from the 1999 catalog is accented with the hand-painted Martha's Rose decoration. In addition, the larger pieces are highlighted with rings and handles of Aquamarine. Hand-decorated animals included in this offering are a mallard, fawn, elephant, and cat.

Lavender Petals is a hand-painted decoration that was new to the 2000 general line. The pattern consists of a violet rose painted on a background of French Opalescent Spiral. All the pieces except the animals are accented with violet crests and handles. Numerous items in the popular hand-painted Trellis decoration were also still in the line.

In 2001, an assortment of hand-painted items was made for the Christmas season using a background of iridized French Opalescent glass. Included in this offering were a Hobnail 12" cake plate and a votive that were not hand painted. The popular regular line hand-painted patterns of Lavender Petals and Daisy Lane were set against a French Opalescent background. These same patterns were still available in the 2002 regular line. An additional pattern, Cottage Roses on French Opalescent, made its appearance in the 2002 line.

Items produced in 1941:	Value
Plate, #175-8" Leaf	$20.00 – 22.00
Plate, #175-11" Leaf	$30.00 – 35.00
Items produced in 1942:	**Value**
Basket, #37-2½" flared, fan. oval, square	$100.00 – 125.00
Bowl, #1942 Butterfly Net finger	UND
Cup plate, #1942-4" Butterfly Net	UND
Goblet, #1942 Butterfly Net water	UND
Jug, #37-2" miniature handled	$100.00 – 110.00
Plate, #175-8" Leaf	$20.00 – 22.00
Plate, #175-11" Leaf	$30.00 – 35.00
Plate, #1942-6" Butterfly Net	UND
Plate, #1942-8" Butterfly Net	UND
Sherbet, #1942 Butterfly Net	UND
Tumbler, #1942-12 oz. Butterfly Net	UND
Items produced in 1942:	**Value**
Vase, #37-2" miniature flared, oval, square, triangle, tulip	$80.00 – 90.00
Vase, #38 miniature hand	$30.00 – 40.00

Items produced in 1946:		Value
Jug, #192-6" handled		$40.00 – 45.00
Items produced 1952 - 1954:	Ware No.	Value
Ashtray, #1728 square	9078-FO	$20.00 – 25.00
Items produced in 1942:	Ware No.	Value
Vase, Mandarin	8251-FO	$100.00 – 125.00
Vase, Empress	8252-FO	$95.00 – 115.00

9078 FO Square Ashtray

#38 Miniature Hand Vase

#38 Miniature Hand Vase

#175-8" Leaf Plate

#37 Miniature Jug

8251 FO Mandarin Vase

#37 Fan Vase

#37 Basket

#1942 Sherbet

#37 Flared Vase

#37 Tulip Vase

#1942 Tumbler

#1942 Water Goblet

Topaz Opalescent

The topaz color first entered the Fenton line in the early 1920s. Some Carnival Glass pieces were made in topaz, and a great variety of shapes were made in iridescent topaz (called stretch glass). Topaz production continued into the 1930s in the Georgian and Daisy and Button patterns. Topaz Opalescent lemonade and guest sets were made in the Rib Optic and Drapery patterns during the 1920s. In the 1930s, pieces of the Dancing Ladies, Basket Weave with Open Edge, Dot Optic, and Leaf Tiers patterns, along with two sizes of Leaf plates, were made with opalescence. Production of the Leaf plates continued until July 1941. Additional information about these patterns may be found in *Fenton Art Glass Patterns 1907 – 1939*.

In the early 1940s, Fenton made numerous pieces of the Hobnail pattern in Topaz Opalescent. The production of this pattern is covered extensively in the book *Fenton Art Glass Patterns 1939 – 1980*. In addition, miniature vases, baskets, a handled jug, and a hand vase were made. Fenton was forced to cease production of this color after 1943 and throughout the remainder of the decade due to the government's restrictions on the civilian use of uranium oxide.

Fenton restricted the Topaz Opalescent color to the manufacture of glass for other companies during much of the fifties. A Hobnail fairy light and a Diamond Lace epergne were made for A. A. Sales Company; a large four-horn epergne was made for L. G. Wright, and a Hobnail lamp base was made for the William F. B. Johnson Company of Philadelphia. In 1959, Fenton resumed production of Topaz Opalescent pieces of the Coin Dot, Cactus, and Hobnail patterns in the regular line. Production of these pieces continued into the early 1960s. In 1960, the 9" Ogee ashtray was made for the regular line and pieces with the Thumbprint pattern were made for the Olde Virginia line. In 1979, Fenton made the Polka Dot pattern for Levay Distributing Company and made the Daisy and Fern pattern for L. G. Wright.

The color was revived in January 1980 with the introduction of nine pieces of the Lily of the Valley pattern into the regular Fenton line. A series of five Collectibells from moulds previously owned by Redcliff was also in the line for a brief period. Special projects in Topaz Opalescent included a few items in Hobnail for Levay Distributing Company and an oval Fenton logo sign for the Fenton Art Glass collectors of America. Fenton continued to make items in Hobnail for Levay in 1981 and 1983. All these later Hobnail pieces were marked with the Fenton logo.

Numerous items were made in Topaz Opalescent in 1988. The Collector's Extravaganza series featured a Cactus water set, a Diamond Lace epergne, four pieces in the Drapery pattern, a Gone with the Wind lamp, a four-piece Regency table set, a butterfly on a stand, a three-toed nut dish, and three pieces in the Butterfly and Berry pattern. Special items included a Butterfly mug for the Fenton Art Glass Collectors of America and a donkey figure for the Duncan Glass Society. Several items were also made for Singleton Bailey. Items produced included the Peacock vase, the Swan and Cattails vase and Swan mug in Topaz Opalescent, and the Butterfly and Rays three-toed basket and a Butterfly and Berry basket in Topaz Opalescent Carnival. In late 1989, a Fine Dot Optic Jack-in-the-Pulpit Vase was made in Topaz Opalescent for Russo.

Topaz Opalescent next appeared in the Fenton catalog in 1997, with a satin iridescent finish. The Family Signature Series was highlighted by a three-piece fairy light with hand-painted hydrangeas that was signed by Frank Fenton. Other general line items included a punch bowl on a metal base with eight cups, a large five-piece epergne set, an 8½" Hobnail basket, a Rose slipper, a Scroll & Eye nut dish, a Wild Rose handkerchief vase, a 6½" Beauty bell, and a 6½" Atlantis vase. Hand-painted Iridized Topaz Opalescent pieces included a 6½" jug, a 9½" vase, an 8" basket, and a 20" lamp with prisms. Numerous additional items were made in hand-painted Iridized Topaz Opalescent for QVC. Special items made for Russo were not iridized. These included the Jack-in-the-Pulpit vase made in the late 1980s, along with Daisy and Fern, Hobnail and Spiral Optic pieces, and numerous animal figures. Singleton Bailey received the Farmyard bowl, Farmyard plate and Poppy Show vase in Iridized Topaz Opalescent. The National Fenton Glass Society and the Fenton Art Glass Collectors of America both had Topaz Opalescent items made. The former chose a Rib Optic cruet with a black handle and black stopper, and the latter claimed a hand-painted Rib Optic egg. Iridized Alley Cats were sold to the collectors at their conventions.

Items produced from the 1930s through July 1941:	Value
Plate, #175-8" Leaf	$35.00 – 40.00
Plate, #175-11" Lea	$55.00 – 60.00

Items produced in 1942 and 1943	Value
Basket, #37-2½" flared, fan. oval, square	$130.00 – 160.00
Jug, #37-2" miniature handled	$120.00 – 140.00
Plate, #175-8" Leaf	$35.00 – 40.00
Plate, #175-11" Leaf	$55.00 – 60.00
Vase, #37-2" miniature flared, oval, square, triangle, tulip	$110.00 – 130.00
Vase, #38 miniature hand	$55.00 – 65.00

Item produced in 1960	Ware No.	Value
Ashtray, 9" Ogee	9178-TO	$100.00 – 125.00

Lily of the Valley (1980)	Ware No.	Value
Basket	8437-TO	$60.00 – 70.00
Bell	8265-TO	$65.00 – 75.00
Candleholder	8475-TO	$40.00 – 45.00
Candy box	8489-TO	$50.00 – 55.00
Candy box, ftd.	8484-TO	$125.00 – 145.00
Fairy light	8404-TO	$120.00 – 140.00
Rose bowl	8453-TO	$40.00 – 45.00
Vase, bud	8458-TO	$30.00 – 35.00
Vase, handkerchief	8450-TO	$40.00 – 50.00

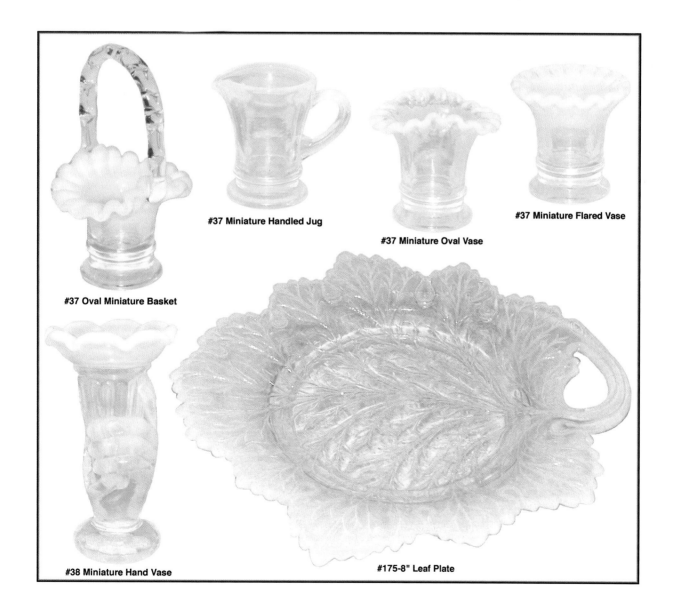

#37 Miniature Handled Jug

#37 Miniature Oval Vase

#37 Miniature Flared Vase

#37 Oval Miniature Basket

#38 Miniature Hand Vase

#175-8" Leaf Plate

Opalescent Collectibells

Fenton introduced an opalescent line of bells, called Collectibells, in January 1980. The moulds from which these bells were made were originally owned by the Red-Cliff Company of Chicago, Illinois. Red-Cliff was a distributor of dinnerware and accessory pieces. In many cases, Fenton and other companies made items for Red-Cliff from moulds that were owned by Red-Cliff. Fenton was making goblets and comports for Red-Cliff during the 1960s and 1970s. When the Red-Cliff Company ran into financial difficulties and discontinued business, Fenton acquired these moulds. Five different shapes of bells were made. Each style of bell was produced in four opalescent colors.

Collectibells	Color	Ware No.	Value
Grape	Blue Opalescent	9062 -BO	$35.00 – 40.00
Grape	Cameo Opalescent	9062-CO	$28.00 – 32.00
Grape	French Opalescent	9066-FO	$25.00 – 28.00
Grape	Topaz Opalescent	9062-TO	$40.00 – 45.00
Knobby Bull's Eye	Blue Opalescent	9061-BO	$35.00 – 40.00
Knobby Bull's Eye	Cameo Opalescent	9061-CO	$27.00 – 30.00
Knobby Bull's Eye	French Opalescent	9061-FO	$25.00 – 28.00
Knobby Bull's Eye	Topaz Opalescent	9061-TO	$40.00 – 45.00
Sable Arche	Blue Opalescent	9065-BO	$35.00 – 40.00
Sable Arche	Cameo Opalescent	9065-CO	$25.00 – 28.00
Sable Arche	French Opalescent	9065-FO	$22.00 – 25.00
Sable Arche	Topaz Opalescent	9065-TO	$35.00 – 40.00
Sydenham	Blue Opalescent	9063-BO	$35.00 – 40.00
Sydenham	Cameo Opalescent	9063-CO	$25.00 – 30.00
Sydenham	French Opalescent	9063-FO	$22.00 – 25.00
Sydenham	Topaz Opalescent	9063-TO	$35.00 – 40.00
Whitton	Blue Opalescent	9064-BO	$35.00 – 40.00
Whitton	Cameo Opalescent	9064-CO	$25.00 – 28.00
Whitton	French Opalescent	9064-FO	$22.00 – 25.00
Whitton	Topaz Opalescent	9064-TO	$35.00 – 40.00

9063 BO "Sydenham"

9062 BO "Grape"

9064 TO "Whitton"

9063 CO "Sydenham"

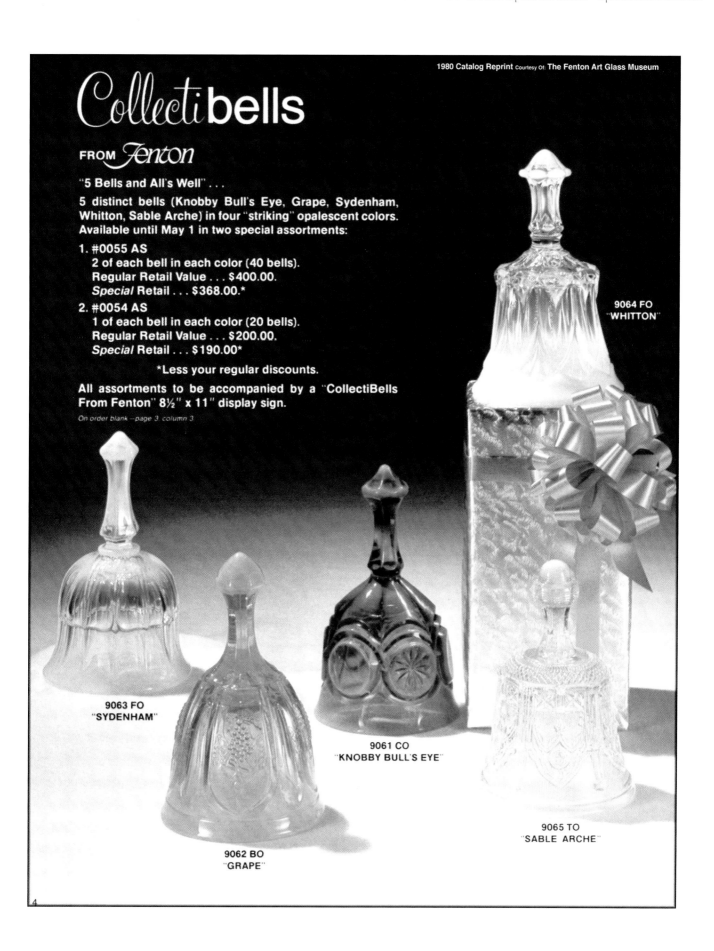

Collectibells

FROM Fenton

"5 Bells and All's Well"...

5 distinct bells (Knobby Bull's Eye, Grape, Sydenham, Whitton, Sable Arche) in four "striking" opalescent colors. Available until May 1 in two special assortments:

1. #0055 AS
   2 of each bell in each color (40 bells).
   Regular Retail Value . . . $400.00.
   Special Retail . . . $368.00.*

2. #0054 AS
   1 of each bell in each color (20 bells).
   Regular Retail Value . . . $200.00.
   Special Retail . . . $190.00*

           *Less your regular discounts.

All assortments to be accompanied by a "CollectiBells From Fenton" 8½" x 11" display sign.

On order blank—page 3. column 3.

9064 FO
"WHITTON"

9063 FO
"SYDENHAM"

9061 CO
"KNOBBY BULL'S EYE"

9065 TO
"SABLE ARCHE"

9062 BO
"GRAPE"

Opalescent Atomizers Made for DeVilbiss

The DeVilbiss Manufacturing Company of Toledo, Ohio, was founded in 1888 by Dr. Allen DeVilbiss, to produce a medical nose and throat sprayer that he had invented. When his son Thomas assumed control of the company in 1907, he began to incorporate the spray technology into fragrance bottles called "perfumizers." DeVilbiss decorated and applied spray parts to glass blanks produced by many of the leading glass houses in the world.

Fenton produced a number of opalescent atomizer parts for DeVilbiss during the 1940s and early 1950s, when bottles from Europe were impossible to obtain due to World War II and the following reconstruction period. These blanks were fitted with an atomizer and a squeeze ball and were sold under the DeVilbiss name. The finished atomizer was embellished with a gold or silver foil paper label that contained the DeVilbiss name, a model number, and a color number.

Atomizers were fashioned from cologne bottles utilizing moulds from the Fenton regular line and from moulds unique to DeVilbiss. DeVilbiss atomizers produced from Fenton moulds such as Hobnail, Coin Dot, and Spiral Optic, etc., are generally referred to by these Fenton pattern names. Atomizers that were produced from the exclusive DeVilbiss moulds were assigned shape or model numbers in the DeVilbiss catalogs. These atomizers have had various names attributed to them by collectors and authors. In the mid-1990s, collector Jackie Shirley, in collaboration with Frank Fenton, did a very detailed investigation of the Fenton relationship with the DeVilbiss company. In her articles published in the *Fenton Nor'wester*, she chose to use descriptive terms from the catalog captions to derive a pattern name. The pattern names of the atomizers appearing here conform to her suggestions. The hardware pictured with these atomizers is the same as the hardware shown in original DeVilbiss catalogs. In some instances, cords and balls may have been replaced.

The first bottles produced by Fenton for DeVilbiss were made during 1940 and 1941. This was followed by a gap from 1942 to 1946, an era when perfumizer production was prohibited due to the restrictions imposed during World War II. In 1947, when this prohibition was lifted, Fenton again began selling bottles to DeVilbiss. Fenton's last sales to DeVilbiss, bottles in the Swirled Feather pattern, were made during 1954.

The tall Green Opalescent spiral design perfumizer at the top left of the photo was dubbed "Tall Opalescent Spiral" by Mrs. Shirley. This bottle is known to exist in French Opalescent, Blue Opalescent, and Green Opalescent. Due to Fenton's switch in color during mid-1941 from Green Opalescent to Topaz Opalescent, there is a possibility this bottle may also be found in Topaz Opalescent.

The bottles at the top center have been named Gem. The DeVilbiss catalog description describes them as "a cologne atomizer with an opalescent gem design on transparent glass." The capacity of the bottle is 2½ oz. These bottles were produced in French Opalescent, Blue Opalescent, and Green Opalescent during 1941.

The Hobnail perfumizer was also in the DeVilbiss line in 1941. This 2¼ oz. bottle was produced in French Opalescent, Blue Opalescent, Green Opalescent, and Topaz Opalescent.

Two other items Fenton sold to DeVilbiss in 1941 were the 7 oz. ball-shaped Dot Optic and Spiral Optic pattern bottles. The Dot Optic bottle was made in French Opalescent, Blue Opalescent, Green Opalescent, and Topaz Opalescent. The ball-shaped Spiral Optic bottle has not yet been reported in Green Opalescent.

Also shown in the 1941 DeVilbiss catalog is a smaller, 2 oz. version of the ball-shaped Dot Optic bottle. This bottle was also made in the same four colors as the larger version.

The Blue Opalescent perfumizer shown at the bottom left of the photo was described as having "an opalescent pillow design on transparent glass" in the 1941 DeVilbiss catalog. This 7 oz. atomizer was listed in French Opalescent, Blue Opalescent, and Green Opalescent colors.

DeVilbiss Perfumizer	French Opal	Blue Opal	Green Opal	Topaz Opal
Tall Opalescent Spiral		$130.00 – 160.00	$160.00 – 180.00	$170.00 – 190.00
Gem	$25.00 – 30.00	$35.00 – 45.00	$35.00 – 45.00	
Hobnail	$25.00 – 35.00	$40.00 – 50.00	$80.00 – 90.00	$90.00 – 110.00
Dot Optic 7 oz.	$25.00 – 35.00	$50.00 – 55.00	$60.00 – 70.00	
Dot Optic 2 oz.	$25.00 – 35.00	$50.00 – 55.00	$60.00 – 70.00	
Spiral Optic 7 oz.	$35.00 – 40.00	$60.00 – 70.00		$80.00 – 90.00
Pillow	$45.00 – 55.00	$70.00 – 80.00	$75.00 – 85.00	

GEM
CS100-8 FO
CS100-9 BO
CS100-10 GO

HOBNAIL
CS100-5 FO
CS100-6 BO
CS100-7 GO
CS100-14 TO

TALL OPALESCENT SPIRAL
CS100-1 FO
CS100-2 BO
CS100-3 GO

DOT OPTIC 7 Oz.
CS150-102 FO
CS150-103 BO
CS150-105 GO

DOT OPTIC 2 Oz.
S150-107 FO
S150-108 BO
S150-109 GO

PILLOW
CS200-4 FO
CS200-5 BO
CS200-6 GO

BALL-SHAPED SPIRAL
CS200-10 FO
CS200-11 BO
CS200-12 TO

A large Cranberry Red with White Beads 7 oz. atomizer was listed in the 1941 DeVilbiss catalog. This color is better known to Fenton collectors as Cranberry Opalescent. The bottle is model No. CS-300 and has been dubbed "Pearls" by collectors.

An opalescent urn-shaped atomizer and dropper pair, commonly called Plume or Leaf by today's collectors, is also shown in the 1941 DeVilbiss catalog. These bottles were described in the catalog as having a "symmetrical urn shape" with an "opalescent leaf design." Both these pieces were made by Fenton. The capacity of both bottles was listed as 2 oz. The colors available were French Opalescent, Blue Opalescent, and Topaz Opalescent. The stopper for the perfume bottle was only made in French Opalescent. Upon the termination of its association with Fenton, DeVilbiss retained the rights to this stopper, since it had provided the funds for having the stopper mould produced.

Another early 1940s atomizer has become known as Scroll among collectors. This tall narrow bottle with scroll-like trim gracing the sides was produced in French Opalescent, Blue Opalescent, and Topaz Opalescent. Bottles of this style are possibly the most elusive of the all of the Fenton shapes produced for DeVilbiss.

The Horizontal Rib pattern perfumizer dates to the early 1940s. Examples have been found in Blue Opalescent, French Opalescent, and Topaz Opalescent. The DeVilbiss model number for this perfumizer was CS-125.

When production of atomizer bottles resumed after World War II, DeVilbiss once again turned to Fenton for a supply of bottles. The first pattern selected was from Fenton's popular Coin Dot line. The Tall Coin Dot model S-350-4 oz. atomizer blank was made in Blue Opalescent and French Opalescent colors for DeVilbiss in 1948.

A tall Spiral Optic perfumizer entered the DeVilbiss line in 1950. This Model S-500-3 oz. atomizer was offered in two colors. The catalog proclaimed these to be "an artistry in glass....with soft spirals of white flowing over a blue or ruby background." Thus, the catalog was describing the colors known to Fenton collectors as Blue Opalescent and Cranberry Opalescent. Notice the difference in shape of the body and the hardware differences between this bottle and the earlier Tall Opalescent Spiral bottle. These bottles remained in the DeVilbiss line through 1952.

New to the DeVilbiss line in 1952, was a three-piece Coin Dot set in Cranberry. The attractively packaged boxed set included an atomizer, an ashtray, and a puff box. The model number for the set was S-1500, and the set sold for $15.00. Notice that the ashtray was designed by crimping the bottom of the powder jar.

The last atomizer blank produced by Fenton for DeVilbiss was from the Swirled Feather pattern in 1954. This Model No. S-750 atomizer was produced in the satin opalescent colors from this era. These colors include blue satin, French Satin, green satin and Rose Satin. Mrs. Shirley found that DeVilbiss received a patent for the safety closure for this bottle in January 1954.

DeVilbiss Perfumizer	French Opal	Blue Opal	Topaz Opal	
Plume atomizer	$40.00 – 45.00	$55.00 – 65.00	$60.00 – 70.00	
Plume dropper				
Scroll	$65.00 – 75.00	$165.00 – 175.00	$185.00 – 200.00	
Horizontal Rib	$45.00 – 55.00	$65.00 – 75.00	$75.00 – 85.00	
Tall Coin Dot	$75.00 – 85.00	$125.00 – 140.00		
Spiral Optic		$125.00 – 150.00		

DeVilbiss Perfumizer	French Satin	Blue Satin	Green Satin	Rose Satin
Swirled Feather	$175.00 – 200.00	$250.00 – 275.00	$250.00 – 275.00	$250.00 – 300.00

DeVilbiss Perfumizer	Cranberry
Pearls	$160.00 – 180.00
Coin Dot Atomizer	$225.00 – 250.00
Coin Dot ashtray	$150.00 – 175.00
Coin Dot Puff Box	$140.00 – 160.00
Spiral Optic	$155.00 – 165.00

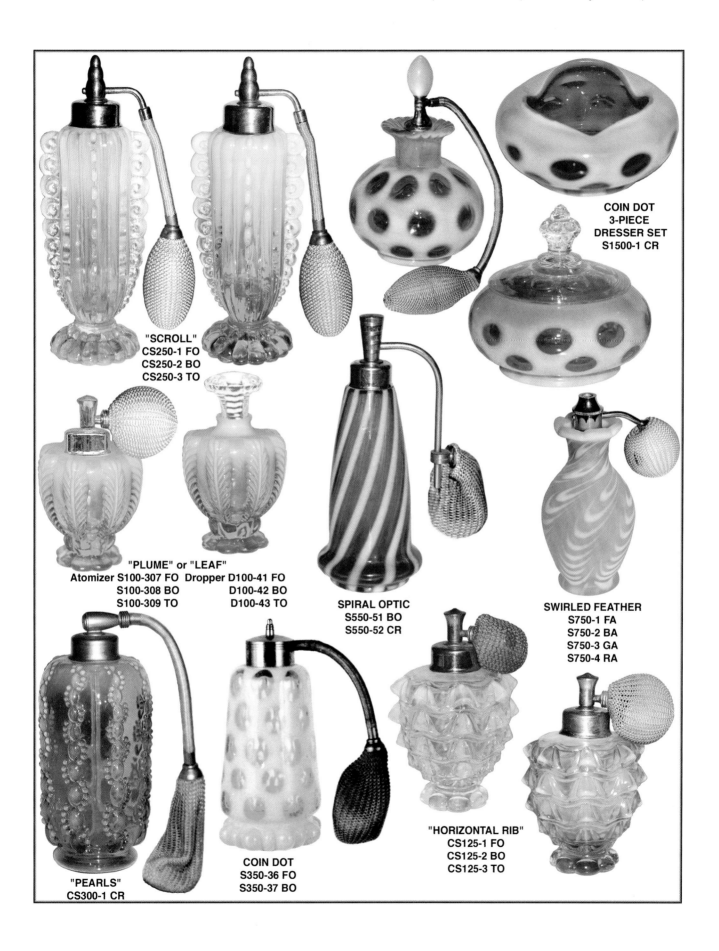

"SCROLL"
CS250-1 FO
CS250-2 BO
CS250-3 TO

**COIN DOT
3-PIECE
DRESSER SET
S1500-1 CR**

"PLUME" or "LEAF"
Atomizer S100-307 FO Dropper D100-41 FO
S100-308 BO   D100-42 BO
S100-309 TO   D100-43 TO

**SPIRAL OPTIC
S550-51 BO
S550-52 CR**

**SWIRLED FEATHER
S750-1 FA
S750-2 BA
S750-3 GA
S750-4 RA**

**"PEARLS"
CS300-1 CR**

**COIN DOT
S350-36 FO
S350-37 BO**

**"HORIZONTAL RIB"
CS125-1 FO
CS125-2 BO
CS125-3 TO**

Catalog Reprint Circa 1969
Courtesy Of:
The Fenton Art Glass Museum

8251 MI
Mandarin Vase

Empress Vase

8252 BK

8252 MI

8226 MI
Bowl (Hexagonal)

8251 BK
Mandarin Vase

Collectors' Group

The Collectors' Group represents a unique dimension in hand glass crafts-manship. Heavy bas-relief, exquisitely sculptured in cameo detail, endows these pieces with classic distinction.

9088 MI
Candy Box

WILD STRAWBERRIES . . . A delightful new pattern. The first of a group of coordinated pieces being developed by our designer. We would appreciate your customer's response.

46

9023 MI
Flared Lattice Bowl

5116 MI
8" Leaf Plate

5118 MI
11" Leaf Plate

Fenton's Non-Transparent Colors

This chapter includes opaque and translucent glassware produced by Fenton. During the 1930s, Fenton produced milk glass and other colors of opaque glassware for patterns such as Dancing Ladies, Lincoln Inn, Georgian, and others. Much of the glass production during the 1940s was opalescent glassware. Another large segment of glassware production consisted of Crest shapes with a milk glass base and a spun colored or crystal trim. Major opalescent patterns and Crest patterns are discussed in the book *Fenton Art Glass Patterns 1939 – 1980*.

During the early 1950s, milk glass Hobnail became a smashing success. As a result, numerous accessory items were produced in that color to accompany the extensive line of tableware. Cigarette sets, hen-on-the-nest boxes, and small animal figures were popular. During the mid-1950s, the pastel colors of blue, green, and rose entered the line. A multitude of satin colors ushered in the 1970s. Pieces in Burmese, Custard Satin, blue satin, Lime Sherbet, and white satin were in production for most of the decade. Several of Fenton's Collector Series limited edition plates were made in blue satin and white satin. Rose Satin and Lavender Satin enjoyed a more limited production during this era.

Sometimes moulds are modified and an item with a similar appearance will come back into the line. For example , the No. 5180 owl decision maker (shown in the catalog reprint below) entered the line in January 1969 in milk glass and Black. The owl remained in the line through the 1972 catalog year. The owl was also sampled in Jonquil Yellow and Pekin Blue II, but the decision was made not to place these colors in production, and the ones that were made were sold through the Fenton Gift Shop. Later, this mould was retooled and the result was the No. 5108 owl fairy light. This piece entered the line in January 1973 in Custard Satin and Lime Sherbet. Later, the owl fairy light was also made in blue satin, Rosalene, Lavender Satin, and Crystal Velvet.

WISE OWL DECISION MAKERS . . . Your customer can't make up her mind? Keep a Decision Maker on your counter. You'll not only help her decide but also sell her one of these winsome little creatures. The Owl is a great gift idea for men — perfect for a desk top conversation piece and, it is designed to hold paper clips, a roll of stamps, etc.

NESTING CHICKENS . . . Hens on the Nest are among the oldest and most popular Milk Glass items ever sold. They are a staple which no Milk Glass selection can afford to be without.

Catalog Reprint Circa 1969 Courtesy Of: The Fenton Art Glass Museum

Black

Fenton's inventory records indicate Fenton first produced black glass about 1911. Various sizes of bases were made for bowls and vases through the 1920s. Production of bowls, vases, and candles encompassed most of the 1920s through the early 1930s. Later, in the 1930s, patterns such as Georgian and Lincoln Inn were made in black.

In 1953, the Happiness bird figure and the fish vase were made in black. The black fish vase was trimmed with a white tail, eyes, and fins. In the late 1960s, Northwood's Old Tobacco Jar mould was used by Fenton to produce a candy jar in black. During this same period the Mandarin and Empress vases were made from old Verly's moulds.

Fenton's first hand-decorated Ebony line, White Daisies on Thumbprint, debuted in 1972. Later, in 1981, an eight-piece Silver Poppies on Ebony assortment was offered in both the general line and through JCPenney. In 1982, several hand-carved pieces were made in Ebony. Later, from 1989 through 1992, another hand-decorated pattern, Copper Rose, was made. Another black hand-decorated pattern, Victorian Bouquet, was in the line during 1995.

Black	Ware No.	Introduced	Discontinued	Value
Bird figure	5197-BK	1953	1955	$45.00 – 55.00
Boy and girl, praying	5100-BK	1973	1974	$45.00 – 55.00
Candy jar, 7¼"				
Grape and Cable	9188-BK	July 1968	1970	$220.00 – 250.00
Owl decision maker	5180-BK	1969	July 1972	$35.00 – 40.00
Toothpick, Paneled Daisy	8924-BK			$20.00 – 25.00
Vase, Empress	8252-BK	July 1968	1970	$90.00 – 120.00
Vase, 7" fish	5156-MK	1953	1954	$650.00 – 800.00
Vase, Mandarin	8251-BK	July 1968	1970	$110.00 – 135.00

9188 BK Grape and Cable Candy Jar

5156 MK Fish Vase

5197 BK Bird Figure

8251 BK Mandarin Vase

8294 BK Paneled Daisy Toothpick

5180 BK Owl Decision Maker

8252 BK Empress Vase

5100 BK Boy & Girl Praying

Blue Marble

Blue Marble, a light blue opaque glass accented with opal swirls, entered the Fenton line in 1970. Patterns such as Hobnail and Rose were made in this color in the early part of the decade. The three decorative accessories listed below were also made during the same period. This original issue of Blue Marble was discontinued at the end of 1973.

In early 1989, several items were sold through the Fenton Gift Shop. The blue color of this issue is darker than the 1970s color. Items we have seen that were included in the sale were the No. 3834 Hobnail basket, No. 3674 Hobnail candleholder, No. 3303 Hobnail pitcher and bowl set, No. 9188 Grape and Cable candy jar and the No. 5228 doll figure.

Black	Ware No.	Introduced	Discontinued	Value
Candy Jar, 7¼"				
Grape and Cable	9188-MB	1971	1972	$215.00 – 235.00
Hen on nest, large	5182-MB	1971	1973	$85.00 – 100.00
Hen on nest, small	5186-MB	1971	1973	$45.00 – 55.00

5186 MB
Small Hen on Nest

9188 MB Grape & Cable Candy Jar

5182 MB Large Hen on Nest

Blue Pastel

Fenton's Blue Pastel was a pale blue opaque color that was produced in the mid-1950s. The color was introduced in 1954 and was used primarily with pieces in the Hobnail and Lacy Edge shapes. Blue Pastel was discontinued at the end of 1954. This short production period virtually assures collectors that items in this color must be scarce. One very hard-to-find item in Blue Pastel is the No. 7302 bathroom set. The set consists of three square bottles with stoppers, and a rectangular tab-handled tray. It was only listed in the catalog for six months. This set was continued in milk and Green Pastel in 1955. Notice the boudoir lamp, which Fenton called a fairy light when it was first listed, was sold in two different styles — as a candle lamp and electrified.

For more information on items in Blue Pastel, see the Hobnail, Daisy & Button, Lamb's Tongue, and Swirl patterns in the book *Fenton Art Glass Patterns 1939 – 1980*.

Blue Pastel	Ware No.	Introduced	Discontinued	Value
Bathroom set	7302-BP	July 1954	1955	$225.00 – 250.00
Cake plate, ftd.	3513-BP	1954	1955	$45.00 – 55.00
Comport, ftd.	7228-BP	1954	1955	$45.00 – 55.00
Hen on basket	5183-BP	1954	1955	$75.00 – 85.00
Lamp, boudoir (candle)	7390-BP	1954	1955	$95.00 – 125.00
Lamp, boudoir (electric)	7392-BP	1954	1955	$95.00 – 125.00
Vase, 6"	7353-BP	July 1954	1955	$35.00 – 45.00
Vase, 6" bud	7348-BP	July 1954	1955	$35.00 – 45.00
Vase, 6½" bud	7349-BP	July 1954	1955	$35.00 – 45.00

Blue Pastel Lacy Edge	Ware No.	Introduced	Discontinued	Value
Bowl, 8" "C"	9026-BP	1954	1955	$20.00 – 25.00
Comport	9028-BP	1954	1955	$40.00 – 50.00
Comport, ftd.	9029-BP	1954	1955	$40.00 – 50.00
Planter, 9" "C" plate	9099-BP	1954	1955	$20.00 – 25.00
Plate, 11"	9011-BP	1954	1955	$20.00 – 25.00
Plate, 9" "C"	9019-BP	1954	1955	$18.00 – 22.00
Plate, #360-8"	9018-BP	1954	1955	$12.00 – 14.00

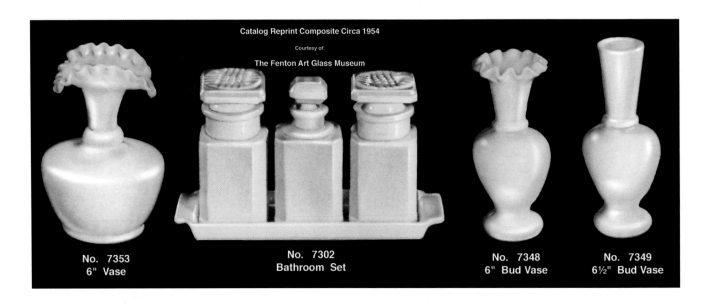

Catalog Reprint Composite Circa 1954

Courtesy of:

The Fenton Art Glass Museum

No. 7353
6" Vase

No. 7302
Bathroom Set

No. 7348
6" Bud Vase

No. 7349
6½" Bud Vase

3513 BP Footed Cake Plate

9028 BP Comport

9019 BP C Plate

9011 BP 11" Plate

7228 BP Footed Comport

5183 BP Hen on Basket

9025 BP 8" Scroll & Eye Bowl

9026 BP 8" C Bowl

**7390 BP Boudoir
Candle Light**

9018 BP 8" Plate

Blue Satin

Fenton has used the *blue satin* designation and the same *BA* color code twice since 1950. An early version of blue satin was made from 1952 to 1954. The only pattern made in this color that had a significant number of pieces was Swirled Feather. For more information on this swirled opalescent blue satin pattern see *Fenton Art Glass Patterns 1939 – 1980*. Other items made during this era included the No. 71-10" shell bowl, the No. 1357-7½" vase, and the No. 1352-8½" Bubble Optic vase.

A medium opaque blue satin color Fenton called blue satin, which used the same color code as the earlier version, appeared in the Fenton line in January 1971. The first item offered was the Happiness Bird. The first of the annual Christmas plates was also produced in this color in July 1971. By January 1972, other small figural items, such as the butterfly, the praying boy and girl, the fish paperweight, and the donkey with the cart, were added to the line in this color. These items proved to sell well and numerous larger pieces were added over the next few years. Blue satin was discontinued at the end of 1984. The No. 7458-11" vase shown in the last photo was not in the regular line in blue satin.

Blue Satin	Ware No.	Introduced	Discontinued	Value
Bowl, #71-10" shell		1952	July 1952	$110.00 – 125.00
Vase, 7½"	1357-BA	July 1952		$40.00 – 50.00
Vase, 8½" Bubble Optic	1352-BA	July 1952		$60.00 – 70.00

Blue Satin	Ware No.	Introduced	Discontinued	Value
Ashtray/Chip 'n Dip/Candle bowl	8478-BA	1975	1977	$30.00 – 40.00
Basket, 3-toed Grape	8438-BA	1978	1980+	$35.00 – 40.00
Basket, 8" Persian Medallion	8238-BA	1973	1978	$45.00 – 55.00
Basket, 7" deep Poppy	9138-BA	1974	1980	$60.00 – 70.00
Basket, 7" Water Lily	8434-BA	1977	1980+	$45.00 – 55.00
Bell, Bride and Groom	9168-BA	1977	1979	$30.00 – 35.00
Bell, Daisy & Button	1966-BA	1973	1980+	$25.00 – 35.00
Bell, Madonna	9467-BA	1975	1980+	$30.00 – 35.00
Bird, Happiness	5197-BA	1971	1980+	$30.00 – 35.00
Bird, small	5163-BA	1978	1980+	$28.00 – 32.00
Bonbon, handled Butterfly	8230-BA	1973	1980	$22.00 – 25.00
Boot, Daisy & Button	1990-BA	1973	1977	$20.00 – 22.00
Bowl, Basket Weave	8222-BA	1974	1980+	$22.00 – 27.00
Bowl, Curtain	8454-BA	1978	1980	$32.00 – 37.00

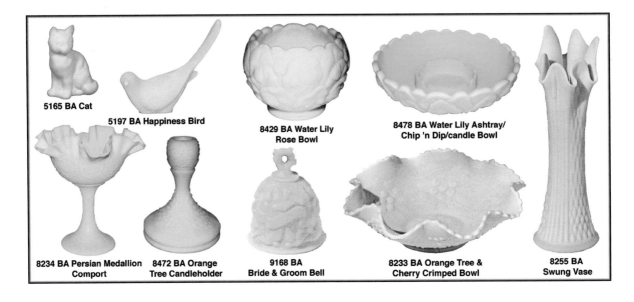

5165 BA Cat

5197 BA Happiness Bird

8429 BA Water Lily Rose Bowl

8478 BA Water Lily Ashtray/ Chip 'n Dip/candle Bowl

8234 BA Persian Medallion Comport

8472 BA Orange Tree Candleholder

9168 BA Bride & Groom Bell

8233 BA Orange Tree & Cherry Crimped Bowl

8255 BA Swung Vase

Blue Satin

Blue Satin is "the compatible color" with all decorator shades. A reproduction of a famous glass treatment that originated about 1880. Each piece is formed by hand and then satinized to give the softness in pattern and subtle colors that blend comfortably with today's homes.

AUTHENTIC
Fenton
HANDMADE

9405 BA
21" POPPY STUDENT LAMP
Antique Brass Finish
Shipping Wgt. —9¾ lbs.

9403 BA
22" OFFSET COLONIAL LAMP
Pewter Finish
Shipping Wgt. —10½ lbs.

8456 BA
WATER LILY BUD VASE

9388 BA
BAROQUE CANDY BOX

8457 BA
3 TOED GRAPE VASE

8454 BA
CURTAIN BOWL

8438 BA
3 TOED GRAPE BASKET

5163 BA
SMALL BIRD

5162 BA
BUNNY

5161 BA
SWAN

Catalog Reprint Circa 1978   Courtesy Of: The Fenton Art Glass Museum

61

Blue Satin	Ware No.	Introduced	Discontinued	Value
Bowl, 3-toed Leaf & Orange Tree	8223-BA	1973	1978	$37.00 – 42.00
Bowl, crimped Orange Tree & Cherry	8233-BA	1973	1977	$40.00 – 45.00
Bowl, cupped Orange Tree & Cherry	8232-BA	1973	1977	$40.00 – 45.00
Bowl, 8" Persian Medallion	8224-BA	1973	1976	$40.00 – 45.00
Bowl, 3-toed Water Lily	8426-BA	1977	1978	$40.00 – 45.00
Bowl, 9" Water Lily	8424-BA	1975	1980+	$40.00 – 45.00
Boy and girl, praying	5100-BA	1972	1980+	$25.00 – 28.00
Bunny	5162-BA	1978	1980+	$37.00 – 42.00
Butterfly	5170-BA	1972	1973	$45.00 – 55.00
Butterfly on Stand	5171-BA	1979	1980+	$30.00 – 35.00
Candleholder, 6" Orange Tree	8472-BA	1974	1976	$20.00 – 25.00
Candleholder, Water Lily	8473-BA	1975	1980	$18.00 – 22.00
Candy box, Baroque	9388-BA	1978	1980+	$45.00 – 55.00
Candy box, Hobnail	3984-BA	1974	1976	$60.00 – 80.00
Candy box, Paneled Daisy	9185-BA	1973	1976	$40.00 – 50.00
Candy box, ftd. Water Lily	8480-BA	1974	1980	$50.00 – 60.00
Candy Jar, 7¼" Grape & Cable	9188-BA	1974	1975	$225.00 – 250.00
Candy jar, ftd. W. Strawberry	9088-BA	1973	1976	$60.00 – 70.00
Cart	5124-BA	1972	1973	$150.00 – 175.00
Cat, sitting	5165-BA	1979	1980+	$45.00 – 55.00
Comport, ftd. flowered	8422-BA	1977	1978	$27.00 – 32.00
Comport, handled fruit	8242-BA	1973	1976	$25.00 – 30.00
Comport, Jefferson	8476-BA	1974	July 1974	$500.00 – 600.00
Comport, Persian Medallion	8234-BA	1973	1980+	$25.00 – 30.00
Comport. Pinwheel	8227-BA	1973	1978	$30.00 – 35.00
Comport, oval Pinwheel	8427-BA	1974	1976	$30.00 – 35.00
Comport, Rose	9222-BA	1974	1977	$20.00 – 22.00
Comport, Water Lily	8431-BA	1977	1978	$27.00 – 32.00
Comport, ftd. Water Lily	8481-BA	1975	1977	$27.00 – 32.00
Donkey	5125-BA	1972	1973	$150.00 – 175.00
Elephant	5123-BA	1972	July 1972	$250.00 – 300.00
Fairy light, Hobnail	3608-BA	1978	1981	$30.00 – 35.00
Fairy light, owl	5108-BA	1975	1980+	$30.00 – 35.00
Fairy light, Persian Medallion	8408-BA	1975	1980+	$55.00 – 65.00
Frog	5166-BA	1979	1980+	$50.00 – 60.00
Hen on nest, small	5186-BA	1974	1976	$55.00 – 65.00
Jardiniere, Water Lily	8498-BA	1975	1978	$30.00 – 35.00
Lamp, 19" Poppy student	9100-BA	1975	1978	$395.00 – 425.00
Lamp, 20" Poppy student	9107-BA	1973	1980+	$225.00 – 245.00
Lamp, 21" Poppy student	9405-BA	1978	1979	$225.00 – 245.00
Lamp, 22" off-set Colonial	9403-BA	1978	1979	$280.00 – 300.00
Lamp, 24" Poppy GWTW	9101-BA	1974	1980+	$275.00 – 300.00
Paperweight, fish	5193-BA	1972	1973	$45.00 – 55.00
Pitcher, 36 oz. Water Lily	8464-BA	1976	1980	$40.00 – 45.00

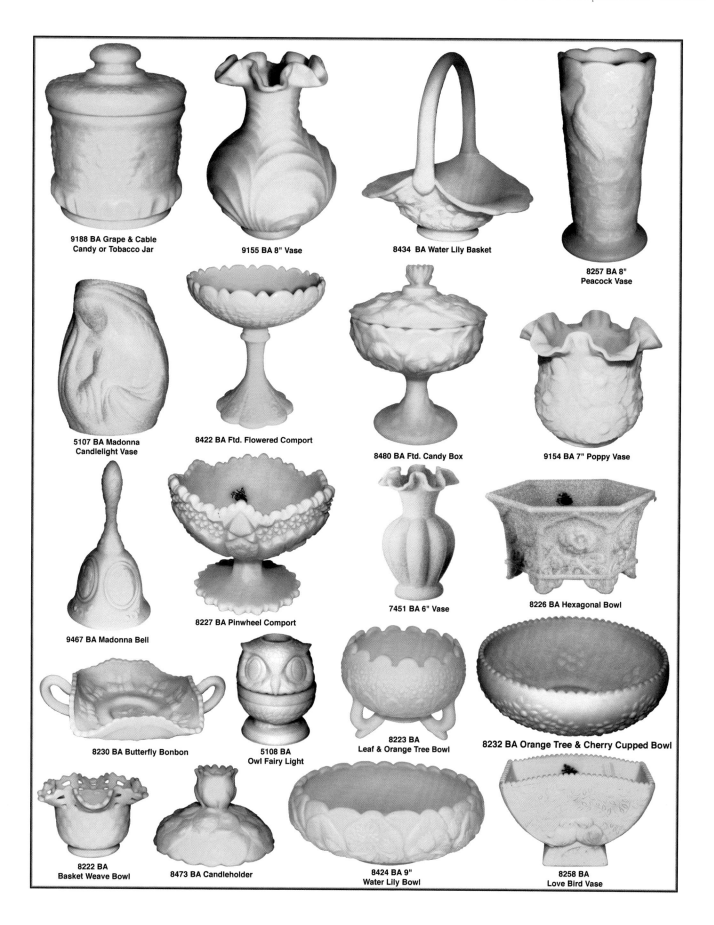

9188 BA Grape & Cable
Candy or Tobacco Jar

9155 BA 8" Vase

8434 BA Water Lily Basket

8257 BA 8"
Peacock Vase

5107 BA Madonna
Candlelight Vase

8422 BA Ftd. Flowered Comport

8480 BA Ftd. Candy Box

9154 BA 7" Poppy Vase

9467 BA Madonna Bell

8227 BA Pinwheel Comport

7451 BA 6" Vase

8226 BA Hexagonal Bowl

8230 BA Butterfly Bonbon

5108 BA
Owl Fairy Light

8223 BA
Leaf & Orange Tree Bowl

8232 BA Orange Tree & Cherry Cupped Bowl

8222 BA
Basket Weave Bowl

8473 BA Candleholder

8424 BA 9"
Water Lily Bowl

8258 BA
Love Bird Vase

Blue Satin	Ware No.	Introduced	Discontinued	Value
Planter bowl, Verly's hexagonal	8226-BA	1974	1979	$45.00 – 55.00
Prayer light, Madonna	5107-BA	July, 1978	1980+	$35.00 – 40.00
Rose bowl, Poppy	9126-BA	1977	1978	$25.00 – 30.00
Rose bowl, Water Lily	8429-BA	1977	1980	$25.00 – 30.00
Swan	5161-BA	1978	1980+	$25.00 – 30.00
Toothpick, Paneled Daisy	8294-BA	1973	1976	$18.00 – 20.00
Vase, 3-toed Grape	8457-BA	1978	1980	$25.00 – 30.00
Vase, 6"	7451-BA	1974	1980+	$25.00 – 30.00
Vase, Love Bird	8258-BA	1974	1976	$40.00 – 45.00
Vase, 7" Poppy	9154-BA	1974	1980	$40.00 – 45.00
Vase, 8"	9155-BA	1974	1980+	$27.00 – 32.00
Vase, 8" Peacock	8257-BA	1973	1977	$40.00 – 45.00
Vase, swung	8255-BA	1973	1976	$40.00 – 50.00
Vase, Water Lily bud	8456-BA	1978	1980+	$25.00 – 27.00

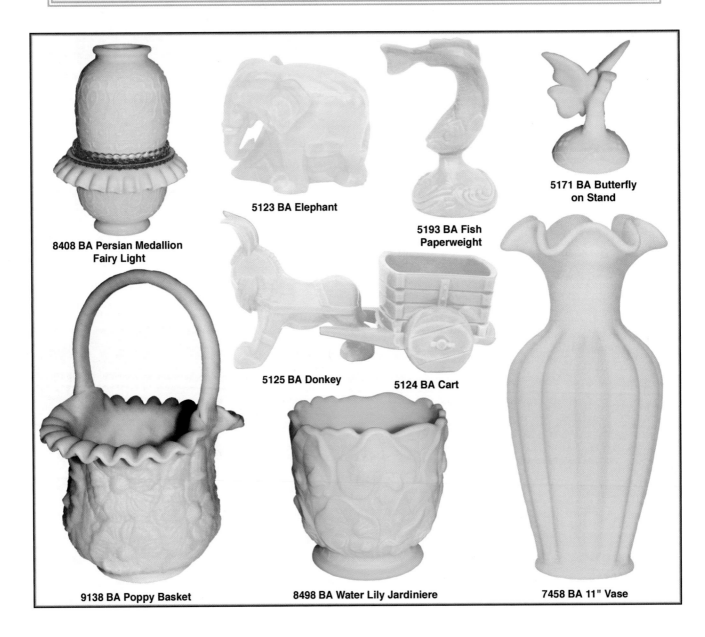

8408 BA Persian Medallion
Fairy Light

5123 BA Elephant

5193 BA Fish
Paperweight

5171 BA Butterfly
on Stand

5125 BA Donkey

5124 BA Cart

9138 BA Poppy Basket

8498 BA Water Lily Jardiniere

7458 BA 11" Vase

Blue Satin Christmas Series Collector Plates

The Christmas in America collection of 12 different plates was available in the catalog supplements from July through December each year from 1970 through 1981. This series was designed by Tony Rosena, and each plate commemorated a historic American church. The first plate was only in the regular line in Fenton's Carnival color. Starting in 1971, each plate in the series was made in blue satin, Carnival, and white satin. Moulds for the plates were destroyed at the end of December each year.

Christmas Plate	Ware No.	Subject	Value
1971 Plate	8271-BA	"The Old Brick Church," Isle of Wright County, Virginia	$12.00 – 14.00
1972 Plate	8272-BA	"The Two Horned Church," Marietta, Ohio	$12.00 – 14.00
1973 Plate	8273-BA	"St. Mary's in the Mountains," Virginia City, Nevada	$12.00 – 14.00
1974 Plate	8274-BA	"The Nation's Church," Philadelphia, Pa.	$12.00 – 14.00
1975 Plate	8275-BA	"Birthplace of Liberty," Richmond, Virginia	$12.00 – 14.00
1976 Plate	8276-BA	"The Old North Church," Boston, Mass.	$12.00 – 14.00
1977 Plate	8277-BA	"San Carlos Borromeo De Carmelo," Carmel, Calif.	$12.00 – 14.00
1978 Plate	8278-BA	"The Church of the Holy Trinity," Philadelphia, Pa.	$12.00 – 14.00
1979 Plate	8279-BA	"San Jose y Miguel De Aguayo," San Antonio, Texas	$12.00 – 14.00
1980 Plate	8280-BA	"Christ Church," Alexandria, Virginia	$12.00 – 14.00
1981 Plate	8281-BA	"Mission of San Xavier Del Bac," Tucson, Arizona	$12.00 – 14.00

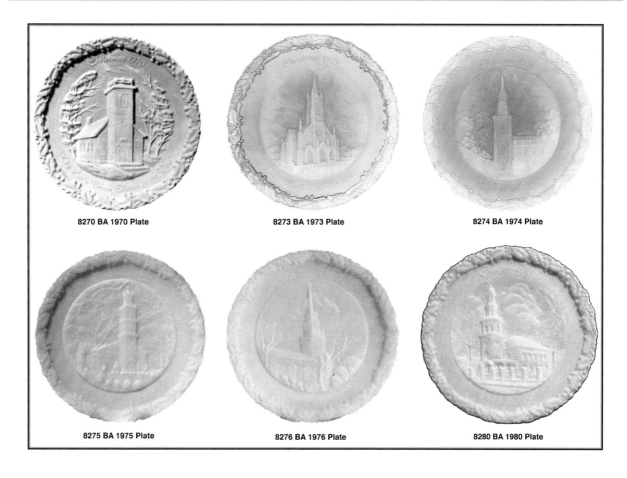

8270 BA 1970 Plate   8273 BA 1973 Plate   8274 BA 1974 Plate

8275 BA 1975 Plate   8276 BA 1976 Plate   8280 BA 1980 Plate

Blue Satin Mother's Day Series Collector Plates

The Madonna Mother's Day series of plates was designed by Tony Rosena and first appeared in 1971. The final plate in this series was issued in 1979. Each year, plates could be ordered from the January catalog supplement. Moulds for each plate were destroyed at the end of June each year. Each plate was also sold in Carnival and white satin and came with a hand-finished wooden holder.

Mother's Day Plate	Ware No.	Subject	Value
1971 Plate	9316-BA	"Madonna with the Sleeping Child"	$12.00 – 14.00
1972 Plate	9317-BA	"Madonna of the Goldfinch"	$12.00 – 14.00
1973 Plate	9318-BA	"The Small Cowpen Madonna"	$12.00 – 14.00
1974 Plate	9319-BA	"Madonna of the Grotto"	$12.00 – 14.00
1975 Plate	9375-BA	"Taddei Madonna"	$12.00 – 14.00
1976 Plate	9376-BA	"The Holy Night"	$12.00 – 14.00
1977 Plate	9377-BA	"Madonna and Child with Pomegranate"	$12.00 – 14.00
1978 Plate	9378-BA	"The Madonnina"	$12.00 – 14.00
1979 Plate	9379-BA	"Madonna of the Rose Hedge"	$12.00 – 14.00

9377 BA 1977 Plate

9318 BA 1973 Plate

9319 BA 1974 Plate

9376 BA 1976 Plate

9375 BA 1975 Plate

Blue Satin Women's Clubs Collector Plates

The General Federation of Women"s Clubs of America commissioned Fenton to produce a series of four annual commemorative plates leading up to the Bicentennial of the United States. The series originated in 1973 and ended in 1976. The plates were made in blue satin and white satin.

Bicentennial Plate	Subject	Value
1973 Plate No. 1	"Give me liberty or give me death"	$14.00 – 16.00
1974 Plate No. 2	"Life, liberty and the pursuit of happiness"	$14.00 – 16.00
1975 Plate No. 3	"In God we trust"	$14.00 – 16.00
1976 Plate No. 4	"Proclaim liberty throughout all the land"	$14.00 – 16.00

Plate No. 1

Plate No. 2

Plate No. 3

Plate No. 4

Burmese

Burmese is a custard-colored glass with a pink blush. The Burmese color is produced by reheating in a manner the glassworkers call "striking the gold." Each piece is formed, stretched and crimped, and bent into shape by hand. Then the glass is reheated. The pure gold in the glass causes the uranium-based yellow to strike pink. Thus, the reheated portion changes from a creamy yellow to a pink blush. The formula and art of production of this glass was developed by Frederick Shirley of the Mt. Washington Glass Company in 1885. However, the cost of production of this type of glassware led the company to discontinue this color in 1900.

The formula and technique for producing this color was lost over the years. Fenton chemist Charles Goe was intrigued with Burmese and spent many years struggling to perfect the formula. Finally, he achieved success in late 1969. Six items of Burmese entered the Fenton line in 1970. All these pieces were offered with a leaf decal decoration also. Burmese was a tremendous success with the public, and eight additional shapes were added in January, 1971. In addition, twenty decorated pieces were available in the line at this time. The first decorations consisted of two patterns — one with a leaf decal and another with hand-painted roses. In 1974, six shapes were hand painted with a tree scene. These original patterns were phased out by the end of the decade, and lamps were the only items continuing into the 1980s.

In 1981, an assortment of 14 pieces was introduced with a hand-painted Pink Dogwood decoration. The collection consisted of the following pieces:

Basket, 5"	7235-PD	Vase 4½"	7546-PD
Basket, 7½"	7535-PD	Vase, 5"	7442-PD
Fairy light, 3-pc.	7501-PD	Vase, 5½"	7547-PD
Lamp, 20" Column	9301-PD	Vase, 6½"	7560-PD
Lamp, 23½" Rochester student	7503-PD	Vase, ½" tulip	7552-PD
Lamp, hanging swag	7506-PD	Vase, 7½"	7559-PD
Vase, bud	7558-PD	Vase, 10" tulip	7255-PD

A special limited edition six-piece set was produced for Cherished Editions of Brownville, New York, in 1982. According to original ads, the hand-painted decoration was inspired by Mary Walrath and consisted of "an arrangement of lilies of the valley, forget-me-nots, one rose and a rosebud." The issue was limited to not more than 500 of each piece as follows:

Basket, 5"	7235-WQ	Vase, 6" bud	7558-WQ
Rose bowl, 4½"	7424-WQ	Vase, 6½" Jack-in-the-Pulpit	7552-WQ
Vase, 4½"	7546-WQ	Vase, 10" Jack-in-the-Pulpit	7255-WQ

The June 1983 supplement featured two Burmese pieces as a part of the Connoisseur Collection. Previously this color had been limited to blown items. The bell and epergne were the first pressed items to be produced in this color. The bell was limited to 2000 pieces and the epergne set was a limited edition of only 500.

Bell, hand-painted Rose	7562-UF	Epergne	7605-BR

More pressed items in Burmese were offered in the 1986 catalog. A hand-painted bell was limited to 2500 pieces and the rest of the undecorated assortment was limited to production in 1986. Items included:

Basket, Butterfly & Berry	9234-BR	Dish, oval	9125-BR
Bear cub/wood base	5151-BR	Epergne, Diamond Lace	4809-BR
Bell, 6½"	7666-EB	Fairy light, Persian Medallion	8408-BR
Bell, Whitton	9066-BR	Fawn/wood base	5160-BR
Bowl, Orange Tree & Cherry	8289-BR	Slipper, Daisy & Button	1995-BR
Candy, Paneled daisey	9185-BR	Toothpick, Paneled Daisy	8294-BR
Comport, Persian Medallion	8234-BR	Vase, 8" Peacock	8257-BR

A hand-painted bell and Mariner's lamp with a marine life Shells decoration were included in the 1987 Connoisseur Collection. The bell, 7666-6½" SB, was limited to 2500; the Mariner's lamp was 7400 SB and was limited in production to 500 pieces.

In the June 1990 supplement, Burmese was offered as part of Fenton's 85th Anniversary Celebration. Four different hand-painted patterns were available — Petite Floral (QJ), Trees Scene (QD), Rose Burmese (RB), and Raspberry

Burmese (QH). These pieces are all marked with the notation, "Fenton — 85th Anniversary." Sales were limited to May through November, and items that were made include:

Basket, 5½"	7732-QD	Lamp, 21" student	7412-QH
Basket, 7"	7731-QH	Vase, 6½"	7791-RB
Cruet and stopper, 7"	7701-QJ	Vase, 9"	7792-QD
Epergne, 9½" 2-pc.	7202-QJ	Vase, 6" fan	7790-RB
Lamp, 20" Classic	9308-RB	Water set, 7-pc.	7700-QH

The 1991 offering featured two items in the Connoisseur Collection. Included were the 6701 RB-20" Rose Burmese Paisley lamp that was limited to 500 pieces and the 7252 QH-7½" Raspberry Burmese vase limited to 1500 pieces.

A hand-panted 10" pitcher was part of the 1994 Limited Edition Collectibles series. The 2729 JI pitcher had a Lattice Rose decoration and was limited in production to 750.

Five hand-decorated Burmese pieces were a part of the 1995, 90th Anniversary Historical Collection. Artists Martha Reynolds and Frances Burton created unique designs for this series. The following pieces were made:

1. Butterfly basket, 2932 UL-8" designed by Martha Reynolds and limited to 790
2. Vintage border bowl and base, 2909 UK-10¼" designed by Martha Reynolds and limited to 790
3. Daybreak Pillar lamp, 7502 UQ-33" designed by Frances Burton and limited to 300
4. Cherry Blossom pitcher, 2968 UN-10" designed by Martha Reynolds and limited to 790
5. Hummingbird vase, 2955 UU-9" designed by Martha Reynolds and limited to 790.

In 1997, production of Burmese continued with the 5141 BG doll figure (limited to 2000) and the 2905 BG vanity set (limited to 2000). Several new special pieces of decorated Burmese appeared with the advent of the new Millennium. The Centennial Collection included a 9" vase with a "lilac bud accented summer bouquet" design created by Frances Burton and signed by Bill Fenton. Production of this piece was limited to sales through November 15, 2000. The Connoisseur Collection contained a Daisy on Burmese ginger jar and a Rose Bed on Burmese 8½" ewer. Both were limited in production to 2750.

Numerous pieces of plain and decorated Burmese were also made for special order customers. Many hand-painted and specially decorated Burmese items were also made for QVC. One of the largest lines for this outlet was floral-decorated Diamond Optic Burmese.

Other colors of Burmese such as Blue Burmese and Lotus Mist Burmese have also been produced in recent years. See the Hand Painted section of this book for more information about decorated Burmese.

7461 BR Pitcher

9055 BR 5" Ribbed Vase

7424 BR Rose Bowl

Burmese	Ware No.	Introduced	Discontinued	Value
Basket	7437-BR	1970	1973	$50.00 – 60.00
Bowl, 8"	7422-BR	1970	July 1972	$55.00 – 65.00
Cruet vase	7462-BR	1971	1972	$70.00 – 80.00
Fairy light	7392-BR	1970	1972	$120.00 – 135.00
Fairy light, 2 pc.	7492-BR	1971	July 1972	$45.00 – 55.00
Lamp, 24" GWTW	9101-BR	1976	1978	$340.00 – 375.00
Lamp, 29" Rose GWTW	9200-BR	1976	1980+	$550.00 – 650.00
Lamp, 37" GWTW	9202-BR	1971	1976	$600.00 – 750.00
Lamp, 38" Pillar	9201-BR	1971	1980+	$550.00 – 650.00
Pitcher	7461-BR	1970	1972	$40.00 – 45.00
Rose bowl	7424-BR	1970	1972	$30.00 – 35.00
Vase, 5" ribbed	9055-BR	1971	1973	$40.00 – 50.00
Vase, 7"	7252-BR	1970	July 1972	$70.00 – 80.00
Vase, 7"	7253-BR	1971	1972	$70.00 – 80.00
Vase, 7½" Empress	8252-BR	1977	1978	$180.00 – 200.00
Vase, 9" Mandarin	8251-BR	1977	1978	$190.00 – 210.00
Vase, 7" pinch	7359-BR	1971	July 1972	$50.00 – 60.00

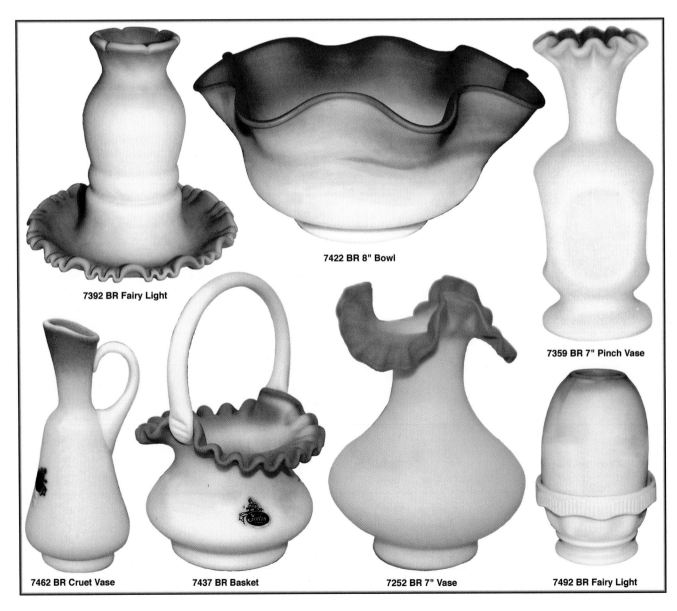

7392 BR Fairy Light

7422 BR 8" Bowl

7359 BR 7" Pinch Vase

7462 BR Cruet Vase   7437 BR Basket   7252 BR 7" Vase   7492 BR Fairy Light

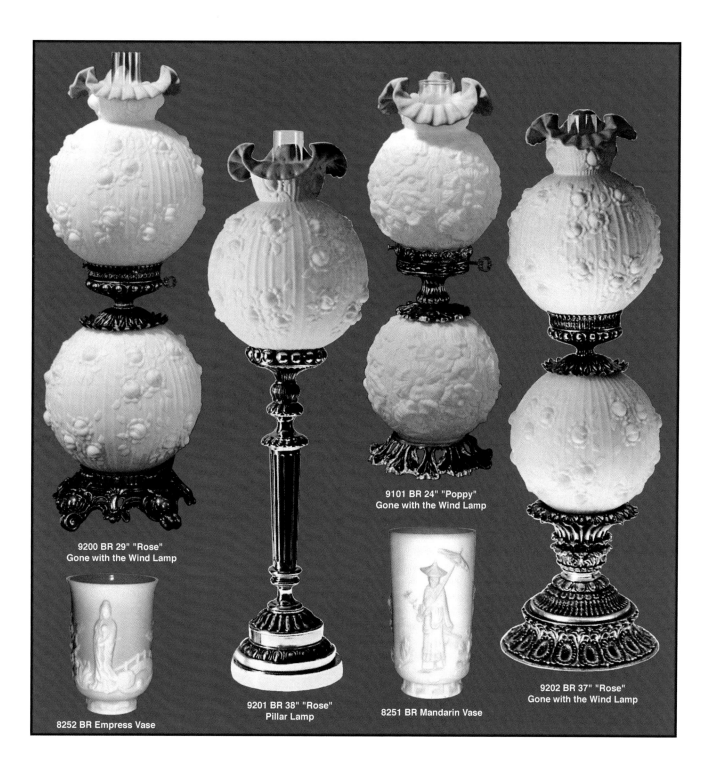

9200 BR 29" "Rose"
Gone with the Wind Lamp

9201 BR 38" "Rose"
Pillar Lamp

9101 BR 24" "Poppy"
Gone with the Wind Lamp

9202 BR 37" "Rose"
Gone with the Wind Lamp

8252 BR Empress Vase

8251 BR Mandarin Vase

Chocolate

Chocolate-colored glassware was re-created for Fenton in 1976, by chief chemist Dr. Subodh Gupta. The color had been made previously at the Greentown plant of the Indiana Tumbler and Goblet Works, but the original Jacob Rosenthal formula was unavailable to Fenton. Therefore chemists Charley Goe and Dr. Gupta spent long hours redeveloping the correct formula. The formula was perfected in time for implementation with the last of the Bicentennial items in January 1976. The seven items in the listing below are the only chocolate items produced in the regular line. The moulds to these items were destroyed at the end of 1976. Chocolate is a heat-sensitive glass and production problems have severely limited attempts to bring the color back into the line. A few other items have been sampled in chocolate and the color was used for some items made for Levay in the 1980s. Included in the Levay grouping were a Lincoln Inn water set, a Cactus-covered cracker jar and cruet, the Craftsman stein, a Cherries cream and sugar, a Button and Arch covered butter, an oval Pinwheel comport, the Kitten slipper, a Strawberry toothpick holder, and the No. 9101 Gone with the Wind lamp.

Chocolate	Ware No.	Introduced	Discontinued	Value
Bell, Patriot's	8467-CK	1976	1977	$25.00 – 30.00
Comport, Jefferson	8476-CK	1976	1977	$110.00 – 130.00
Paperweight, Eagle	8470-CK	1976	1977	$22.00 – 27.00
Planter, Patriot's	8499-CK	1976	1977	$28.00 – 32.00
Plate, Eagle	9418-CK	1976	1977	$20.00 – 22.00
Plate, Lafayette	9419-CK	1976	1977	$20.00 – 22.00
Stein, Bicentennial	8446-CK	1976	1977	$30.00 – 35.00

8470 CK
Eagle Paperweight

8499 CK
Patriot's Planter

9419 CK
Lafayette Plate

8467 CK
Patriot's Bell

9418 CK Eagle Plate

8476 CK Jefferson Comport

8446 CK
Bicentennial Stein

Crystal Satin

Crystal Satin was a line of small figurals made of frosted crystal glass that was introduced in 1972. A few of the animals were out of production by July 1972. The Praying Boy and Girl figures were the last to be discontinued at the end of 1974. This crystal satinized glass line was not expanded, but was replaced by another softer translucent crystal line called Crystal Velvet in 1977. For an example of the difference in appearance between Crystal Satin and Crystal Velvet, examine the Praying Boy and Girl in the photo below. The boy is Crystal Satin and the girl is Crystal Velvet.

Crystal Satin	Ware No.	Introduced	Discontinued	Value
Bird figure	5197-CS	1972	1974	$18.00 – 20.00
Boy and girl, praying	5100-CS	1973	1975	$35.00 – 40.00
Butterfly	5170-CS	1972	July 1972	$18.00 – 20.00
Cart	5124-CS	1972	1973	$90.00 – 100.00
Donkey	5125-CS	1972	1973	$125.00 – 150.00
Elephant	5123-CS	1972	July 1972	$130.00 – 150.00
Paperweight, fish	5193-CS	1972	1973	$18.00 – 22.00

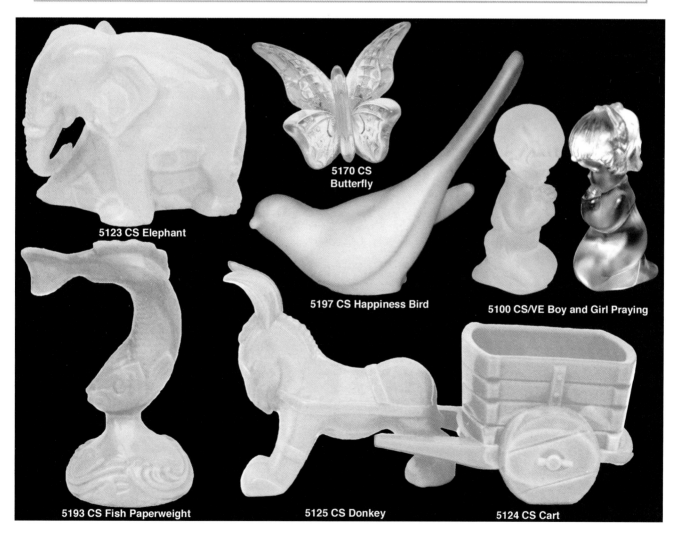

5123 CS Elephant

5170 CS Butterfly

5197 CS Happiness Bird

5100 CS/VE Boy and Girl Praying

5193 CS Fish Paperweight

5125 CS Donkey

5124 CS Cart

Crystal Velvet

Crystal Velvet is the Fenton name for a type of softly satinized crystal glassware that entered the line in 1977. Fenton described this treatment as having an "unusual clarity of pattern and a gentle softness." The initial offering consisted of fifteen popular shapes. Crystal Velvet was a great success, and fifteen additional items were placed in the line in 1978. The popularity of Crystal Velvet resulted in numerous items being produced with this finish well into the 1980s.

In July 1980, Fenton introduced the first in a series of four annual Currier & Ives plates. The first edition of these plates was produced in Crystal Velvet, Antique Blue (TB), Antique Brown (TN), and Antique White (AW). These plates were introduced with a matching bell, lamp, and fairy light/vase. In the order of production, the plates depicted Winter in the Country, The Old Grist Mill, Harvest, The Old Homestead, and Winter Pastime.

Crystal Velvet Praying Boy and Girl bells were included in the 1983/84 general catalog. Although many of the earlier Crystal Velvet items disappeared from the line by the mid-1980s, some new pieces were still being added in this treatment. New items in the 1985/86 catalog included small animals such as a mouse, a mallard, a whale, a bear cub, an elephant, a kitten, spaniels, and a snail. A Scottie, Squirrel, and a set of two Praying Angels were added to the line in 1986.

Twelve new items in 1987 included the following:

Basket, Butterfly and Berry	9234-VE	Plate, 11¾" Tassel	9718-VE
Basket, Tulip	9737-VE	Puppy figure	5225-VE
Bowl, Tulip	9722-VE	Vase, Mandarin	8251-VE
Comport, Daisy	9782-VE	Vase, 8¼" Spring/Autumn	9259-VE
Mint dish, Tulip	9721-VE	Vase, 8¼" Summer/Winter	9258-VE
Pig figure	5220-VE	Vase, Thistle	9257-VE

In addition to these new items, the animals that were introduced in 1985 still remained in production. Earlier items still in production included the swan, bunny, small bird, fawn, cat, butterfly on stand, kissing kids, Madonna prayer light, Poppy student lamp, and candy with butterfly knob.

A new item in Crystal Velvet for Christmas in the June 1988 supplement was the 5¾" Cross Bell (9761-VE). Crystal Velvet no longer was in the regular Fenton line by the end of the decade.

Crystal Velvet	Ware No.	Introduced	Discontinued	Value
Ashtray, Rose	9271-VE	1981		$5.00 – 7.00
Basket, 3-toed Grape	8438-VE	July, 1978	1980+	$30.00 – 35.00
Basket, Miniature Faberge	9431-VE	1981		$32.00 – 37.00
Basket, 7" Strawberry	9437-VE	1980		$30.00 – 35.00
Basket, 7" Water Lily	8434-VE	1977	1980+	$30.00 – 35.00
Basket, ftd. Water Lily	8433-VE	1977	1980+	$35.00 – 40.00
Bell, Bride and Groom	9168-VE	1977	1980+	$18.00 – 22.00
Bell, Craftsman	9660-VE	1979	1980+	$18.00 – 20.00
Bell, Currier & Ives	8461-VE	July, 1980		$18.00 – 22.00
Bell, Faberge	8466-VE	1977	1980+	$18.00 – 20.00
Bell, Nativity	9463-VE	July, 1980		$18.00 – 22.00
Bell, Praying Boy	9661-VE	1983		$18.00 – 20.00
Bell, Praying Girl	9662-VE	1983		$18.00 – 20.00
Bell, Strawberry	9465-VE	1980		$22.00 – 27.00
Bird, Happiness	5197-VE	1977	1980+	$20.00 – 25.00
Bird, small	5163-VE	July, 1978	1980+	$20.00 – 25.00
Bowl, Basket Weave	8222-VE	1977	1980+	$16.00 – 18.00
Bowl, cupped ftd.	8439-VE	July, 1978	1979	$18.00 – 22.00
Bowl, Curtain	8454-VE	July, 1978	1980	$22.00 – 25.00
Bowl, 7" Strawberry	9427-VE	1980		$18.00 – 22.00
Bowl, crimped ftd. Water Lily	8423-VE	July, 1978	1980	$27.00 – 30.00

the unusual clarity of pattern and elegant soft look of handcrafted glass!

The great success story of Fenton Crystal Velvet has inspired the creation of a number of beautiful new pieces for '78. Fifteen entirely new Fenton pieces. The new pelican ash tray, the butterfly, the lotus nut dish, the water lily cake plate and footed bowls are available only in this treatment. So you can sell more Crystal Velvet by Fenton.

other Crystal Velvet items shown on pages 40-41 in 1977-78 catalog. On order blank—page 2, column 1

8439 VE
WATER LILY FTD. BOWL (CUPPED)

9388 VE
BAROQUE CANDY BOX

9405 VE
21" POPPY STUDENT LAMP
Antique Brass Finish
Shipping Wgt.—9¾ lbs.

8457 VE
3 TOED GRAPE VASE

5175 VE
PELICAN TRAY

8410 VE
12½" WATER LILY CAKE PLATE

5163 VE
SMALL BIRD

5162 VE
BUNNY

Catalog Reprint Circa 1978   Courtesy Of: The Fenton Art Glass Museum

Crystal Velvet	Ware No.	Introduced	Discontinued	Value
Bowl, 9"	8424-VE	1977	1980+	$30.00 – 35.00
Boy and girl, praying	5100-VE	1977	1980+	$25.00 – 30.00
Bunny	5162-VE	July, 1978	1980+	$28.00 – 32.00
Butterfly on stand	5171-VE	July, 1978	1980+	$25.00 – 28.00
Cake plate, 12½" Water Lily	8410-VE	July, 1978	1980	$35.00 – 40.00
Candleholder, Water Lily	8473-VE	1977	1980+	$14.00 – 16.00
Candy box, Baroque	9388-VE	July, 1978	1980+	$30.00 – 35.00
Candy box, Butterfly/Rose	9280-VE	1983		$25.00 – 30.00
Candy box, ftd. Water Lily	8480-VE	1977	1980+	$35.00 – 45.00
Cat	5165-VE	1979	1980+	$35.00 – 40.00
Comport, Oval Pinwheel	8427-VE	1980		$25.00 – 28.00
Comport, Strawberry	9428-VE	1980		$22.00 – 25.00
Comport, ftd. Water Lily	8430-VE	1977	1980+	$20.00 – 25.00
Duckling	5169-VE	1981		$27.00 – 30.00
Fairy light, beaded	8405-VE	July, 1978	1980+	$28.00 – 30.00
Fairy light, Currier & Ives	8409-VE	1977	1980+	$30.00 – 35.00
Fairy light, Nativity	9401-VE	July, 1980		$28.00 – 30.00
Fairy light, Owl	5108-VE	1981		$25.00 – 30.00
Fairy light, Strawberry	9407-VE	1980		$25.00 – 30.00
Fawn	5160-VE	1983		$30.00 – 35.00
Frog	5166-VE	1979	1980+	$30.00 – 35.00
Hen on Nest, small	5186-VE	1981		$30.00 – 35.00
Kissing Kids	5101-VE	1981		$30.00 – 35.00
Lamp, Chou Ting ceremonial	8407-VE	1977	1978	$55.00 – 65.00
Lamp, 22" off-set Colonial	9403-VE	1978	1979	$225.00 – 250.00
Lamp, 11" Currier & Ives	8400-VE	July, 1980		$200.00 – 225.00
Lamp, 21" Poppy student	9405-VE	1978	1980+	$180.00 – 200.00
Nut dish, Lotus	8441-VE	July, 1978	1980+	$8.00 – 10.00
Owl	5168-VE	1980		$18.00 – 22.00
Pelican tray	5175-VE	July, 1978	1979	$40.00 – 45.00
Pitcher, 36 oz. Water Lily	8464-VE	1977	1980	$30.00 – 35.00
Prayer light, Madonna	5107-VE	July, 1978	1980+	$30.00 – 35.00
Ring tree, Owl	9299-VE	1980		$18.00 – 22.00
Rose bowl, Water Lily	8429-VE	1977	1980+	$18.00 – 20.00
Soap dish, Rose	9126-VE	1981		$14.00 – 16.00
Stein, Craftsman	9640-VE	1979	1980+	$18.00 – 20.00
Sunfish	5167-VE	1979	1980+	$18.00 – 22.00
Swan	5161-VE	July, 1978	1980+	$22.00 – 25.00
Tumbler, Rose bathroom	9242-VE	1981		$20.00 – 22.00
Turtle	5164-VE	1979	1980+	$27.00 – 32.00
Vase, miniature Faberge bud	9451-VE	1981		$15.00 – 17.00
Vase, 3-toed Grape	8457-VE	July, 1978	1980+	$25.00 – 27.00
Vase, Strawberry bud	9454-VE	1980		$18.00 – 20.00
Vase, Water Lily bud	8456-VE	July, 1978	1980+	$18.00 – 20.00

9427 VE Bowl

5169 VE Duckling

9465 VE Bell

9428 VE Comport

9407 VE Fairy Light

5108 VE Owl
Fairy Light

5168 VE Owl

9454 VE Bud Vase

9168 VE Bride & Groom Bell

5165 VE Cat

9437 VE Basket

8441 VE
Lotus Nut Dish

8438 VE 3-toed
Grape Basket

5107 VE Madonna
Prayer Light

8222 VE Basketweave Bowl

5161 VE Swan

5101 VE Kissing Kids

9660 VE Craftsman Bell

Custard Satin

Fenton introduced custard-colored glass in 1972 as a reproduction of "a glass treatment that originated in 1880." Most of the glassware produced for the regular line in this color was made with a satin finish. Numerous items were made in this color for over a decade. Also during this period, several hand-painted decorations were applied to this background color. For more information on hand-painted Custard Satin decorations, see the hand-painted chapter of this book. A number of shapes may also be found in Shiny Custard. Some of these pieces are planters and vases made for the wholesale florist trade. Other items were produced and sold through the Fenton Gift Shop.

Custard	Ware No.	Introduced	Discontinued	Value
Ashtray/Chip 'n Dip/Candle bowl	8478-CU	1975	1977	$27.00 – 32.00
Basket, 3-toed Grape	8438-CU	1978	1980+	$27.00 – 32.00
Basket, Persian Medallion	8238-CU	1972	1978	$35.00 – 40.00
Basket, 7" deep Poppy	9138-CU	1973	1980	$40.00 – 50.00
Basket, Water Lily	8434-CU	1977	1980+	$30.00 – 35.00
Bell, Daisy & Button	1966-CU	1972	1980+	$20.00 – 22.00
Bird, Happiness	5197-CU	1974	1980+	$22.00 – 25.00
Bird, small	5163-CU	1978	1980+	$22.00 – 25.00
Bonbon, handled Butterfly	8230-CU	1973	1980	$18.00 – 20.00
Boot, Daisy & Button	1990-CU	1972	1977	$12.00 – 15.00
Bowl, Basket Weave	8222-CU	1974	1980+	$18.00 – 20.00
Bowl, Curtain	8454-CU	1978	July 1979	$25.00 – 27.00
Bowl, 3-toe Leaf and Orange Tree	8223-CU	1972	1978	$27.00 – 30.00
Bowl, crimped Orange Tree and Cherry	8233-CU	1973	1977	$30.00 – 35.00
Bowl, cupped Orange Tree and Cherry	8232-CU	1973	1976	$30.00 – 35.00
Bowl, 8" Persian Medallion	8224-CU	1972	1976	$30.00 – 35.00
Bowl, 3-toed Water Lily	8426-CU	1977	1978	$30.00 – 35.00
Bowl, 9" Water Lily	8424-CU	1975	1980+	$30.00 – 35.00
Boy and girl, praying	5100-CU	1973	1980+	$22.00 – 27.00
Bunny	5162-CU	1978	1980+	$25.00 – 30.00
Butter, Cactus	3477-CU	1974	1975	$27.00 – 32.00
Butterfly on stand	5171-CU	1979	1980+	$22.00 – 25.00
Candle bowl, Orange Tree	9173-CU	1973	1976	$20.00 – 25.00
Candleholder, 6" Orange Tree	8472-CU	1974	1976	$14.00 – 16.00
Candleholder, Water Lily	8473-CU	1975	1980	$15.00 – 18.00
Candy box, Baroque	9388-CU	1978	1980+	$30.00 – 35.00
Candy box, heart-shaped	8200-CU	1973	1975	$40.00 – 45.00
Candy box, ftd. Water Lily	8480-CU	1974	1980	$25.00 – 30.00
Candy box, Paneled Daisy	9185-CU	1972	1976	$25.00 – 30.00
Candy box or sugar, Cactus	3488-CU	1974	1975	$20.00 – 22.00
Candy jar, 7¼" Grape & Cable	9188-CU	1974	1975	$125.00 – 150.00
Candy jar, ftd. W. Strawberry	9088-CU	1972	1976	$35.00 – 40.00
Cat	5165-CU	1979	1980+	$35.00 – 40.00
Chalice, Persian Medallion	8241-CU	1972	1974	$25.00 – 30.00
Comport, ftd. flowered	8422-CU	1977	1978	$20.00 – 22.00
Comport, ftd. Water Lily	8481-CU	1975	1977	$18.00 – 22.00

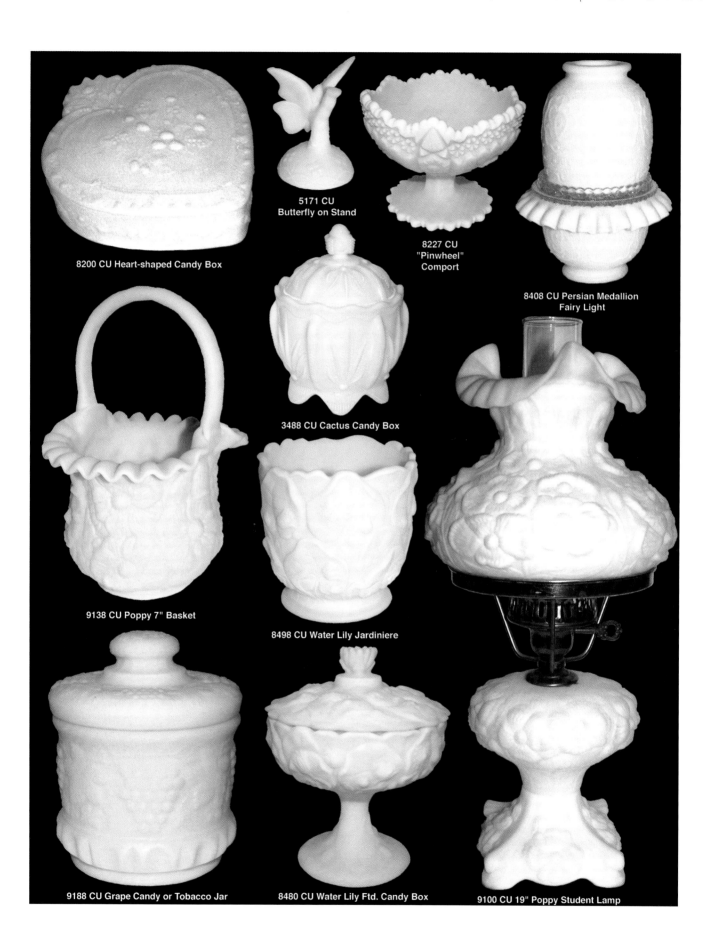

8200 CU Heart-shaped Candy Box

5171 CU
Butterfly on Stand

8227 CU
"Pinwheel"
Comport

8408 CU Persian Medallion
Fairy Light

3488 CU Cactus Candy Box

9138 CU Poppy 7" Basket

8498 CU Water Lily Jardiniere

9188 CU Grape Candy or Tobacco Jar

8480 CU Water Lily Ftd. Candy Box

9100 CU 19" Poppy Student Lamp

Custard	Ware No.	Introduced	Discontinued	Value
Comport, handled fruit	8242-CU	1973	1976	$18.00 – 20.00
Comport, Persian Medallion	8234-CU	1972	1980+	$18.00 – 22.00
Comport, Pinwheel	8227-CU	1972	1978	$20.00 – 25.00
Comport, oval Pinwheel	8427-CU	1974	1976	$20.00 – 25.00
Comport, Rose	9222-CU	1973	1977	$12.00 – 14.00
Comport, Water Lily	8431-CU	1977	1978	$18.00 – 20.00
Cream pitcher, 10 oz. Cactus	3468-CU	July 1974	1975	$15.00 – 18.00
Fairy light, owl	5108-CU	1973	1980+	$22.00 – 27.00
Fairy light, Persian Medallion	8408-CU	1974	1980+	$40.00 – 45.00
Frog	5166-CU	1979	1980+	$25.00 – 30.00
Hen on nest, small	5186-CU	1974	1976	$30.00 – 40.00
Jardiniere, Water Lily	8498-CU	1975	1978	$25.00 – 30.00
Lamp, 22" off-set Colonial	9402-CU	1978	1979	$125.00 – 150.00
Lamp, 18" electric	9105-CU	1974	1978	$225.00 – 250.00
Lamp, 18" oil	9104-CU	1974	July 1976	$225.00 – 250.00
Lamp, 24" Poppy GWTW	9101-CU	1973	1980+	$180.00 – 200.00
Lamp, 19" Poppy student	9100-CU	1975	July 1976	$225.00 – 250.00
Lamp, 20" Poppy student	9107-CU	July 1972	1980+	$100.00 – 125.00
Lamp, 21" Poppy student	9405-CU	1978	1979	$125.00 – 150.00
Nappy, Grape	8225-CU	1972	1975	$16.00 – 18.00
Pitcher, 36 oz Water Lily	8464-CU	1976	1980	$30.00 – 35.00
Planter bowl, Verly's hexagonal	8226-CU	1974	1979	$28.00 – 32.00
Prayer light, Madonna	5107-CU	July, 1978	1980+	$30.00 – 35.00
Rose bowl, Poppy	9126-CU	1977	1978	$20.00 – 25.00
Rose bowl, Water Lily	8429-CU	1977	1980	$20.00 – 25.00
Salt and pepper, Cactus	3406-CU	1974	1975	$18.00 – 20.00
Santa candle light*	5106-CU	July 1973	1975	$30.00 – 35.00
Swan	5161-CU	1978	1980+	$18.00 – 22.00
Toothpick, Paneled Daisy	8294-CU	1973	1976	$14.00 – 16.00
Toothpick, Strawberry	8295-CU	1972	1976	$15.00 – 18.00
Vase, bud Water Lily	8456-CU	1978	1980+	$18.00 – 22.00
Vase, 6"	7451-CU	1974	1980+	$16.00 – 18.00
Vase, 8"	9155-CU	1973	1980+	$20.00 – 25.00
Vase, 3-toed Grape	8457-CU	1978	1980	$20.00 – 22.00
Vase, Love Bird	8258-CU	1974	1976	$30.00 – 35.00
Vase, 8" Peacock	8257-CU	1972	1977	$30.00 – 35.00
Vase, 7" Poppy	9154-CU	1973	1978	$30.00 – 35.00
Vase, swung	8255-CU	1973	1976	$30.00 – 35.00

*Only offered from July through December of the years indicated.

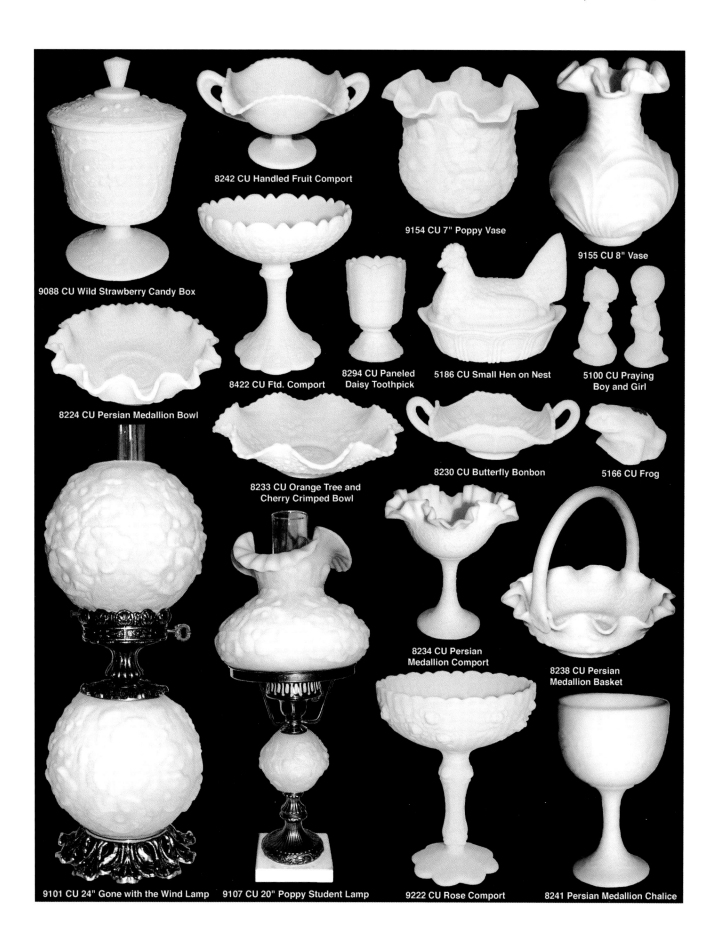

8242 CU Handled Fruit Comport

9154 CU 7" Poppy Vase

9155 CU 8" Vase

9088 CU Wild Strawberry Candy Box

8224 CU Persian Medallion Bowl

8422 CU Ftd. Comport

8294 CU Paneled Daisy Toothpick

5186 CU Small Hen on Nest

5100 CU Praying Boy and Girl

8233 CU Orange Tree and Cherry Crimped Bowl

8230 CU Butterfly Bonbon

5166 CU Frog

8234 CU Persian Medallion Comport

8238 CU Persian Medallion Basket

9101 CU 24" Gone with the Wind Lamp

9107 CU 20" Poppy Student Lamp

9222 CU Rose Comport

8241 Persian Medallion Chalice

Green Pastel

Green Pastel is a very pale opaque green that may almost appear to be a very light blue. This color was introduced in January 1954, along with two other pastel opaque colors — blue and rose. Green Pastel was in the line for two years — until the end of 1955. Pieces in the Lacy Edge and Hobnail patterns and a few novelty items were made in this color. The boudoir lamps and the bathroom set are seldom found.

More pieces in Green Pastel may be found in the Hobnail, Daisy & Button, Lamb's Tongue, and Swirl sections of the book *Fenton Art Glass Patterns 1939 – 1980*.

Green Pastel	Ware No.	Introduced	Discontinued	Value
Bathroom set	7302-GP	July 1954	1956	$225.00 – 250.00
Cake plate, ftd.	3513-GP	1954	1956	$45.00 – 55.00
Comport, ftd.	7228-GP	1954	1956	$45.00 – 55.00
Hen on basket	5183-GP	1954	1955	$80.00 – 90.00
Lamp, boudoir (candle)	7390-GP	1954	1955	$100.00 – 125.00
Lamp, boudoir (electric)	7392-GP	1954	1955	$100.00 – 125.00
Plate, 8" Leaf	5116-GP	1955	1956	$18.00 – 22.00
Plate, 11" Leaf	5118-GP	1955	1956	$25.00 – 30.00
Tidbit, 2-tier Leaf	5196-GP	July 1955	1956	$50.00 – 60.00
Vase, 6"	7353-GP	July 1954	1955	$35.00 – 40.00
Vase, 6" bud	7348-GP	July 1954	1956	$35.00 – 40.00
Vase, 6½" bud	7349-GP	July 1954	1956	$35.00 – 40.00

Lacy Edge	Ware No.	Introduced	Discontinued	Value
Bowl, Banana	9024-GP	1955	1956	$50.00 – 55.00
Bowl, 8" "C"	9026-GP	1954	1956	$20.00 – 25.00
Bowl, Scroll & Eye	9025-GP	1955	1956	$20.00 – 25.00
Comport	9028-GP	1954	1956	$40.00 – 50.00
Comport, ftd.	9029-GP	1954	1956	$40.00 – 50.00
Comport, Scroll & Eye	9021-GP	1955	1956	$35.00 – 45.00
Planter, "C" plate 9"	9099-GP	1954	1956	$20.00 – 25.00
Plate, 11"	9011-GP	1954	1956	$20.00 – 25.00
Plate, 9" "C"	9019-GP	1954	1956	$18.00 – 22.00
Plate, Scroll & Eye	9015-GP	1955	1956	$12.00 – 14.00
Plate, #360-8"	9018-GP	1954	1956	$12.00 – 14.00

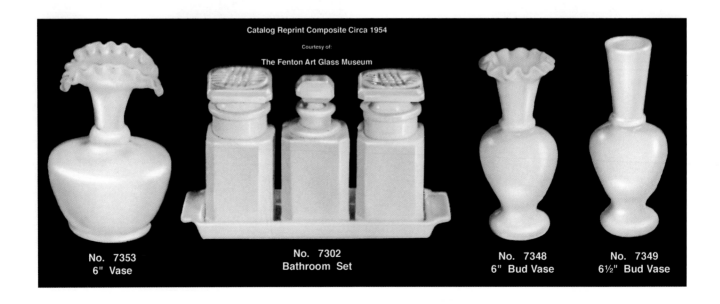

Catalog Reprint Composite Circa 1954

Courtesy of:

The Fenton Art Glass Museum

No. 7353
6" Vase

No. 7302
Bathroom Set

No. 7348
6" Bud Vase

No. 7349
6½" Bud Vase

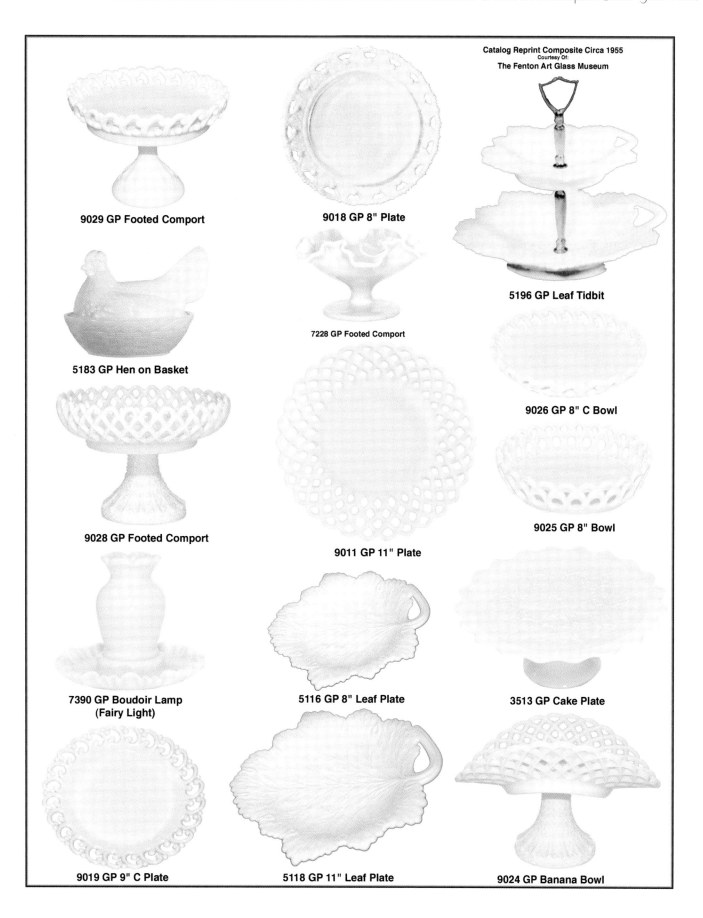

9029 GP Footed Comport

9018 GP 8" Plate

Catalog Reprint Composite Circa 1955
Courtesy Of:
The Fenton Art Glass Museum

5196 GP Leaf Tidbit

5183 GP Hen on Basket

7228 GP Footed Comport

9026 GP 8" C Bowl

9028 GP Footed Comport

9025 GP 8" Bowl

9011 GP 11" Plate

**7390 GP Boudoir Lamp
(Fairy Light)**

5116 GP 8" Leaf Plate

3513 GP Cake Plate

9019 GP 9" C Plate

5118 GP 11" Leaf Plate

9024 GP Banana Bowl

Lavender Satin

Fenton's Lavender Satin color appeared in the line at the beginning of 1977. This color was discontinued at the end of 1978. Some glossy pieces that escaped the satinizing process may also be found. Items such as this were often sold through the Fenton Gift Shop. An expensive element, neodymium was used to produce this opaque satin color and its transparent sister color, Wisteria, also produced during this period. Both of these colors are dichroic. This means the pieces change hue depending upon the type of light source they are exposed to. The best appearance occurs under natural, incandescent, or warm fluorescent lighting conditions. Other light sources may cause these colors to appear either gray or almost colorless.

Lavender Satin	Ware No.	Introduced	Discontinued	Value
Basket, 7" Water Lily	8434-LN	1977	1979	$140.00 – 160.00
Bell, Faberge	8466-LN	1978	1979	$60.00 – 70.00
Bird	5197-LN	1977	1979	$70.00 – 80.00
Bird, small	5163-LN	1978	1979	$65.00 – 75.00
Bowl, Basket Weave	8222-LN	1977	1979	$40.00 – 45.00
Boy and girl, praying	5100-LN	1977	1979	$120.00 – 140.00
Bunny	5162-LN	1978	1979	$75.00 – 85.00
Candy box, Baroque	9388-LN	1978	1979	$180.00 – 200.00
Candy box, ftd. Water Lily	8480-LN	1977	1979	$200.00 – 225.00
Fairy lamp, owl	5108-LN	1977	1979	$80.00 – 90.00
Lamp, 20" student	9107-LN	1977	1979	$500.00 – 600.00
Lamp, 24" GWTW	9101-LN	1977	1979	$700.00 – 800.00
Swan	5161-LN	1978	1979	$70.00 – 80.00
Vase, 6"	7451-LN	1977	1979	$30.00 – 40.00
Vase, Water Lily bud	8456-LN	1978	1979	$30.00 – 40.00

8456 Water Lily Bud Vase

8480 Water Lily Candy Box

8434 Water Lily 7" Basket

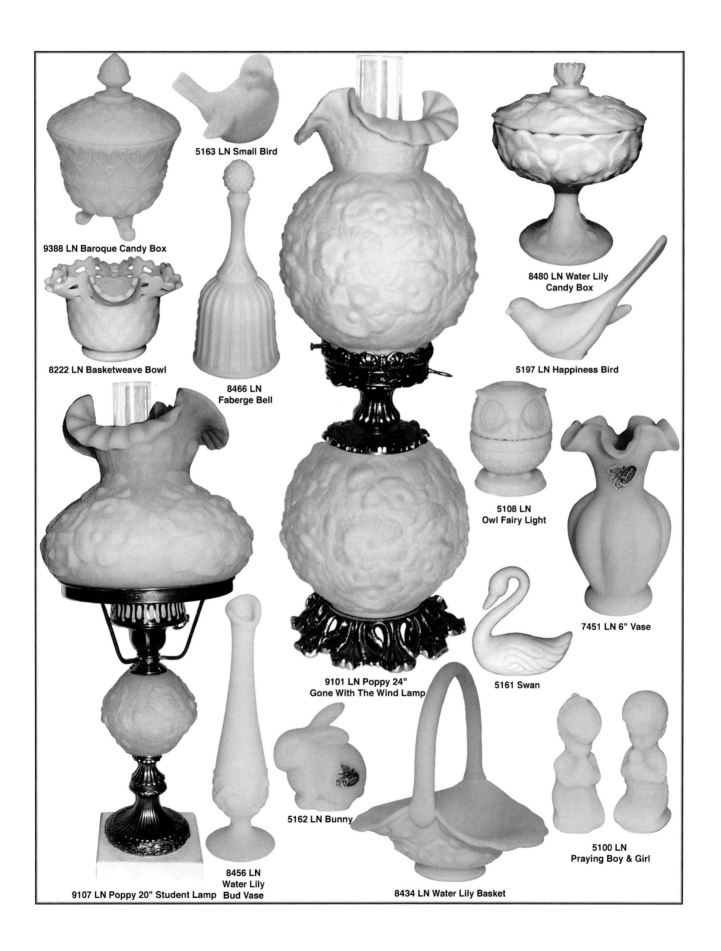

5163 LN Small Bird

9388 LN Baroque Candy Box

8222 LN Basketweave Bowl

8466 LN
Faberge Bell

8480 LN Water Lily
Candy Box

5197 LN Happiness Bird

5108 LN
Owl Fairy Light

7451 LN 6" Vase

9101 LN Poppy 24"
Gone With The Wind Lamp

5161 Swan

5162 LN Bunny

8456 LN
Water Lily
Bud Vase

9107 LN Poppy 20" Student Lamp

8434 LN Water Lily Basket

5100 LN
Praying Boy & Girl

Lime Sherbet

Fenton's light opaque green satin glass called Lime Sherbet was introduced in January 1973. The color was discontinued at the end of 1980. Numerous items were added and discontinued during the span of years the color was produced. Special interest items include animal figures and pieces made from the Verly's moulds. The Santa figural candle light was only produced from July through December during the years 1973 through 1978. In addition to the pieces listed below, a few items were also made in the Hobnail pattern.

Another green satin color produced by Fenton was green satin (GA). This color was made between 1952 and 1954 and is opalescent. See *Fenton Art Glass Patterns 1939 – 1980* for more information.

Lime Sherbet	Ware No.	Introduced	Discontinued	Value
Ashtray/Chip 'n Dip/Candle bowl	8478-LS	1975	1977	$32.00 – 37.00
Basket, Persian Medallion	8238-LS	1973	1978	$47.00 – 52.00
Basket, 3-toed "Grape"	8438-LS	1978	1980	$32.00 – 37.00
Basket, 7" deep Poppy	9138-LS	1973	1978	$57.00 – 65.00
Basket, 7" Water Lily	8434-LS	1977	1980	$40.00 – 50.00
Bell, Daisy & Button	1966-LS	1973	1980	$20.00 – 25.00
Bird, Happiness	5197-LS	1974	1980	$27.00 – 30.00
Bird, small	5163-LS	1978	1980	$26.00 – 29.00
Bonbon, handled Butterfly	8230-LS	1973	1979	$22.00 – 25.00
Boot, Daisy & Button	1990-LS	1973	1977	$15.00 – 20.00
Bowl, Basket Weave	8222-LS	1974	1980	$22.00 – 25.00
Bowl, Curtain	8454-LS	1978	1980	$30.00 – 35.00
Bowl, 3-toe Leaf and Orange Tree	8223-LS	1973	1978	$32.00 – 35.00
Bowl, crimped Orange Tree and Cherry	8233-LS	1973	1977	$37.00 – 42.00
Bowl, cupped Orange Tree and Cherry	8232-LS	1973	1976	$37.00 – 42.00
Bowl, 8" Persian Medallion	8224-LS	1973	1976	$37.00 – 42.00
Bowl, 3-toed Water Lily	8426-LS	1977	1978	$35.00 – 40.00
Bowl, 9" Water Lily	8424-LS	1975	1979	$37.00 – 42.00
Boy and girl, praying	5100-LS	1973	1980	$25.00 – 28.00
Bunny	5162-LS	1978	1980	$30.00 – 35.00
Butterfly on Stand	5171-LS	1979	1980	$28.00 – 32.00
Candleholder, 6" Orange Tree	8472-LS	1974	1976	$20.00 – 22.00
Candleholder, Water Lily	8473-LS	1975	1979	$18.00 – 20.00
Candy box, Baroque	9388-LS	1978	1980	$45.00 – 50.00
Candy box, Paneled Daisy	9185-LS	1973	1977	$40.00 – 45.00
Candy box, ftd. Water Lily	8480-LS	1974	1980	$45.00 – 50.00
Candy jar, 7¼" Grape & Cable	9188-LS	1974	1975	$180.00 – 200.00
Candy jar, ftd. W. Strawberry	9088-LS	1973	1976	$50.00 – 60.00
Cat, sitting	5165-LS	1979	1980	$40.00 – 50.00
Comport, ftd. flowered	8422-LS	1977	1978	$25.00 – 28.00
Comport, handled fruit	8242-LS	1973	1976	$22.00 – 25.00
Comport, Persian Medallion	8234-LS	1973	1980	$22.00 – 27.00
Comport, Pinwheel	8227-LS	1973	1978	$22.00 – 27.00
Comport, oval Pinwheel	8427-LS	1974	1976	$28.00 – 32.00
Comport, Rose	9222-LS	1974	1977	$20.00 – 22.00

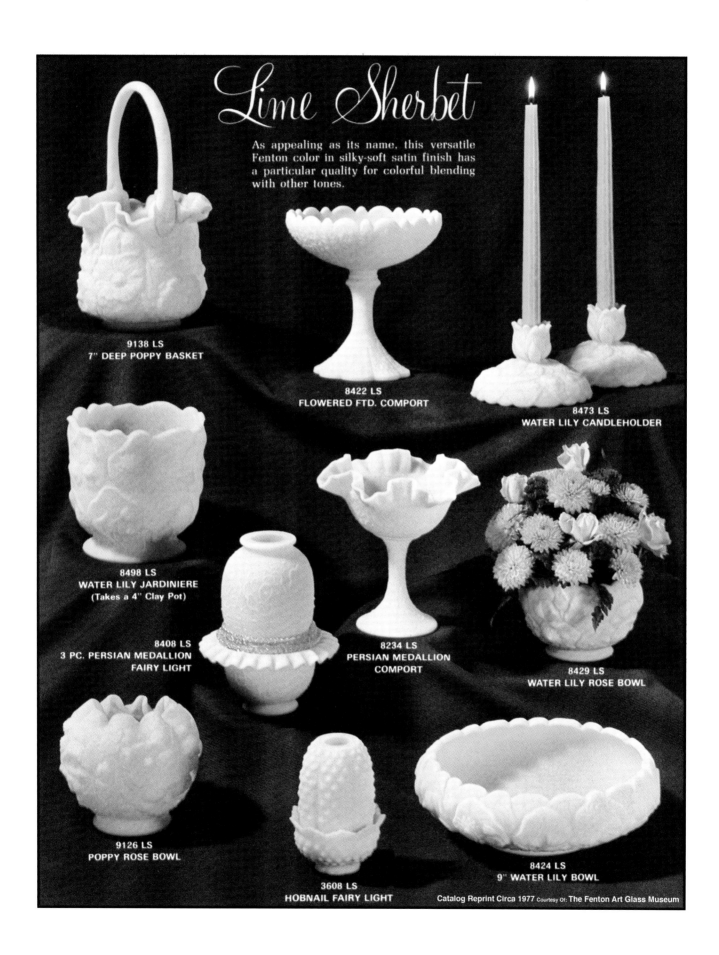

Lime Sherbet

As appealing as its name, this versatile Fenton color in silky-soft satin finish has a particular quality for colorful blending with other tones.

9138 LS
7" DEEP POPPY BASKET

8422 LS
FLOWERED FTD. COMPORT

8473 LS
WATER LILY CANDLEHOLDER

8498 LS
WATER LILY JARDINIERE
(Takes a 4" Clay Pot)

8408 LS
3 PC. PERSIAN MEDALLION
FAIRY LIGHT

8234 LS
PERSIAN MEDALLION
COMPORT

8429 LS
WATER LILY ROSE BOWL

9126 LS
POPPY ROSE BOWL

3608 LS
HOBNAIL FAIRY LIGHT

8424 LS
9" WATER LILY BOWL

Catalog Reprint Circa 1977 Courtesy Of: **The Fenton Art Glass Museum**

Lime Sherbet	Ware No.	Introduced	Discontinued	Value
Comport, Water Lily	8431-LS	1977	1978	$27.00 – 30.00
Comport, ftd. Water Lily	8481-LS	1975	1977	$25.00 – 28.00
Fairy light, owl	5108-LS	1973	1980	$28.00 – 32.00
Fairy light, Persian Medallion	8408-LS	1974	1980	$50.00 – 55.00
Frog	5166-LS	1979	1980	$40.00 – 45.00
Hen on nest, small	5186-LS	1974	1976	$45.00 – 55.00
Jardiniere, Water Lily	8498-LS	1975	1978	$30.00 – 32.00
Lamp, 22" off-set Colonial	9402-LS	1978	1979	$200.00 – 250.00
Lamp, 24" GWTW	9101-LS	1973	1980	$200.00 – 250.00
Lamp, 19" Poppy student	9100-LS	1975	1978	$300.00 – 350.00
Lamp, 20" Poppy student	9107-LS	1973	1980	$180.00 – 200.00
Pitcher, 36 oz.	8464-LS	1976	1980	$30.00 – 35.00
Planter bowl, Verly's hexagonal	8226-LS	1974	1979	$40.00 – 45.00
Rose bowl, Poppy	9126-LS	1977	1978	$22.00 – 27.00
Rose bowl, Water Lily	8429-LS	1977	1980	$22.00 – 27.00
Santa candle light	5106-LS	July 1973	1978	$40.00 – 50.00
Swan	5161-LS	1978	1980	$25.00 – 30.00
Toothpick, Paneled Daisy	8294-LS	1973	1976	$16.00 – 18.00
Vase, 6"	7451-LS	1974	1980	$22.00 – 27.00
Vase, 8"	9155-LS	1973	1979	$25.00 – 30.00
Vase, 3-toed Grape	8457-LS	1978	1980	$22.00 – 27.00
Vase, Love Bird	8258-LS	1974	1976	$37.00 – 42.00
Vase, 8" Peacock	8257-LS	1973	1977	$37.00 – 42.00
Vase, 7" Poppy	9154-LS	1973	1978	$37.00 – 42.00
Vase, swung	8255-LS	1973	1976	$40.00 – 45.00
Vase, Water Lily bud	8456-LS	1978	1980	$22.00 – 25.00

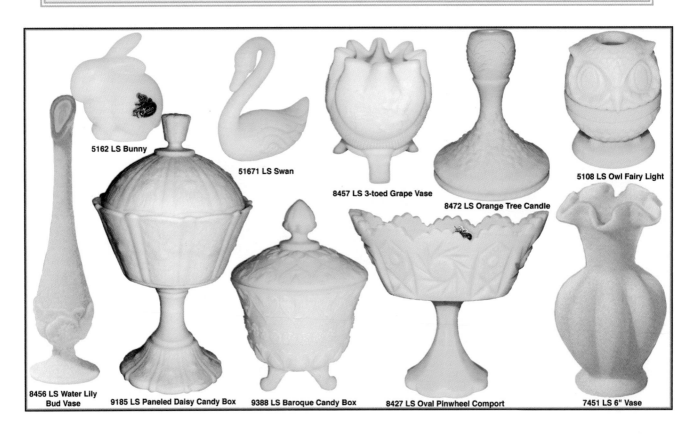

5162 LS Bunny

51671 LS Swan

8457 LS 3-toed Grape Vase

8472 LS Orange Tree Candle

5108 LS Owl Fairy Light

8456 LS Water Lily Bud Vase

9185 LS Paneled Daisy Candy Box

9388 LS Baroque Candy Box

8427 LS Oval Pinwheel Comport

7451 LS 6" Vase

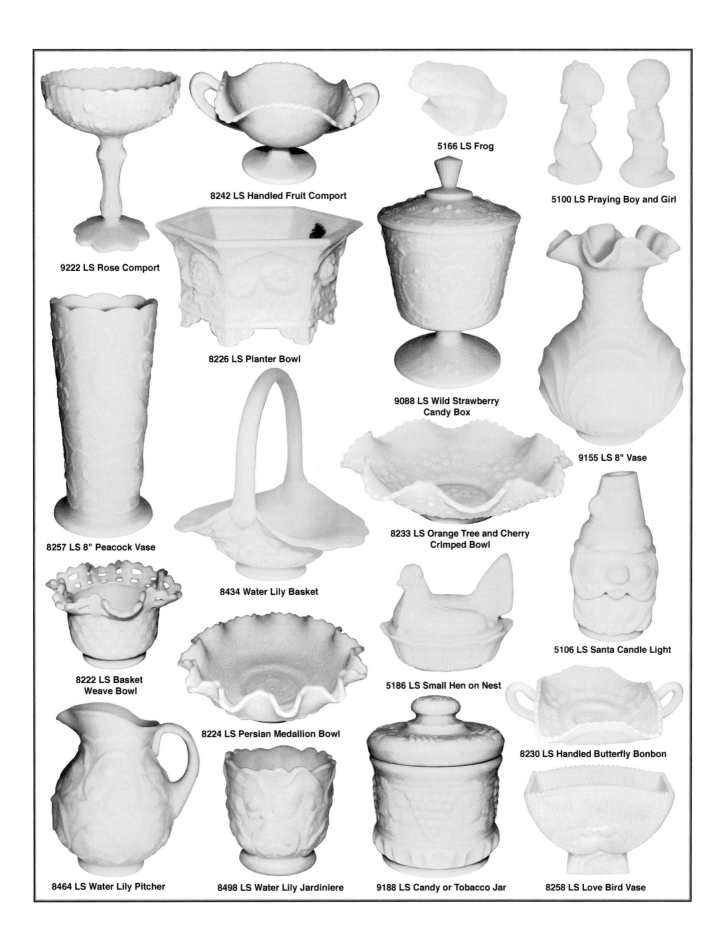

9222 LS Rose Comport

8242 LS Handled Fruit Comport

5166 LS Frog

5100 LS Praying Boy and Girl

8226 LS Planter Bowl

9088 LS Wild Strawberry
Candy Box

9155 LS 8" Vase

8257 LS 8" Peacock Vase

8434 Water Lily Basket

8233 LS Orange Tree and Cherry
Crimped Bowl

5106 LS Santa Candle Light

8222 LS Basket
Weave Bowl

8224 LS Persian Medallion Bowl

5186 LS Small Hen on Nest

8230 LS Handled Butterfly Bonbon

8464 LS Water Lily Pitcher

8498 LS Water Lily Jardiniere

9188 LS Candy or Tobacco Jar

8258 LS Love Bird Vase

Milk Glass

A few bowls and plates in milk glass first appeared in the Fenton line about 1924. There appears to then have been a lapse in production until about 1933, when an assortment of bowls, plates, and vases was introduced. Also, pieces in the Georgian pattern, kitchenware items, and bases for bowls were made during the 1930s. In 1938, some of the swan novelty items were made in milk glass. The 1939 inventory records list the #1900 bootee, slipper, and hats in this color. Also, the nymph figure and flower block were produced at this same time. For more information on the production of early milk glass see the Milk Glass section in *Fenton Art Glass 1907 – 1939.*

With the exception of some kitchenware, which may have been produced under private contract, milk glass disappeared from the line during most of the 1940s. In 1950, Fenton revived production of milk glass with optimistic enthusiasm. The 1948-A apartment-size epergne set and numerous pieces of #389 Hobnail were added to the line. Public acceptance was favorable, and in the following years, many more pieces of milk glass Hobnail were added. During the 1950s, milk glass became Fenton's best seller, and pieces in patterns such as Block and Star, Daisy and Button, and Lacy Edge were made in this color. Various accessory items including ashtrays, cigarette sets, vases, planters, bowls, condiment jars, and shakers were also made. Utility servers in the shape of chickens were especially popular.

Fenton also produced items in milk glass under private contract for Rubel. Rubel's moulds were sent to Fenton when Paden City ceased operating in the early 1950s. Rubel pieces listed in milk glass from the 1951 inventory records include the P-28 mustard, the P-38 punch bowl, and the P-50 bottle. For more information on Rubel shapes, see *Fenton Art Glass Patterns 1939 – 1980.* This book also provides additional information on milk glass with the patterns Lacy Edge, Hobnail, Daisy & Button, Block & Star, Rose, and Thumbprint.

1951 New Milk Glass Accessory Items

The #752 console set was sold as both a three–piece and a five-piece set. The three-piece set consisted of a planter bowl and a pair of candleholders; the larger set added another pair of candleholders.

1952 New Milk Glass Accessory Items

Fenton often combined individual items to produce sets. Cigarette sets, beverage sets, and console sets were among the most popular items offered in milk glass.

Fenton's 5808-MI canasta (cigarette) set, introduced in January 1952, consisted of a #5889 cigarette box and one each of the following ashtrays: #5887 heart ashtray, #5878 spade ashtray, #5875 club ashtray, and #5876 diamond ashtray. The #68 console set was produced by combining a #66-11½" bowl with a pair of #67 candleholders. The #380 cigarette set was made by adding a pair of #379 ashtrays to a #378 cigarette box. The #1562 clusterette set was a four-piece set containing two straight sections and two curved sections. A seven-piece beverage set with the Ware No. 9007 contained one No. 9067 jug and six No. 9047 tumblers. A pair of dark green No. 9078 ashtrays was combined with a pair of milk No. 9078 ashtrays to produce the No. 9009 four-piece ashtray set.

The ivy ball vase introduced in July 1952 combined a colored ball vase with a milk glass foot. Colors of balls offered in 1952 included amber (MA), Amethyst (MY), and green (MG).

1953 New Milk Glass Accessory Items

In addition to solid milk glass, the chick, hen on basket, and chicken server came in various color combinations. The color combinations, ware numbers, and color codes of the chick, hen on basket, and chicken server are as follows:

5182 hen on basket has a white body and a green (GM), black (KM), or Amethyst (YM) head.
5183 hen on basket has a white head, colored body — green (MG), or Amethyst (MY) — and a white base.
5185 chick has a white base — with a green (GM) top or an Amethyst (YM) top.
5188 chicken server has a white body with a green (GM), black (KM), or Amethyst (YM) head.
5189 chicken server has a white head, colored top — green (MG) or Amethyst (MY) — and a white base.

Many of the above items have been made in other colors over the years. The No. 5182 hen on nest was made in milk glass (MI) from 1968 to 1973, in Carnival (CN) from 1970 to 1974, and in Blue Marble (MB) from 1971 to 1973. In 1983 this hen was produced in Country Peach (RT) and Forget-Me-not Blue (KL).

The No. 5183 hen was also made in Rose Pastel (RP) and Blue Pastel (BP) in 1954.

The No. 5186 small hen on nest was produced in a variety of colors for over two decades. From 1970 – 1974, this piece was made in Carnival (CN). Between 1974 and 1976, this hen was made in Lime Sherbet (LS), blue satin (BA) and Custard Satin (CU). In 1981, the hen was in the line in Crystal Velvet (VE). During 1983, the small hen was made in crystal (CR), Forget-Me-Not Blue (KL), Country Peach (RT), Candleglow Yellow (YL) and Heritage Green (HG). From 1985 through 1987, the hen appeared in Dusty Rose (DK). From 1986 until 1988, the hen was produced in pink opalescent Peaches 'N Cream (UO) and blue opalescent Minted Cream (EO). This small hen in milk glass with a blue head (EU) was part of the Elizabeth collection from 1989 until 1991. Fenton's 1992 Easter assortment included Jade Pearl (EZ) and Pink Pearl (HZ) hens. The Easter Collection in 1993 featured this hen in

8226 MI
Hexagonal Bowl

8253 MI
Vessel of Gems Vase

8251 MI
Mandarin Vase

8252 MI
Empress Vase

8299 MI Rectangular Planter

8221 MI
Nut Dish

1021 MG
Ftd. Ivy Ball

1021 MY
Ftd Ivy Ball

1021 MA
Ftd. Ivy Ball

7390 MI Fairy Lamp
or
7392 MI Electric
Fairy Lamp

6674 MI
Petite Epergne

6674 CY
Petite Epergne

2 in 1 Candle and Flower Holder

Although you can't see the Petite Epergne in the illustration above, we show below 3 of the infinite varieties of uses for these practical and versatile aids to attractive flower arranging.

The Petite Epergne is available in Crystal or Milk Glass. It is deep and large enough for sizable bouquets and a plastic ring (with each epergne) keeps it secure in any type holder.

Rose Pearl (DN), Ocean Blue (OB), and Iridized Opal (BT). The 1997 Easter Folk Art collection included a hen in green, brown, and red airbrushed earth tone colors. Misty Blue Satin (LR) and Champagne Satin (PQ) hens were also in the 1997 Easter assortment. In 1997, the small hen was also made for QVC in Dusty Rose Carnival with a milk glass head. In 1998, a hen was produced in a combination of sage, rose, and rust colors for the Easter Folk Art series. In 1999, the small hen was included in the regular line in Empress Rose (CP), Ice Blue (LC), French Opalescent (FZ), cobalt (KN), Aquamarine (AI), and Champagne Satin (PQ).

The No. 5185 chick was a part of the 1993 Easter Collection in Rose Pearl (DN) and Ocean Blue (OB). The No. 5188 chicken server was produced for the Easter collection in 1997. It was made in a hand-painted iridized pearl color and was limited to 950 pieces.

The 5156-MK fish vase has a white body with black tail and eyes. The fish vase with a black body and white trim will be found listed in the section on black glass.

1954 New Milk Glass Accessory Items

Fenton introduced the company's first fairy light in the Swirled Feather pattern in 1953. The same shape candle and an electrified version of the light appeared in milk glass, Blue Pastel, Green Pastel, and Rose Pastel colors in Fenton's January 1954 catalog. This new solid-colored version of fairy light was listed in the catalog as a boudoir light. The No. 3513 Spanish Lace design footed cake plate with a scalloped edge made an appearance in milk and pastel colors. Two new bud vases were unveiled in the July supplement. The No. 7348-6" and No. 7349-6½" bud vases were made in milk glass, Blue Pastel, Green Pastel, and Rose Pastel.

1955 New Milk Glass Accessory Items

Leaf pattern plates were first produced in the 1930s. Numerous transparent and opalescent colors were made during that era. Plates in milk glass are also indicated in 1930s inventory records. The Leaf line was discontinued in the mid-1940s, but plates in milk glass and pastel colors reappeared in January 1955. A tidbit server was added in July 1955. This server was produced by drilling holes in the center of both sizes of plates and joining them in a layered fashion with a metal rod. A four-piece bathroom set was also new this year. The No. 7302 set consisted of three vanity bottles and a rectangular tray. This set was also made in Blue Pastel and Green Pastel and will sometimes be found with a Charleton decoration. Another new item was a footed ivy ball with a ruby Coin Dot globe and a milk glass foot. Two new vases and three handled jugs were added to the line in the July supplement. The swirled-base No. 6066 and No. 6068 handled jugs were also made in turquoise, Peach Crest, and Silver Crest. In addition, the No. 6068 handled jug, the No. 7264 handled jug, and the No. 7255 vase were in the line in Cased Lilac.

1956 New Milk Glass Accessory Items

New items in the January catalog included the No. 3523 shallow footed bowl with Spanish Lace design, the No. 6080 candy box, and the No. 6006 shakers. Three new vases were introduced in July. The new vases were the No. 7360-10" two-handled vase, the No. 7364-11½" vase, and the No. 7361-12" vase.

1957 New Milk Glass Accessory Items

New offerings in 1957 included an ashtray set and a footed ivy ball in a new color. The new color for the globe of the footed ivy ball was Jamestown Blue. The petal-shaped three-piece No. 9010 ashtray set consisted of No. 9075-5½", No. 9076-7", and No. 9077-8½" ashtrays.

1958 New Milk Glass Accessory Items

This was an active year for the introduction of new pieces in milk glass. Five new shapes, inspired by an early Beatty ribbed pattern, were included in the January catalog. This narrow vertical ribbed group consisted of a No. 6621-4½" bonbon, a No. 6620-10" rectangular bowl, a No. 6601 covered sugar and creamer set and a No. 6681 covered nut dish. The two bowls were no longer in the line in 1959, and the other pieces of this pattern were were discontinued at the end of 1959. Another addition this year featured a condiment set with a lacy-edge triangular plate. The No. 6206 salt and pepper and No. 6289 mustard rested upon a drilled No. 6219 triangular plate that was fitted with a chrome handle, to produce the No. 6209 condiment set. Also new this year was the No. 3511-12" footed, piecrust-crimped cake plate with a Spanish Lace pattern on the top. Also new to the line was the No. 6674 petite epergne. This small combination candle and flower holder came with a plastic ring designed to keep it secure in various types of holders.

1960 - 1966 New Milk Glass Accessory Items

The new decade was ushered in with the introduction of the now elusive 9" Ogee ashtray. The ashtray remained in production until 1965. The only new item added to the regular line in 1961 was the No. 9080 honey jar. There was a void in new milk glass introductions until 1965, when the No. 9195 high-button shoe was added. The No. 9199 Turtle ring tree was a new item for 1966. This ring tree was made for two years in milk glass.

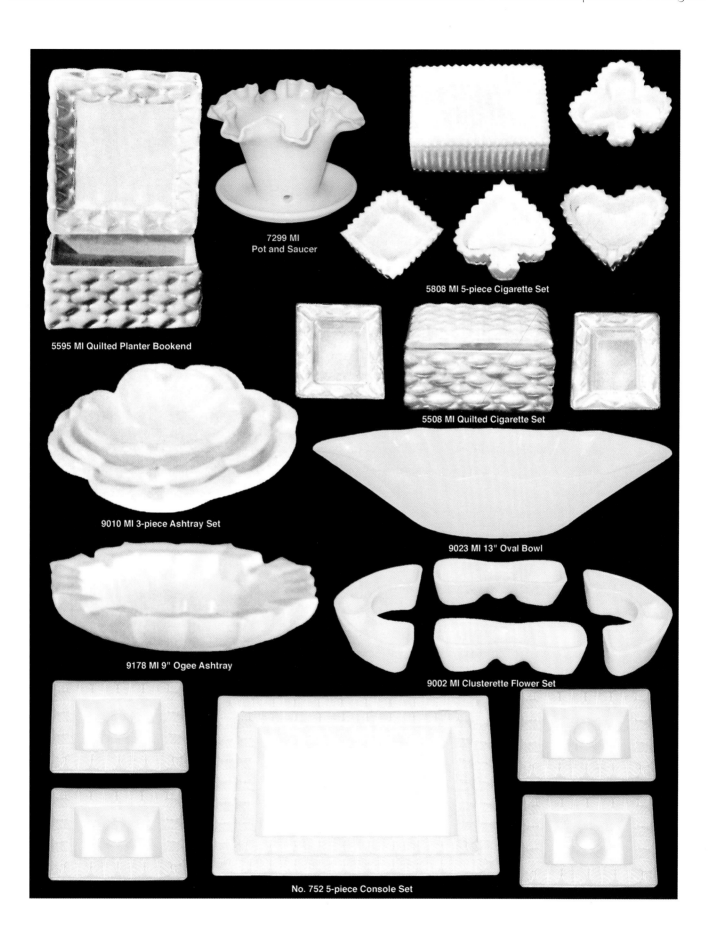

7299 MI
Pot and Saucer

5808 MI 5-piece Cigarette Set

5595 MI Quilted Planter Bookend

5508 MI Quilted Cigarette Set

9010 MI 3-piece Ashtray Set

9023 MI 13" Oval Bowl

9178 MI 9" Ogee Ashtray

9002 MI Clusterette Flower Set

No. 752 5-piece Console Set

1967 New Milk Glass Accessory Items

New milk glass items in 1967 were illustrated in a special lamp supplement catalog. In addition to lamps in the traditional Rose and Hobnail patterns, new lamps were made in Fenton's Poppy pattern. The three latest lamps consisted of the No. 9107-20" student lamp, the No. 9108-21½" double ball lamp and the No. 9109-23" crimped double ball lamp.

1968 New Milk Glass Accessory Items

Numerous new milk glass pieces were presented in the 1968 catalog. A tobacco jar/candy jar in the Grape pattern was described in the Fenton general catalog as an "accurate reproduction of an old Northwood tobacco jar."

The large No. 5182 hen on nest returned to the line in solid milk glass. It had been made previously with a colored head. It was now accompanied by the smaller No. 5186-5½" hen on nest. Other new items in milk glass were made from recently acquired Verly's moulds. Items produced from the Verly's moulds included the No. 8226 hexagonal bowl, the No. 8299 rectangular planter, the No. 8252 Empress vase, the No. 8251 Mandarin vase, and the No. 8253 Vessel of Gems vase.

1969 New Milk Glass Accessory Items

Milk glass items introduced in January 1969 were the No. 5180 Owl Decision Maker and the No. 9088 Wild Strawberries footed candy jar. The No. 5106 Santa candle light entered the line in July. This Christmas item was produced from July through December each year until 1977. The candle light was also made in ruby and in Lime Sherbet.

1972 - 1980 New Milk Glass Accessory Items

By 1972, most new milk glass items were being produced in white satin. For more information on these pieces, see the white satin section of this book. In 1972, the No. 5170 butterfly figure was made in milk glass. The butterfly was only made for one year in this color. A few lamps were made in milk glass during this period. In 1974, a replica of an early American oil lamp was introduced in the Poppy pattern. This 18" lamp with an all-glass base was available as either an oil lamp (No. 9104) or an electric lamp (No. 9105). In 1975, the No. 9490 picture frame with easel was made in milk glass. A new 19" No. 9100 Poppy student lamp was also introduced.

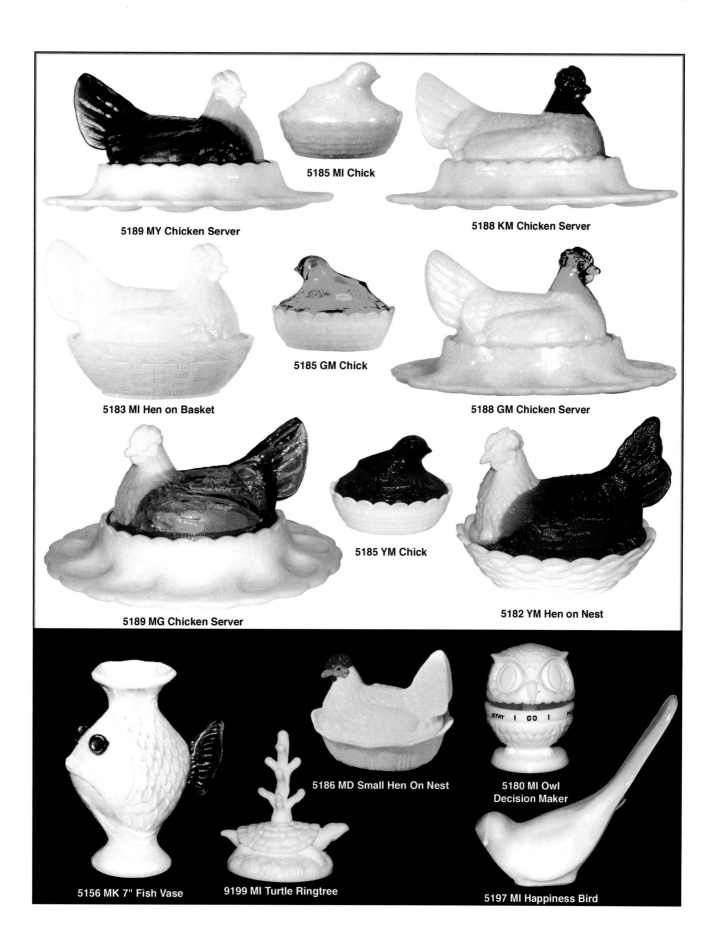

5185 MI Chick

5189 MY Chicken Server

5188 KM Chicken Server

5185 GM Chick

5183 MI Hen on Basket

5188 GM Chicken Server

5185 YM Chick

5189 MG Chicken Server

5182 YM Hen on Nest

5186 MD Small Hen On Nest

5180 MI Owl
Decision Maker

5156 MK 7" Fish Vase

9199 MI Turtle Ringtree

5197 MI Happiness Bird

Milk Glass	Ware No.	Introduced	Discontinued	Value
Ashtray, 5½"	9075-MI	1957	1959	$6.00 – 8.00
Ashtray, 7"	9076-MI	1957	1959	$8.00 – 10.00
Ashtray, 8½"	9077-MI	1957	1959	$10.00 – 12.00
Ashtray, 9" Ogee	9178-MI	1960	1965	$20.00 – 30.00
Ashtray, #379 quilted		1952	1958	$6.00 – 8.00
Ashtray, #1728 square	9078-MI	1952	1954	$10.00 – 12.00
Ashtray, #1800 Club	5875-MI	1952	1957	$6.00 – 8.00
Ashtray, #1800 Diamond	5876-MI	1952	1957	$6.00 – 8.00
Ashtray, #1800 Heart	5877-MI	1952	1957	$6.00 – 8.00
Ashtray, #1800 Spade	5878-MI	1952	1957	$6.00 – 8.00
Ashtray set	9010-MI	1957	1959	$24.00 – 30.00
Ashtray set, 4-piece	9009	1952	1954	$40.00 – 48.00
Basket, 4" handled	7331-MI	1953	1956	$27.00 – 32.00
Bathroom set	7302-MI	1955	1956	$90.00 – 125.00
Bird, Happiness	5197-MI	1953	1956	$18.00 – 20.00
Bonbon, 4½" Ribbed	6621-MI	1958	1959	$8.00 – 10.00
Bowl, 10" rect. Ribbed	6620-MI	1958	1959	$45.00 – 55.00
Bowl, shallow	3523-MI	1956	1959	$12.00 – 14.00
Bowl, #65-6"		1952	July 1952	$10.00 – 12.00
Bowl, #66-11½" oval		1952	July 1952	$25.00 – 30.00
Bowl, #680 high ftd.	7328-MI	1952	1959	$25.00 – 30.00
Bowl, #752-13" rect. planter		1951	July 1952	$45.00 – 55.00
Bowl, #1562-13" oval	9023-MI.	1952	July 1952	$25.00 – 35.00
Butterfly	5170-MI	July 1970	1971	$10.00 – 12.00
Cake plate, ftd.	3513-MI	1954	1965	$25.00 – 30.00
Cake plate, ftd.	3511-MI	1958	1967	$25.00 – 30.00
Canasta set, #1800 5-pc.	5808-MI	1952	1957	$50.00 – 62.00
Candleholder, #67		1952	July 1952	$9.00 – 11.00
Candleholder, #752		1951	July 1952	$12.00 – 14.00
Candy box, Wave Crest	6080-MI	1956	1960	$40.00 – 45.00
Candy jar (tobacco jar)	9188-MI	1968	1970	$100.00 – 125.00
Candy jar, ftd.				
Wild Strawberries	9088-MI	1969	1971	$40.00 – 45.00
Chick	5185-MI	1953	July 1956	$22.00 – 27.00
Chick	5185-GM	1953	1955	$50.00 – 60.00
Chick	5185-YM	1953	1955	$50.00 – 60.00
Chicken server	5188-GM	1953	July 1954	$275.00 – 300.00
Chicken server	5188-KM	1953	1954	$325.00 – 350.00
Chicken server	5188-YM	1953	1955	$275.00 – 300.00
Chicken server	5189-MG	1953	1954	$325.00 – 350.00
Chicken server	5189-MY	1953	1954	$325.00 – 350.00
Chicken server	5189-MI	July 1953	July 1954	$225.00 – 250.00
Cigarette box, #378 quilted		1952	1958	$30.00 – 35.00
Cigarette box, #1800	5889-MI	1952	1954	$25.00 – 30.00
Cigarette set, #380 quilted	5508-MI	1952	1958	$38.00 – 47.00
Clusterette, #1952 4-pc.	9002-MI	1952	1954	$40.00 – 45.00
Condiment set	6209-MI	1958	1960	$47.00 – 57.00
Console set, #68		1952	July 1952	$40.00 – 50.00
Creamer and sugar, Ribbed	6601-MI	1958	1960	$25.00 – 30.00
Epergne, petite	6674-MI	1958	1960	$6.00 – 8.00
Fairy lamp	7390-MI	1954	1955	$40.00 – 50.00
Fairy lamp (electric)	7392-MI	1954	1955	$40.00 – 50.00
Hen on basket	5183-MG	July 1953	1954	$120.00 – 140.00
Hen on basket	5183-MI	July 1953	1957	$75.00 – 85.00
Hen on basket	5183-MY	July 1953	1954	$120.00 – 140.00
Hen on basket, large	5182-YM	July 1953	1955	$150.00 – 175.00

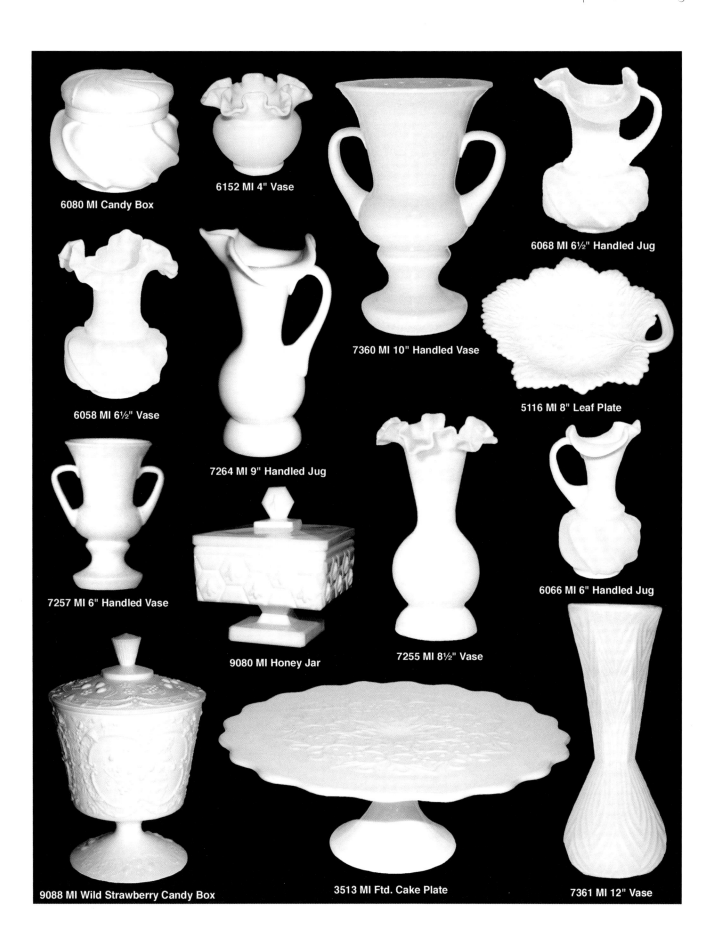

6080 MI Candy Box

6152 MI 4" Vase

7360 MI 10" Handled Vase

6068 MI 6½" Handled Jug

6058 MI 6½" Vase

5116 MI 8" Leaf Plate

7264 MI 9" Handled Jug

7257 MI 6" Handled Vase

9080 MI Honey Jar

6066 MI 6" Handled Jug

7255 MI 8½" Vase

9088 MI Wild Strawberry Candy Box

3513 MI Ftd. Cake Plate

7361 MI 12" Vase

Milk Glass	Ware No.	Introduced	Discontinued	Value
Hen on basket, large	5182-KM	July 1953	1954	$150.00 – 175.00
Hen on basket, large	5182-MI	1968	1973	$90.00 – 110.00
Hen on basket, large	5182-MD	1971	1973	$120.00 – 140.00
Hen on nest, small	5186-MI	1968	1973	$22.00 – 27.00
Hen on nest, small	5186-MD	1971	1973	$50.00 – 60.00
Honey jar	9080-MI	1961	1965	$20.00 – 25.00
Ivy ball ftd.	1021-JM	1957	1960	$95.00 – 110.00
Ivy ball ftd.	1021-MA	July 1952	1955	$50.00 – 60.00
Ivy ball ftd.	1021-MG	July 1952	1957	$75.00 – 85.00
Ivy ball ftd.	1021-MY	July 1952	1955	$75.00 – 85.00
Ivy ball, ftd.	1021-MR	1955	1967	$95.00 – 115.00
Jug, 6" handled	6066-MI	July 1955	July 1956	$22.00 – 27.00
Jug, 6½" handled	6068-MI	July 1955	July 1956	$30.00 – 35.00
Jug, 9" handled	7264-MI	July 1955	July 1956	$40.00 – 50.00
Jug, 50 oz.	9067-MI	July 1952	1953	$55.00 – 65.00
Ladle, punch	9527-MI	July 1952	1954	$50.00 – 60.00
Ladle, punch	9520-MI	1955	July 1959	$45.00 – 55.00
Lamp, GWTW	9101-MI	1971	1980+	$180.00 – 200.00
Lamp, 21½" Poppy ball	9108-MI	1967	1974	$160.00 – 180.00
Lamp, 23" Poppy ball	9109-MI	1967	1975	$180.00 – 200.00
Lamp, 18" Poppy electric	9105-MI	1974	1978	$240.00 – 260.00
Lamp, 18" Poppy oil	9104-MI	1974	July 1976	$240.00 – 260.00
Lamp, 19" Poppy student	9100-MI	1975	1977	$230.00 – 250.00
Lamp, 20" Poppy student	9107-MI	1967	1980+	$125.00 – 145.00
Mustard	6289-MI	1958	1960	$18.00 – 20.00
Nut dish	8221-MI	1968	1969	$15.00 – 18.00
Nut dish, covered "Ribbed"	6681-MI	1958	1960	$20.00 – 25.00
Owl decision maker	5180-MI	1969	1973	$30.00 – 35.00
Picture frame w/easel	9490-MI	1975	1976	$25.00 – 30.00
Planter bookend, Quilted	5595-MI	1952	1954	$45.00 – 55.00
Planter bowl, Verly's hexagonal	8226-MI	1968	1970	$18.00 – 22.00
Planter bowl, 10" Verly's rect.	8299-MI	1968	1969	$50.00 – 60.00
Plate, 8" Leaf	5116-MI	1955	1970	$7.00 – 9.00
Plate, 11" Leaf	5118-MI	1955	1970	$12.00 – 14.00
Plate, triangle	6219-MI	1958	1960	$13.00 – 15.00
Pot and saucer, #400	7299-MI	1951	1959	$25.00 – 30.00
Ring tree, turtle	9199-MI	1966	1969	$14.00 – 16.00
Salt and pepper	7205-MI	1953	1955	$18.00 – 20.00

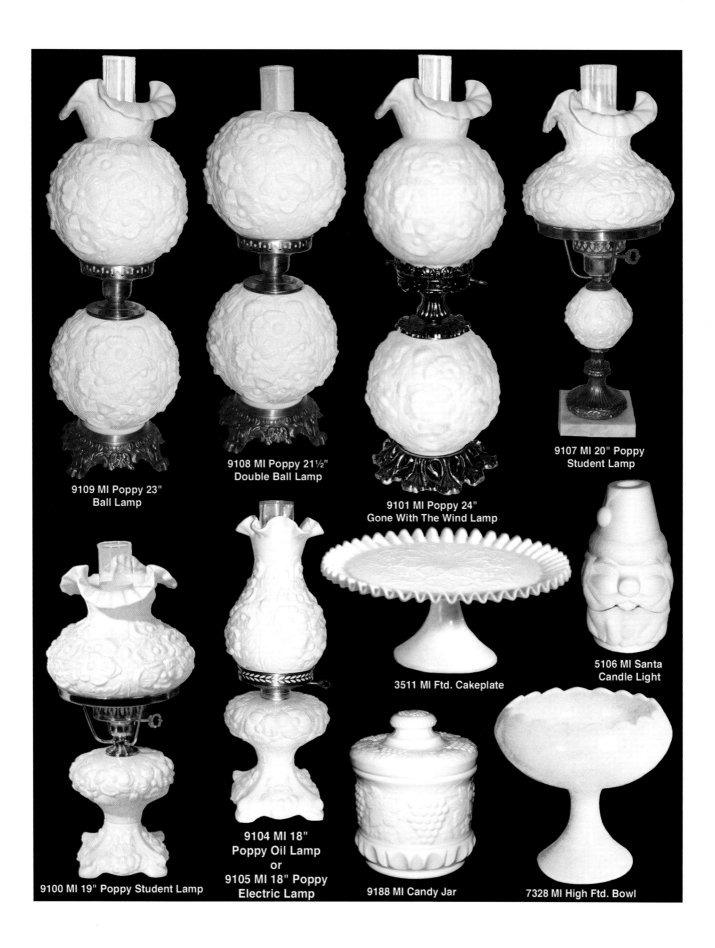

9109 MI Poppy 23"
Ball Lamp

9108 MI Poppy 21½"
Double Ball Lamp

9101 MI Poppy 24"
Gone With The Wind Lamp

9107 MI 20" Poppy
Student Lamp

3511 MI Ftd. Cakeplate

5106 MI Santa
Candle Light

9100 MI 19" Poppy Student Lamp

9104 MI 18"
Poppy Oil Lamp
or
9105 MI 18" Poppy
Electric Lamp

9188 MI Candy Jar

7328 MI High Ftd. Bowl

Milk Glass	Ware No.	Introduced	Discontinued	Value
Salt and pepper	6206-MI	1958	1969	$18.00 – 22.00
Salt and pepper, Wave Crest	6006-MI	1956	1965	$20.00 – 25.00
Santa candle light*	5106-MI	July 1969	1978	$30.00 – 35.00
Shoe, high button	9195-MI	1965	1966	$25.00 – 30.00
Tidbit, 2-tier Leaf	5196-MI	July 1955	1965	$25.00 – 35.00
Tumbler, 5 oz. Georgian	6545-MI	July 1953	1954	$6.00 – 8.00
Tumbler, 9 oz. Georgian	6550-MI	July 1952	1958	$5.00 – 7.00
Tumbler, 12 oz. Georgian	6547-MI	July 1953	1954	$6.00 – 8.00
Tumbler	9047-MI	July 1952	1953	$7.00 – 9.00
Vase, 3"	7351-MI	1953	1960	$14.00 – 16.00
Vase, 4"	6152-MI	1960	1961	$16.00 – 18.00
Vase, 8½"	7255-MI	July 1955	July 1956	$40.00 – 45.00
Vase, 11½"	7364-MI	1956	July 1956	$55.00 – 65.00
Vase, 12"	7361-MI	1956	July 1956	$55.00 – 65.00
Vase, 7" handled	7257-MI	July 1955	July 1956	$35.00 – 40.00
Vase, 10" handled	7360-MI	1956	July 1956	$75.00 – 85.00
Vase, 6" bud	7348-MI	July 1954	July 1956	$20.00 – 25.00
Vase, 6½" bud	7349-MI	July 1954	1956	$20.00 – 25.00
Vase, Empress	8252-MI	1968	1970	$70.00 – 80.00
Vase, 7" fish	5156-KM	1953	1954	$600.00 – 750.00
Vase, Madonna	5157-MI	1953	1957	$35.00 – 40.00
Vase, Mandarin	8251-MI	1968	1970	$80.00 – 90.00
Vase, Vessel of Gems	8253-MI	1968	1969	$40.00 – 45.00

*Offered from July through December each year.

Lacy Edge	Ware No.	Introduced	Discontinued	Value
Bowl, Banana	9024-MI	1955	1959	$40.00 – 50.00
Bowl, 8" "C"	9026-MI	1954	1959	$18.00 – 22.00
Bowl, Lattice	9031-MI	1957	1960	$25.00 – 28.00
Bowl, flared Lattice	9023-MI	1957	1970	$25.00 – 28.00
Bowl, Scroll & Eye	9025-MI	1955	1957	$15.00 – 18.00
Comport	9028-MI	1953	July 1961	$25.00 – 35.00
Comport, ftd.	9029-MI	July 1952	1965	$25.00 – 35.00
Comport, Scroll & Eye	9021-MI	1955	1959	$25.00 – 35.00
Planter, 9" "C" plate	9099-MI	July 1952	1960	$15.00 – 18.00
Plate, 11"	9011-MI	1953	1960	$14.00 – 16.00
Plate, 12"	9012-MI	1954	1958	$20.00 – 25.00
Plate, 9" "C"	9019-MI	July 1952	July 1961	$10.00 – 12.00
Plate, ftd.	9017-MI	1954	1959	$40.00 – 50.00
Plate, Scroll & Eye	9015-MI	1955	July 1959	$7.00 – 9.00
Plate, #360-8"	9018-MI	1952	1956	$7.00 – 9.00
Shell	9030-MI	1955	1966	$6.00 – 8.00

Milk Glass
Lacy Edge

9029 MI Ftd Comport

9018 MI 8" Plate

9030 MI Lacy Edge Shell

9015 MI Scroll & Eye Plate

9026 Mi 8" C Bowl

9025 MI 8" Scroll & Eye Bowl

9021 MI Scroll & Eye Comport

9011 MI 11" Plate

9028 MI Comport

9520 MI Ladle

9017 MI Ftd. Plate

9019 MI 9" C Plate

9024 MI Banana Bowl

9031 MI Lattice Bowl

9023 MI Flared Lattice Bowl

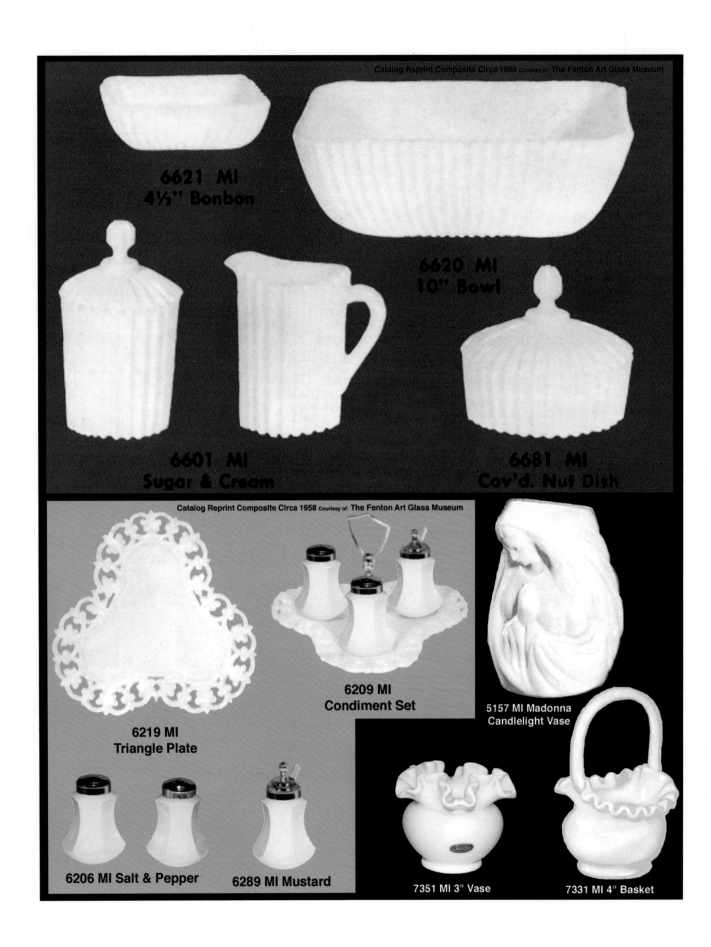

Catalog Reprint Composite Circa 1958 courtesy of: The Fenton Art Glass Museum

6621 MI
4½" Bonbon

6620 MI
10" Bowl

6601 MI
Sugar & Cream

6681 MI
Cov'd. Nut Dish

Catalog Reprint Composite Circa 1958 Courtesy of: The Fenton Art Glass Museum

6219 MI
Triangle Plate

6209 MI
Condiment Set

5157 MI Madonna
Candlelight Vase

6206 MI Salt & Pepper

6289 MI Mustard

7351 MI 3" Vase

7331 MI 4" Basket

102

Fenton Commemorates the Bicentennial of the United States of America
1776-1976
in "Patriot Red"

THE JEFFERSON COMPORT

This distinctive hand made Fenton bowl was commissioned as a commemorative piece for the bicentennial of the signing of The Declaration of American Independence. Designed upon the theme of Thomas Jefferson, it includes in bas-relief a bust of Jefferson and two different views of his beloved Monticello. The cover of the bowl is engraved with four of the many quotes from the pen of this great man.

This bowl is one of a limited edition of 3600 pieces to be made in Patriot Red only in 1975. In 1976, a limited number will be made in a different color. The moulds will then be destroyed forever.

Both as an attractive decorative composition and as a collector's piece, the appreciation of this bowl will grow with the years. Hand-crafted by some of America's finest glass artists, the Jefferson Bowl will take its rightful place among the treasured memorabilia designed for the bicentennial of the founding of The United States of America.

"Patriot Red" is a "new-old" color recreated especially for the occasion. (Antique collectors call it Fenton Red Slag.)

8476 PR
THE JEFFERSON COMPORT

Maximum of 3600 pieces to be produced. Customers who bought this comport in Independence Blue will be given priority on orders placed by February 1. Limited to 2 per store. See enclosed letter.

8470 PR
EAGLE PAPERWEIGHT

8467 PR
PATRIOTS BELL
Cameos of Washington, Adams, Jefferson and Franklin.

9418 PR
EAGLE PLATE
Inscribed on back with quotation from Daniel Webster's eulogy of Adams and Jefferson.

64

Patriot Red

Patriot Red is a brilliant opaque red similar to Fenton's Mandarin Red from the early 1930s. The color was adapted by Fenton, in 1975, especially for the production of pieces commemorating the celebration of America's Bicentennial.

The Eagle paperweight and the Lafayette plate were not offered in the January 1976 price listing. However, they were listed as being available "in limited quantities" in the July price list. Production of the Jefferson comport was limited to 3600 pieces. All the Bicentennial items were discontinued at the end of 1976, and the moulds for the pieces were destroyed.

Patriot Red	Ware No.	Introduced	Discontinued	Value
Bell, Patriot's	8467-PR	1975	1976	$30.00 – 35.00
Comport, Jefferson	8476-PR	1975	1976	$120.00 – 150.00
Paperweight, Eagle	8470-PR	1975	1977	$28.00 – 32.00
Plate, Eagle	9418-PR	1975	1976	$18.00 – 22.00
Plate, Lafayette	9419-PR	July 1975	1977	$18.00 – 22.00
Stein, Bicentennial	8446-PR	July 1975	1976	$27.00 – 32.00

8467 PR Jefferson Comport

8470 PR Eagle Paperweight

9419 PR Lafayette Plate

9418 PR Eagle Plate

8467 PR Patriot's Bell

8446 PR Bicentennial Stein

Rosalene . . .

A dramatic new glass from Fenton. Lovely translucent opaline gently blushing from the warm red glow of pure gold ruby. This demure beauty is offered in seven completely new pieces never offered before in any color or treatment.

8480 RE
Water Lily Candy Box

8452 RE
Fan Vase

8406 RE
Heart Fairy Light

8226 RE
Floral Planter Bowl

8466 RE
Faberge Bell

5197 RE
Bird

8222 RE
Basket Weave Bowl

5108 RE
Fairy Light

Catalog Reprint Circa 1976 Courtesy Of: The Fenton Art Glass Museum

105

Rosalene and Rosalene Satin

Rosalene is a heat-sensitive opaque pink glass with white swirls that Fenton introduced in January 1976. Fenton made 27 different items in Rosalene during the three years this color was in production. This type of glassware was first made around the turn of the twentieth century. Glassware of this type from that era is often referred to as "slag" glass. During the late 1960s and early 1970s, Fenton chemist Charley Goe and Frank M. Fenton worked together to re-create glassware with this pink slag appearance. After numerous trials, success was achieved in 1972. The formula and process were refined, and the first pieces of Rosalene entered the line in 1976.

Although the color was attractive and sold well, production problems limited Fenton's ability to produce this type of glassware. Early batches that were made in 1976 were bright pink in color. Formula changes, made in an effort to prevent the molten glassware from eating through the melting pots, resulted in later runs of Rosalene having a paler pink color.

Acid-dipped, satin-finished Candy Stripe Satin Rosalene lamps entered the line in July 1976. Two of the lamps were discontinued in mid-1977, and the last one remained in production through the end of the year.

Although it is difficult to produce, the Rosalene color has reappeared on occasion. In the June 1989 supplement a limited number of pieces appeared as part of the Connoisseur Collection. Three pieces of Rosalene and two pieces of hand-painted Rosalene Satin were made:

Rosalene	Ware No.	Number Produced
Epergne set, 5-pc.	7605-RE	2000
Pitcher, Diamond	7060-RE	2500
Vase, Basket Weave	8354-RE	2500
Rosalene Satin	Ware No.	Number Produced
Bell	9667-KT	3500
Lamp, 21" Classic student	9308-TT	1000

In 1992, several limited edition pieces were made. The No. 4647 Empress basket was limited to 1500 pieces. The No. 6761 Paisley bell and the No. 5193 Fish paperweight were both made in a number limited to 2000. More recently, in 1998, an opal rung Rosalene bell was used as the background for a Fairy Roses limited edition hand-painted bell. This special bell was limited to 2500 pieces. In 1999, a hand-painted Rosalene No. 6833-8" basket was included in the Family Signature Series. This basket was signed by Lynn Fenton Erb and was limited in production to sales through April 30, 1999.

Several items of hand-painted Rosalene appeared in the 2002 *General Catalog* as a part of the strictly limited and numbered Honor Collection. This collection was created as a tribute to former Fenton chemist Charley Goe. The hand-painted design on this Rosalene background was named Trailing Flower on Rosalene. The pattern was designed by Fenton artist Diane Gessel and featured a "blush rose framed in a cascade of heart-shaped leaves and tiny berries." Items in the collection included:

Trailing Floral on Rosalene	Ware No.	Number Produced
Basket, 10½"	6531-R4	1950
Cat figure, 5"	5065-R4	2750
Fairy light, 3-pc	7610-R4	1750
Rose bowl, 3"	2759-R4	2500
Vase, 6"	7515-R4	2500
Vase, 11" Feather	2782-R4	1750

Additional Rosalene items have been produced for QVC. In 1988, a No. C7532-QX rose-decorated hand-painted basket with William C. Fenton's signature was made. Items made in 1991 included a rose-decorated hand-painted Rosalene Satin No. C7255-QX tulip vase with William C. Fenton signature, a No. C7370-QX rose-decorated hand-painted Beaded Melon small pitcher, a No. C7124-QX rose-decorated hand-painted rose bowl, and a pair of No. C5101-RE Kissing Kids. Rosalene items produced in 1992 for QVC were a No. C9435-R7 satin Curtain basket, a No. C5487-RE Holly plate, a hand-painted No. C6572-R5 basket, a No. C8462-RE Hanging Cherries small jug, a No. C7551-QX hand-painted Dolphin fan vase and a No. C5127-RJ iridescent swan. The popularity of Rosalene continued in 1993 with the production of a No. CV024-QX hand-painted Wave Crest small jug, a hand-painted No. C7501-6V three-piece fairy, light, a No. C5140-6K hand-painted egg, a No. C5165-6R satin hand-painted cat, a No. C1220-R7 satin Spiral Optic 14" vase, a No. CV026-RE Orange Tree basket with

Candy Stripe Lamps

Three stunning new lamps in bright new Fenton CANDY STRIPE pattern. A French Colonial, Gone with the Wind, and large Student Lamp, each fitted with entirely new metal fittings, each in beautiful Fenton Satin Rosalene. CANDY STRIPE is an adaptation of an early Fenton Swirl or Spiral pattern glass. You can be sure these unusual lamps will catch your customer's eye.

2606 SR
20" STUDENT LAMP

2601 SR
21" STUDENT LAMP

Fenton

5197 RE
BIRD

2602 SR
22" GONE WITH THE WIND LAMP

Lions interior, a hand-painted No. CV036-6R satin pinch vase, a hand-painted No. 7660-6R satin ribbed vase, a hand-painted No. C3995-6R satin slipper, a hand-painted No. C5228-6R satin doll figure, and a hand-painted No. C5114-1N satin Girl Angel. Items produced in 1994 included a No. CV05-RE Lamb's Tongue basket, a No. C9020-RJ iridescent shell bowl, a hand-painted No. C7259-4U satin vase with George Fenton's signature, a No. C3801-RJ iridescent mini epergne, a No. C5151-8T satin hand-painted bear figure, and a No. C5160-8I hand-painted satin fawn. Items made in 1995 included a No. C9752-R7 satin Daffodil vase and a hand-painted No. C5197-8I satin Happiness Bird. In 1997, a No. 8464-RE Water Lily pitcher with Bill Fenton's signature was offered. A No. CV248-R7 satin Spiral Optic epergne and a No. C5144-HV satin hand-painted Girl Angel bell were produced in 1998. Items made in 1999 for QVC were a hand-painted No. CV295-QY Spiral Optic tulip vase and a No. CV256 R7 satin Spiral Optic three-piece fairy light. In 2000, a hand-painted No. CV282-TR basket with an opal edge and handle was made as part of the Glass Legacy Collection. This basket had Bill Fenton's signature. Other items made this year included a No. C5162 iridescent hand-painted bunny, a No. C5146-TR iridescent hand-painted egg, and a No. C1500-QY hand-painted Rib Optic handled guest set.

Rosalene	Ware No.	Introduced	Discontinued	Value
Basket, 7" Threaded Diamond Optic	8435-RE	1976	1978	$130.00 – 150.00
Bell, Faberge	8466-RE	1976	1979	$28.00 – 32.00
Bird, Happiness	5197-RE	1976	1979	$30.00 – 35.00
Bird, small	5163-RE	1978	1979	$30.00 – 35.00
Bonbon, handled Butterfly	8230-RE	1976	1978	$30.00 – 35.00
Bowl, Basket Weave	8222-RE	1976	1979	$20.00 – 25.00
Bowl, Carolina Dogwood	9424-RE	1977	1978	$80.00 – 90.00
Bowl, Curtain	8454-RE	July 1978	1979	$40.00 – 50.00
Bowl, 3-toed Leaf and Orange Tree	8223-RE	1976	1978	$50.00 – 60.00
Bowl, 3-toed Water Lily	8426-RE	1976	1978	$60.00 – 65.00
Bunny	5162-RE	1978	1979	$35.00 – 40.00
Candleholder, Water Lily	8473-RE	1976	1978	$25.00 – 30.00
Candy box, Chessie	9480-RE	1977	1978	$175.00 – 190.00
Candy box, covered Ogee	9394-RE	1976	1978	$220.00 – 250.00
Candy box, ftd. Water Lily	8480-RE	1976	1978	$120.00 – 140.00
Comport, ftd. flowered	8422-RE	1976	1978	$60.00 – 65.00
Fairy light, Heart	8406-RE	1976	1978	$80.00 – 90.00
Fairy light, owl	5108-RE	1976	1979	$80.00 – 85.00
Lamp, Chou Ting ceremonial	8407-RE	1977	July 1977	$200.00 – 225.00
Planter bowl, Verly's hexagonal	8226-RE	1976	1978	$65.00 – 75.00
Plate, 8" Leaf	5116-RE	1977	1978	$30.00 – 35.00
Swan, open	5127-RE	1977	1979	$40.00 – 45.00
Swan, solid	5161-RE	1978	1979	$35.00 – 40.00
Vase, bud	9056-RE	1977	1979	$70.00 – 80.00
Vase, fan	8452-RE	1976	July 1976	$100.00 – 125.00
Vase, 3-toed Grape	8457-RE	July 1978	1979	$45.00 – 50.00

Satin Rosalene	Ware No.	Introduced	Discontinued	Value
Lamp, 20" Candy Stripe	2606-SR	July 1976	1978	$600.00 – 800.00
Lamp, 21" Candy Stripe	2601-SR	July 1976	July 1977	$800.00 – 1000.00
Lamp, 22" Candy Stripe	2602-SR	July 1976	July 1977	$700.00 – 850.00

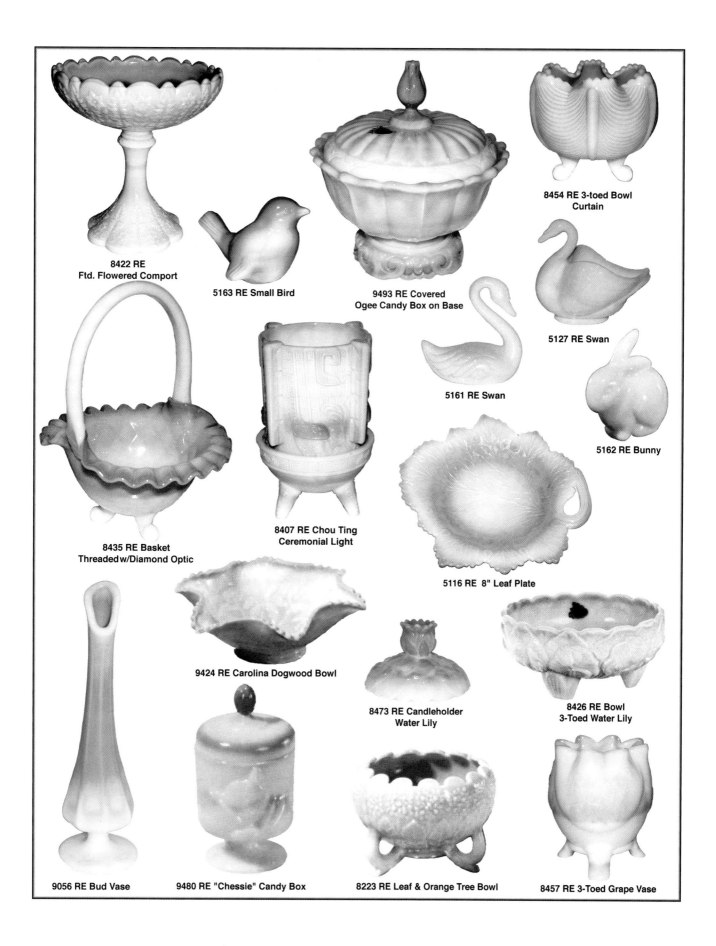

8422 RE
Ftd. Flowered Comport

5163 RE Small Bird

9493 RE Covered
Ogee Candy Box on Base

8454 RE 3-toed Bowl
Curtain

5127 RE Swan

5161 RE Swan

5162 RE Bunny

8435 RE Basket
Threaded w/Diamond Optic

8407 RE Chou Ting
Ceremonial Light

5116 RE 8" Leaf Plate

9424 RE Carolina Dogwood Bowl

8473 RE Candleholder
Water Lily

8426 RE Bowl
3-Toed Water Lily

9056 RE Bud Vase

9480 RE "Chessie" Candy Box

8223 RE Leaf & Orange Tree Bowl

8457 RE 3-Toed Grape Vase

Rose Pastel

Pastel blue, green, and pink opaque colors were put into the line by Fenton in January 1954. Fenton's name for the pink opaque pastel color was Rose Pastel. Of the three pastel colors, Rose Pastel remained in production for the longest period and was used in the widest assortment of items. Rose Pastel was discontinued at the end of 1957 when production of the last remaining item — the No. 3513 footed cake plate — ended. Some pieces, such as the No. 7353-6" vase, the No. 5183 hen, and the boudoir lamps were only made for a short time. As a result, they are not easily found today. The boudoir lamps were originally listed as fairy lamps when they were introduced. In a later catalog they were called boudoir lamps. They were sold either with a candle insert or with an electric fitting.

In addition to the items listed below, Rose Pastel was also used in the Daisy & Button, Hobnail, Lamb's Tongue, and Swirl patterns. For more information on pieces in these patterns see the appropriate listings in the book *Fenton Art Glass Patterns 1939 – 1980*.

Rose Pastel	Ware No.	Introduced	Discontinued	Value
Bowl, shallow	3523-RP	1956	1957	$40.00 – 45.00
Cake plate, ftd.	3513-RP	1954	1958	$40.00 – 45.00
Comport, ftd.	7228-RP	1954	1957	$40.00 – 45.00
Hen on basket	5183-RP	1954	1955	$70.00 – 80.00
Lamp, boudoir (candle)	7390-RP	1954	1955	$95.00 – 120.00
Lamp, boudoir (electric)	7392-RP	1954	1955	$95.00 – 120.00
Plate, 8" Leaf	5116-RP	1955	July 1956	$18.00 – 20.00
Plate, 11" Leaf	5118-RP	1955	July 1956	$25.00 – 30.00
Tidbit, 2-tier Leaf	5196-RP	1955	July 1956	$50.00 – 55.00
Vase, 6"	7353-RP	July 1954	1955	$30.00 – 35.00
Vase, 6" bud	7348-RP	July 1954	1956	$30.00 – 35.00
Vase, 6½" bud	7349-RP	July 1954	1956	$30.00 – 35.00

Lacy Edge	Ware No.	Introduced	Discontinued	Value
Bowl, Banana	9024-RP	1955	1957	$50.00 – 55.00
Bowl, 8" "C"	9026-RP	1954	1957	$20.00 – 25.00
Bowl, Scroll & Eye	9025-RP	1955	1957	$20.00 – 25.00
Comport	9028-RP	1954	1957	$40.00 – 50.00
Comport, ftd.	9029-RP	1954	1957	$40.00 – 50.00
Comport, Scroll & Eye	9021-RP	1955	1957	$35.00 – 40.00
Planter, 9" "C" plate	9099-RP	1954	1957	$20.00 – 25.00
Plate, 11"	9011-RP	1954	1955	$20.00 – 25.00
Plate, 12"	9012-RP	1955	1957	$25.00 – 30.00
Plate, 9" "C"	9019-RP	1954	1957	$18.00 – 22.00
Plate, #360-8"	9018-RP	1954	1955	$12.00 – 14.00
Plate, Scroll & Eye	9015-RP	1955	July 1956	$12.00 – 14.00

5183 RP Hen on Basket   **9026 RP 8" C Bowl**   **7390 RP Boudoir Lamp (Fairy Light)**   **7228 RP Ftd. Comport**

9029 RP Footed Comport

9018 RP 8" Plate

Catalog Reprint Composite Circa 1955
Courtesy Of:
The Fenton Art Glass Museum

9025 RP 8" Bowl

5196 RP Leaf Tidbit

**7348 RP 6"
Bud Vase**

**7349 RP 6 1/2"
Bud Vase**

7353 RP 6" Vase

9028 RP Footed Comport

9011 RP 11" Plate

3513 RP Cake Plate

3523 RP Shallow Bowl

5116 RP 8" Leaf Plate

9019 RP 9" C Plate

5118 RP 11" Leaf Plate

9024 RP Banana Bowl

Rose Satin

Rose Satin (RS) glassware was brought into the Fenton general line in 1974. It was advertised as "rose hued glass made with pure gold." As a result of the heat-sensitive nature of this color, shapes were limited to blown pieces. Several new items were added to the line in 1975. The first item discontinued was the No. 7434-11" basket, after only six months of production. A few more pieces were discontinued at the end of 1976, and the color was discontinued at the end of 1977. Several items, such as the lamps, fairy light, rose bowl, and 11" basket, are not easily found today.

An earlier, opalescent version of Rose Satin (RA) was made in the mid-1950s in the Diamond Optic, Fern, and Rib Optic patterns. For more information about these patterns, see the book *Fenton Art Glass Patterns 1939 – 1980.*

Rose Satin	Ware No.	Introduced	Discontinued	Value
Basket	7437-RS	1975	1978	$45.00 – 55.00
Basket, 11"	7434-RS	1974	July 1974	$50.00 – 60.00
Basket, 7" deep Poppy	9138-RS	1974	1978	$65.00 – 75.00
Fairy lamp, 2-pc.	7492-RS	1975	1977	$40.00 – 50.00
Lamp, Poppy GWTW	9101-RS	1974	1978	$300.00 – 350.00
Lamp, 20" Poppy student	9107-RS	1974	1978	$250.00 – 290.00
Pitcher	7464-RS	1974	1977	$30.00 – 40.00
Pitcher, 36 oz. Water Lily	8464-RS	1976	July 1977	$40.00 – 45.00
Rose bowl	7424-RS	1975	1977	$22.00 – 27.00
Vase, 6"	7451-RS	1974	1978	$25.00 – 30.00
Vase, 7"	7252-RS	1975	1978	$35.00 – 40.00
Vase, 8"	9155-RS	1974	1978	$27.00 – 32.00
Vase, 11"	7458-RS	1974	July 1977	$40.00 – 50.00
Vase, 7" Poppy	9154-RS	1974	1978	$40.00 – 50.00

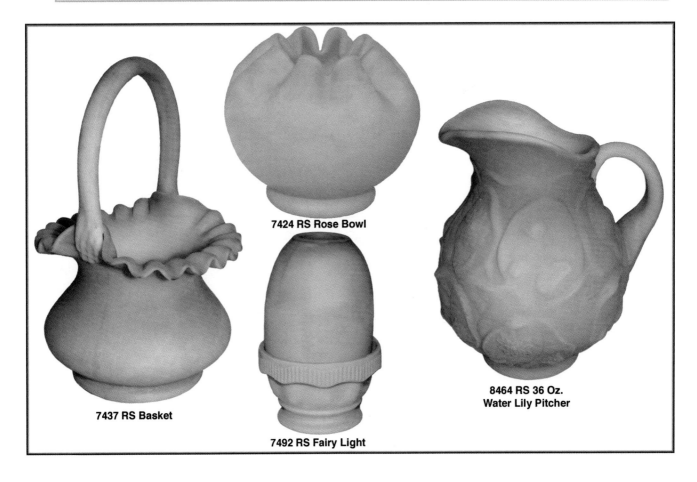

7437 RS Basket

7424 RS Rose Bowl

7492 RS Fairy Light

8464 RS 36 Oz.
Water Lily Pitcher

Catalog Reprint
Courtesy Of:
The Fenton Art Glass Museum

7458 RS 7451 RS 9138 RS

9107 RS 7434 RS 9154 RS 7464 RS

CATALOG SUPPLEMENT • JANUARY 1974

Rose Satin

An exquisite rose hued glass made
with pure gold. Hand formed
and satinized to an alluring
blush. The newest in
Fenton Satin color creations.

Fenton

The Fenton Art Glass Company
Williamstown, West Virginia 26187

9155 RS

9101 RS

Turquoise

Fenton's opaque Turquoise color was introduced in July 1955 and remained in the line through 1957. The more aqua-colored turquoise replaced Blue Pastel as the opaque blue color that was made to complement Rose Pastel and Green Pastel during their final years of production.

Cased Lilac is an interesting cased variation of this color made by using Turquoise as the outer layer and Lilac as the interior layer. For items made in the Cased Lilac color, see page 130.

Turquoise	Ware No.	Introduced	Discontinued	Value
Bowl, shallow	3523-TU	1956	July 1956	$40.00 – 50.00
Cake plate	3513-TU	1955	1957	$45.00 – 55.00
Comport, ftd.	7228-TU	1955	1957	$45.00 – 55.00
Jug, 6" handled	6066-TU	1956	July 1956	$40.00 – 45.00
Jug, 6½" handled	6068-TU	1956	July 1956	$55.00 – 65.00
Plate, 8" Leaf	5116-TU	1955	July 1956	$18.00 – 22.00
Plate, 11" Leaf	5118-TU	1955	1957	$25.00 – 30.00
Tidbit, 2-tier Leaf	5196-TU	July 1955	July 1956	$50.00 – 60.00
Vase, 11½"	7364-TU	1956	July 1956	$150.00 – 180.00
Vase, 12"	7361-TU	1956	July 1956	$150.00 – 180.00
Vase, 10" handled	7360-TU	July 1955	July 1956	$120.00 – 150.00

Lacy Edge	Ware No.	Introduced	Discontinued	Value
Bowl, Banana	9024-TU	1955	1957	$50.00 – 55.00
Bowl, 8" "C"	9026-TU	1955	July 1956	$20.00 – 25.00
Bowl, Scroll & Eye	9025-TU	1955	1957	$20.00 – 25.00
Comport	9028-TU	1955	1957	$40.00 – 50.00
Comport, ftd.	9029-TU	1955	1957	$40.00 – 50.00
Comport, Scroll & Eye	9021-TU	1955	1957	$35.00 – 45.00
Planter, 9" "C" plate	9099-TU	1955	July 1956	$20.00 – 25.00
Plate, #360-8"	9018-TU	1955	1956	$12.00 – 14.00
Plate, 11"	9011-TU	1955	July 1956	$20.00 – 25.00
Plate, 9" "C"	9019-TU	1955	July 1956	$18.00 – 22.00
Plate, Scroll & Eye	9015-TU	1955	1957	$12.00 – 14.00
Shell	9030-TU	1955	July 1956	$12.00 – 15.00

7361 TU 12" Vase   **7360 TU 10" Handled Vase**   **7364 TU 11 1/2" Vase**   **6068 TU 6 1/2" Handled Jug**

3513 TU Footed Cake Plate

9024 TU Banana Bowl

6066 TU 6" Handled Jug

9028 TU Comport

9011 TU 11" Plate

7228 TU Footed Comport

9018 TU 9" C Plate

5116 TU 8" Leaf Plate

9030 TU Shell

9026 TU 8" C Bowl

9018 TU 8" Plate

9015 TU Scroll & Eye 8" Plate

Valley Forge White

Valley Forge White was Fenton's patriotic name for its white opaque satinized glassware produced to commemorate America's Bicentennial. The color was introduced with two items in July 1975, and five additional pieces were made in 1976 to complete the line. The Bicentennial items were discontinued at the end of 1976, and the moulds were destroyed.

Valley Forge White	Ware No.	Introduced	Discontinued	Value
Bell, Patriot's	8467-VW	1976	1977	$1800 – 22.00
Comport, Jefferson	8476-VW	1976	1977	$90.00 – 110.00
Paperweight, Eagle	8470-VW	1976	1977	$18.00 – 22.00
Plate, Eagle	9418-VW	1976	1977	$14.00 – 16.00
Plate, Lafayette	9419-VW	July 1975	1977	$16.00 – 18.00
Planter, Patriot's	8499-VW	1976	1977	$25.00 – 30.00
Stein, Bicentennial	8446-VW	July 1975	1977	$20.00 – 25.00

8470 VW Eagle Paperweight

8446 VW Stein

9418 VW Eagle Plate

8467 VW Patriot's Bell

8499 Patriot's Planter

8476 Jefferson Comport

116

White Satin

Fenton added satin milk glass to the general line in 1971. This new version of soft colored milk glass was called white satin (WS). All items except the prayer children were discontinued by the end of the decade. In addition to the pieces listed below, Fenton produced numerous collector plates during this era. More information about these plates is presented in the next few pages.

White Satin	Ware No.	Introduced	Discontinued	Value
Ashtray/Chip' n dip/Candle bowl, Water Lily	8478-WS	1975	1978	$27.00 – 30.00
Bell, Bride & Groom	9168-WS	1977	1979	$20.00 – 25.00
Bell, Madonna	9467-WS	1975	1977	$20.00 – 25.00
Bird	5197-WS	1972	1979	$18.00 – 22.00
Bookends, Girl and Fawn	5102-WS	1972	1973	$100.00 – 125.00
Bowl, 9" Water Lily	8424-WS	1975	July 1976	$27.00 – 32.00
Boy and girl, praying	5100-WS	1972	1980+	$22.00 – 27.00
Butterfly	5170-WS	1972	July 1972	$15.00 – 18.00
Candleholder, Water Lily	8473-WS	1975	July 1976	$15.00 – 18.00
Candy box, ftd. Water Lily	8480-WS	1975	1977	$25.00 – 30.00
Cart	5124-WS	1972	1973	$100.00 – 120.00
Comport, ftd. Water Lily	8481-WS	1975	1977	$18.00 – 22.00
Donkey	5125-WS	1972	1973	$140.00 – 160.00
Elephant	5123-WS	1972	July 1972	$180.00 – 200.00
Jardiniere, Water Lily	8498-WS	1975	1977	$25.00 – 30.00
Lamp, 24" GWTW	9101-WS	1976	1979	$175.00 – 200.00
Lamp, 37" Rose GWTW	9202-WS	1971	1976	$180.00 – 200.00
Lamp, 38" Rose pillar	9201-WS	1971	1973	$160.00 – 180.00
Light, Chou Ting Ceremonial	8407-WS	1977	July 1977	$125.00 – 150.00
Paperweight, fish	5193-WS	1972	1973	$20.00 – 24.00
Pitcher, 36 oz. Water Lily	8464-WS	1976	1978	$27.00 – 32.00

8473 WS Candleholder

8480 WS Footed Candy Box

5125 WS Donkey

5124 WS Cart

8498 WS Jardiniere

8478 WS Ashtray/Chip 'n Dip/Candle Bowl

AUTHENTIC
Fenton
HANDMADE

White Satin

For the soft touch, in handmade glass.

9101 WS
24" GONE WITH THE WIND LAMP
Shipping Weight 13 lbs.

9416 SL
ANNIVERSARY PLATE

8464 WS
36 OZ. PITCHER

8407 WS
CHOU TING CERE. LIGHT

9168 WS
BRIDE & GROOM BELL

5100 WS
PRAYING BOY & GIRL

5197 WS
BIRD

Catalog Reprint courtesy of: The Fenton Art Glass Museum

White Satin Anniversary Plates

The Anniversary plate in white satin was incorporated into the Fenton line in July 1971. The white satin 25th Anniversary plate was added a year later. Both versions of plates in plain white satin were discontinued at the end of 1974. In 1975, the Anniversary plate appeared with gold, silver, and blue trim, and the 25th Anniversary plate was marketed with silver trim. The Anniversary plate with blue trim was discontinued at the end of 1975. The Anniversary plate with silver decoration was discontinued at the end of 1977, and the two remaining plates were discontinued at the end of 1978.

White Satin	Ware No.	Introduced	Discontinued	Value
Plate, Anniversary	9416-WS	July 1971	1975	$10.00 – 12.00
Plate, Anniversary (blue trim)	9416-BL	1975	1976	$18.00 – 22.00
Plate, Anniversary (gold trim)	9416-GL	1975	1979	$12.00 – 15.00
Plate, Anniversary (silver trim)	9416-SL	1975	1978	$12.00 – 15.00
Plate, 25th Anniversary	9417-WS	July 1972	1975	$11.00 – 13.00
Plate, 25th Anniversary (silver trim)	9417-SL	1975	1979	$11.00 – 13.00

Catalog Reprint
Courtesy Of:
The Fenton Art Glass Museum

Anniversary Plates w/Stand

9416 GL

9416 SL

9416 BL

9417 SL

White Satin Christmas Series Collector Plates

Fenton's Christmas in America collection of 12 different plates was available in the catalog supplements from July through December each year from 1970 through 1981. The first plate was only in the regular line in Fenton's Carnival. color. Starting in 1971, each plate in the series was made in blue satin, Carnival, and white satin. Moulds for the plates were destroyed at the end of each year. The subject of each plate is listed below.

Christmas Plate	Ware No.	Subject	Value
1972 Plate	8272-WS	"The Two Horned Church," Marietta, Ohio	$12.00 – 14.00
1973 Plate	8273-WS	"St. Mary's in the Mountains," Virginia City, Nevada	$11.00 – 13.00
1974 Plate	8274-WS	"The Nation's Church," Philadelphia, Pa.	$11.00 – 13.00
1975 Plate	8275-WS	"Birthplace of Liberty," Richmond, Virginia	$11.00 – 13.00
1976 Plate	8276-WS	"The Old North Church," Boston, Mass.	$11.00 – 13.00
1977 Plate	8277-WS	"San Carlos Borromeo De Carmelo," Carmel, Calif.	$11.00 – 13.00
1978 Plate	8278-WS	"The Church of the Holy Trinity," Philadelphia, Pa.	$11.00 – 13.00
1979 Plate	8279-WS	"San Jose y Miguel De Aguayo," San Antonio, Texas	$11.00 – 13.00
1980 Plate	8280-WS	"Christ Church," Alexandria, Virginia.	$11.00 – 13.00
1981 Plate	8281-WS	"Mission of San Xavier Del Bac," Tucson, Arizona	$11.00 – 13.00

1972 WS Christmas Plate

Back of
1972 Christmas Plate

1974 WS Christmas Plate

1975 WS Christmas Plate

Back of
1980 Christmas Plate

1980 WS Christmas Plate

White Satin Mother's Day Series Collector Plates

The Madonna Mother's Day series of plates first appeared in 1971. The final plate in this series was issued in 1979. Each year plates could be ordered from the January catalog supplement. Moulds for each plate were destroyed at the end of June each year. Each plate was also sold in Carnival and blue satin and came with a hand-finished wooden holder. Plates were offered in white satin beginning in 1972.

Mother's Day	Ware No.	Subject	Value
1972 Plate	9317-BA	"Madonna of the Goldfinch"	$11.00 – 13.00
1973 Plate	9318-BA	"The Small Cowpen Madonna"	$11.00 – 13.00
1974 Plate	9319-BA	"Madonna of the Grotto"	$11.00 – 13.00
1975 Plate	9375-BA	"Taddei Madonna"	$11.00 – 13.00
1976 Plate	9376-BA	"The Holy Night"	$11.00 – 13.00
1977 Plate	9377-BA	"Madonna and Child with Pomegranate"	$11.00 – 13.00
1978 Plate	9378-BA	"The Madonnina"	$11.00 – 13.00
1979 Plate	9379-BA	"Madonna of the Rose Hedge"	$11.00 – 13.00

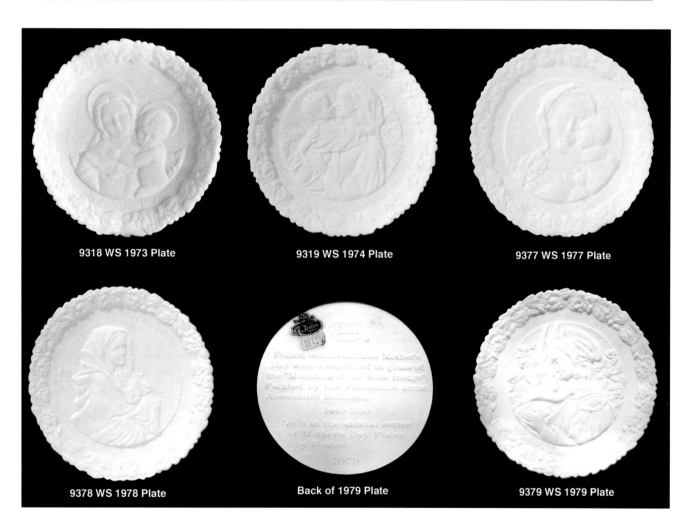

9318 WS 1973 Plate   9319 WS 1974 Plate   9377 WS 1977 Plate

9378 WS 1978 Plate   Back of 1979 Plate   9379 WS 1979 Plate

Miscellaneous Opaque Colors

Numerous items were made in colors as samples or for special orders, Except for the pipe ashtray, the items pictured below were not in the regular Fenton line. The opaque green color shown below has been dubbed "Kitchen Green" for lack of an official name. This color was used primarily for lamp parts made for the E. P. Paul Co.

Opaque Colored Item	Value
1. Jonquil Yellow No. 5193 fish paperweight	$80.00 – 90.00
2 Green Marble No. 9070 pipe ashtray (in the regular line from July 1952 through December 1954)	$90.00 – 110.00
3. Hexagonal No. 8226 planter bowl made in Jonquil Yellow and from Verly's mould	$100.00 – 120.00
4. No. 5180 Owl Decision Maker in Pekin Blue II	$75.00 – 85.00
5. Blue opaque No. 848 3-ftd. candleholder	$40.00 – 45.00
6. No. 848 3-ftd. candleholder in Kitchen Green	$28.00 – 35.00
7. Blue opaque lamp made for the E. P. Paul Company	$115.00 – 135.00
8. Milady pattern vase made in Kitchen Green	$220.00 – 245.00
9. Hexagonal No. 8226 planter bowl made in Pekin Blue II from Verly's mould	$90.00 – 110.00
10. No. 3264-11½" vase made in Kitchen Green	$100.00 – 120.00
11. Kitchen Green lamp made for the E. P. Paul Company, with the original Paulix label	$95.00 – 115.00

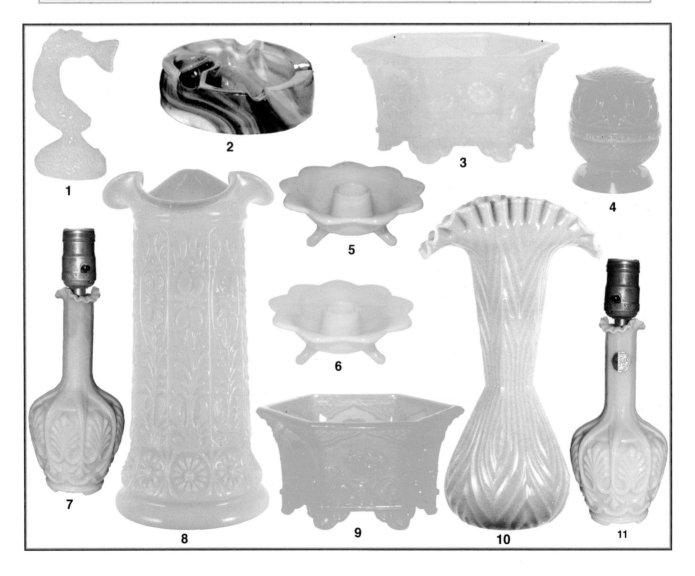

INTRODUCING

Tiara

in

Crests

and

• • •

Overlays

Catalo Reprint Circa 1949

Courtesy Of:

The Fenton Art Glass Museum

DESCRIPTION OF ITEM AND COLOR IN WHICH SHOWN.

Top Row:—Left to Right
711—5" Vase—Ivy
711—4" Rose Bowl—
　　　　　　Gold Overlay
711—5½" Hdl. Jug—
　　　　　　Blue Overlay
711—Covered Candy Jar—
　　　　　　Silver Crest
711—4" Handled Creamer—
　　　　　　Green Overlay

Middle Row:
711—6" Handled Jug—
　　　　　　Gold Overlay
711—Miniature Vase—
　　　　　　Peach Crest
711—8" Vase—Green Overlay
711—Miniature Vase—
　　　　　　Gold Overlay
711—7" Handled Basket—
　　　　　　Peach Crest

Bottom Row:
711—9" Vase—Peach Crest
711—Miniature Vase—
　　　　　　Blue Overlay
711—3 pc. Vanity Set—
　　　　　　Green Overlay
711—Miniature Vase—
　　　　　　Silver Crest
711—4" Handled Creamer—
　　　　　　Blue Overlay

COMPLETE LIST OF ITEMS MADE IN THE NEW TIARA LINE IS CONTAINED IN PRICE LIST.

The art of the Fenton craftsmen is beautifully displayed in these five new Fenton overlay colors. The Milk Glass inner lining mirrors the outside layer of glass in creating the colors of Wild Rose, Coral, Powder Blue, Honey Amber and Apple Green.

*5858 BV
8" DC Vase

Catalog Reprint Circa 1961
Courtesy Of:
The Fenton Art Glass Museum

*5858 WR
8" DC Vase

*5858 AG
8" DC Vase

*5858 HA
8" DC Vase

*5858 CL
8" DC Vase

Fenton's Overlay Colors

Overlay glassware, or cased glassware as it is sometimes called, is composed of more than one layer of glass. During the 1800s, this type of glassware was popular in the Bohemian area of Europe. Many of the finished overlay pieces were cut, allowing the underlying layer to show clearly. Overlay glass in the United States was first produced in New England in the 1880s.

Cased glass is blown ware that is produced through the cooperative efforts of a team of glassworkers. The process is initiated when a casing boy gathers a small quantity of molten glass on a punty from a pot furnace. The glass is rolled into a thin shaft on a marver (a small table with a smooth steel top). The gob of glass is kept pliable by being reheated as necessary in a small furnace called a glory hole. The next worker, called a caser, cuts a small piece of this pliable glass from the shaft and attaches it to a blow pipe. The caser moulds the glass to the proper shape around the tip of the blow pipe. Any necessary reheating is performed by a warming-in boy who reheats the glass in the glory hole. After the initial gather has been properly shaped, the warming-in boy, takes the blow pipe with the hot gob of glass to a gatherer. This individual gathers a new layer of glass over the first layer on the end of the blow pipe. The blow pipe is then passed to the striker, who inserts the glass into the glory hole. The glass is reheated to the proper temperature for blowing. When this is accomplished, the blow pipe is passed to the blower, who places the glass into a mould. The blower forces the glass to conform to the shape of the mould by either blowing with his mouth or, in some cases, using compressed air. After the piece is shaped, it is removed from the mould and sent to the finisher or handler. After the piece has been finished or a handle has been applied, the piece is sent to the annealing lehr for a controlled cool down.

Records indicate Fenton first produced overlay glassware in 1939. Ruby Overlay, Peach Blow, and Cranberry Opalescent were the first overlay colors to enter the line. Ruby Overlay was used primarily with the Diamond Optic pattern during this era. Spiral Optic shapes were produced in Cranberry Opalescent. The addition of a spun crystal edge to Peach Blow resulted in the Peach Crest pattern in 1940. All of these colors used Gold Ruby as the interior layer. During the 1940s, the Hobnail, and Coin Dot patterns were made in Cranberry Opalescent. Blue Overlay and Rose Overlay also had prominent places in the line during the decade. Many of the pieces in these two colors were made in Fenton's popular Melon Rib shapes. Another overlay color that used the Diamond Optic pattern was Mulberry. This color was made in 1942, and was the result of a light blue overlay of Gold Ruby. More information about these colors in the Coin Dot, Hobnail and Diamond Optic patterns may be found in the book *Fenton Art Glass Patterns 1939 – 1980*.

In 1949, Fenton retooled the Melon Rib moulds and introduced the Beaded Melon shape. This new Tiara line included the new overlay colors of Ivy, Green Overlay, and Gold Overlay. Gold Overlay was short lived and was no longer in the line by 1950. Green Overlay and Ivy fared somewhat better, with some pieces of these colors remaining in the line until the end of 1953.

During the mid-1950s, a Turquoise overlay color called Cased Lilac was produced for one year. This color was made by casing Turquoise with an interior layer of Gold Ruby. Shortly afterward, a yellow overlay color called Goldenrod was made. There were serious color control and other production problems, so this color was only in the line for six months. Ruby Overlay revived the Polka Dot pattern and was also popular with several lamp styles. Production of Jamestown Blue Overlay, a transparent peacock blue color over milk glass, finished out the overlay production near the end of the decade.

Customers in the early 1960s were offered a choice of colorful light overlay colors. Apple Green Overlay, Coral, Powder Blue Overlay, and Wild Rose Overlay all appeared in the line in 1961. The Bubble Optic and Jacqueline patterns were produced in these colors. The No. 6080 Wave Crest candy boxes and the Wheat Sheaf vases appeared in all of these colors, and several different lamps in Fenton's Rose pattern were also made in Wild Rose Overlay. The darker overlay colors, Plated Amberina and Opaque Blue Overlay, followed in 1962. Plated Amberina was limited to only a few items and was out of the line by the end of 1963. Opaque Blue Overlay fared somewhat better. Although most pieces were discontinued by the end of 1963, some lamps in this color were made into the early 1970s. Fenton introduced Vasa Murrhina–style glassware into the line in 1964. This is a cased glassware that incorporates variegated glass flakes, called frit, into the layers. Fenton made nine different colors of Vasa Murrhina glass before production ended at the end of 1968. Between the end of the production of Vasa Murrhina and 1980, overlay production for the regular line was limited to lamps.

No. 1923 6" Basket

No. 711 10½" Basket

No. 192 10½" Basket

No. 1924 5" Basket

No. 711 6" Jug

No 203 7" DC Bowl

No. 203 7" Basket

No. 711 5 Oz. Tumbler

No. 711 8" Jug

No. 192 6" Jug

No. 711 4" Creamer

No. 1924 Creamer

No. 192 Squat Candleholder

No. 711 5½" Jug

No. 192-A 9" Jug

No. 1924 5" Top Hat

No. 192 6" Squat Jug

No. 192 8" Jug

No 192 Candy or Bath Powder Jar

Blue Overlay	Ware No.	Introduced	Discontinued	Value
Tumbler, #711 5 oz.		1949	1951	$35.00 – 40.00
Vanity set, #192-A 3-pc.		1943	1948	$132.00 – 157.00
Vanity set, #711-3-pc.		1949	1951	$195.00 – 225.00
Vase, 7½"	1357-BV	July 52	1953	$50.00 – 55.00
Vase, 8½"	1352-BV	July 52	1954	$60.00 – 65.00
Vase, #192-5" double crimped, oval		1943	1948	$20.00 – 25.00
Vase, #192-5" square, triangular		1943	1948	$20.00 – 25.00
Vase, #192-5½" double crimped, square		1943	1948	$20.00 – 25.00
Vase, #192-5½" triangular, tulip		1943	1948	$22.00 – 27.00
Vase, #192-6" double crimped, regular		1943	1948	$25.00 – 30.00
Vase, #192-6" square, triangular, tulip		1943	1948	$32.00 – 35.00
Vase, #192-8" double crimped, square		1943	1948	$45.00 – 55.00
Vase, #192-8" triangular, tulip		1943	1948	$50.00 – 60.00
Vase, #192-10" double crimped, square		1943	1946	$50.00 – 60.00
Vase, #192-10" triangular, tulip		1943	1946	$60.00 – 70.00
Vase, #192-A-9" double crimped, square		1943	1948	$45.00 – 55.00
Vase, #203-5" double crimped				$30.00 – 35.00
Vase, #192-A-9" triangular, tulip		1943	1948	$55.00 – 65.00
Vase, #711 miniature crimped, triangular, tulip		1949	1951	$27.00 – 32.00
Vase #711-4½" cupped crimped, double crimped		1949	1951	$27.00 – 32.00
Vase, #711-5" double crimped	7155-BV	1949	1953	$35.00 – 40.00
Vase, #711-5½" crimped, triangular, tulip		1949	1951	$40.00 – 45.00
Vase, #711-6" double crimped	7156-BV	1949	1953	$35.00 – 42.00
Vase, #711-6" tulip	7157-BV	1949	1953	$40.00 – 45.00
Vase, #711-8" double crimped, tulip		1949	1951	$65.00 – 75.00
Vase, #711-9" double crimped, tulip		1949	1951	$70.00 – 80.00
Vase, #1924-5"		1949	1951	$20.00 – 25.00
Vase, #3001-5"		1950	1952	$60.00 – 65.00
Vase, #3001-7"		1950	1952	$70.00 – 75.00
Vase, #3003-6"		1950	1952	$60.00 – 70.00
Vase, #3003-7"		1950	1952	$70.00 – 80.00

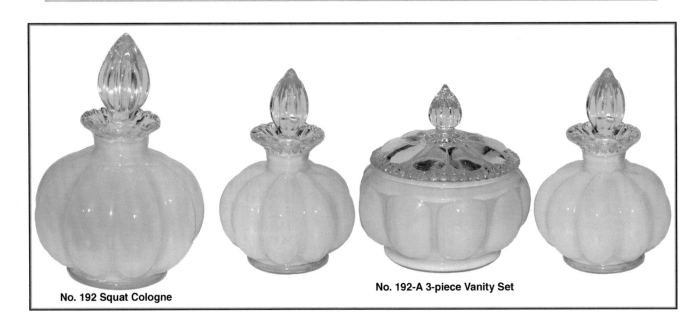

No. 192 Squat Cologne

No. 192-A 3-piece Vanity Set

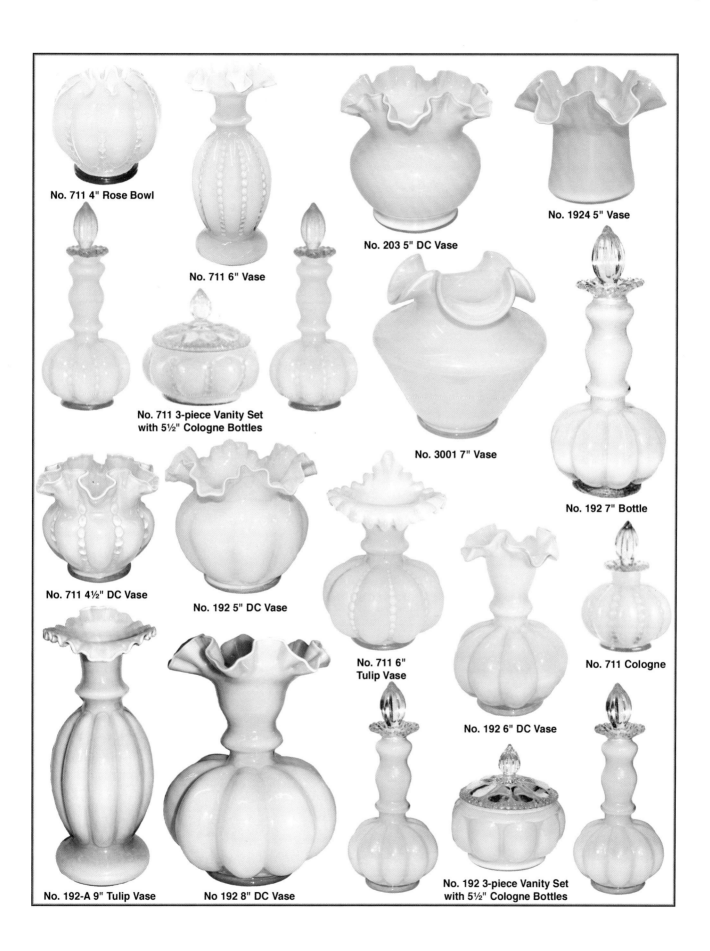

No. 711 4" Rose Bowl

No. 711 6" Vase

No. 203 5" DC Vase

No. 1924 5" Vase

No. 711 3-piece Vanity Set
with 5½" Cologne Bottles

No. 3001 7" Vase

No. 192 7" Bottle

No. 711 4½" DC Vase

No. 192 5" DC Vase

No. 711 6"
Tulip Vase

No. 711 Cologne

No. 192 6" DC Vase

No. 192-A 9" Tulip Vase

No 192 8" DC Vase

No. 192 3-piece Vanity Set
with 5½" Cologne Bottles

Cased Lilac

Cased Lilac is an overlay color that was made from July 1955 through June 1956. The exterior color is Fenton's Turquoise, and the interior color was formed using Gold Ruby. As the listing below indicates, only a handful of pieces were made in this color during the year it was in production.

Cased Lilac	Ware No.	Introduced	Discontinued	Value
Bowl, shell	9020-LC	July 1955	July 1956	$125.00 – 150.00
Jug, 6½" handled	6068-LC	July 1955	July 1956	$75.00 – 95.00
Jug, 9" handled	7264-LC	July 1955	July 1956	$100.00 – 125.00
Vase, 6½"	6058-LC	July 1955	July 1956	$65.00 – 75.00
Vase, 8½"	6059-LC	1956	July 1956	$75.00 – 85.00
Vase, 8½"	7255-LC	July 1955	July 1956	$75.00 – 85.00

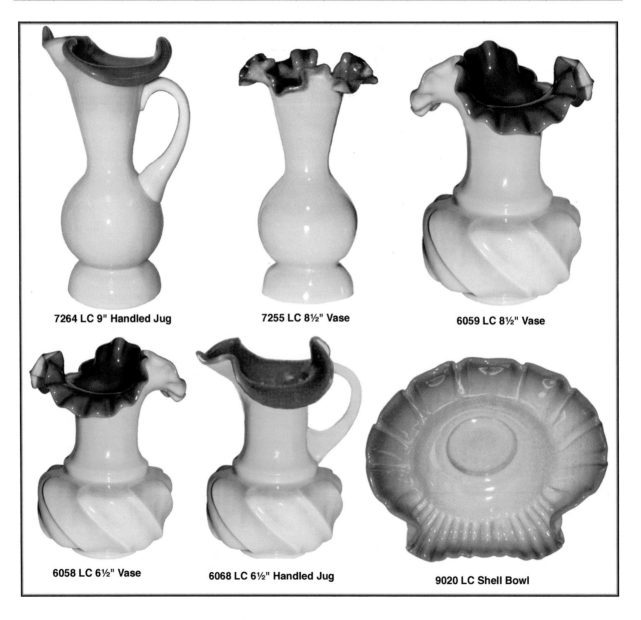

7264 LC 9" Handled Jug   **7255 LC 8½" Vase**   **6059 LC 8½" Vase**

6058 LC 6½" Vase   **6068 LC 6½" Handled Jug**   **9020 LC Shell Bowl**

Coral

Fenton's Coral Overlay (CL) consists of glass with a light pinkish-orange exterior cased with an opal interior. This color was only made during 1961. It was used primarily with the Bubble Optic, Jacqueline, Hobnail, and Wild Rose with Bowknot patterns. For more information about these patterns, see the book *Fenton Art Glass Patterns 1939 – 1980*. Other items produced in this color include the No. 6080 Wave Crest candy box and the No. 5858 Wheat Sheaf vase.

Coral	Ware No.	Introduced	Discontinued	Value
Candy box, Wave Crest	6080-CL	1961	1962	$95.00 – 115.00
Vase, 8" Wheat Sheaf	5858-CL	1961	1962	$60.00 – 70.00

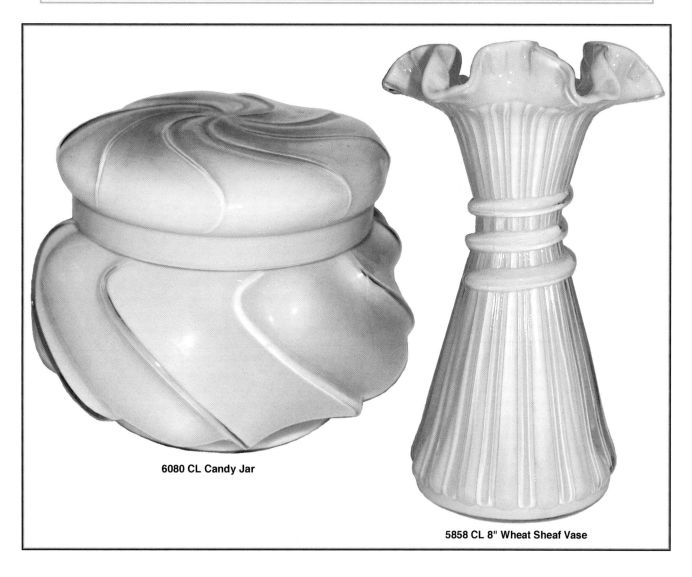

6080 CL Candy Jar

5858 CL 8" Wheat Sheaf Vase

Goldenrod

A yellow overlay color called Goldenrod was marketed for a brief period starting in July 1956. Difficulties producing the color resulted in discontinuation of the color in December 1956. Color variations may range from a bright yellow to almost a deep reddish-amber. This color was used to produce a few vases, a large bowl, and a candleholder for the regular line. The vases have a yellow exterior and white interior, while the bowl and candleholder are yellow on the inside with a white exterior. In addition, a number of experimental items were produced, and a few other Goldenrod-colored pieces appeared in the regular line. A condiment set — salt, pepper, mustard, and holder with a metal handle — was made in the Teardrop pattern, and the No. 3859 vase was made in the Hobnail pattern. For more information about the Teardrop pattern, see *Fenton Art Glass Patterns 1939 – 1980*.

Goldenrod	Ware No.	Introduced	Discontinued	Value
Bowl, 13"	7223-GD	July 1956	1957	$225.00 – 275.00
Candleholder	7272-GD	July 1956	1957	$75.00 – 85.00
Vase, 7½"	7266-GD	July 1956	1957	$70.00 – 80.00
Vase, 8" Hobnail	3859-GD	July 1956	1957	$250.00 – 275.00
Vase, 11"	7251-GD	July 1956	1957	$125.00 – 150.00
Vase, 12"	7265-GD	July 1956	1957	$275.00 – 325.00

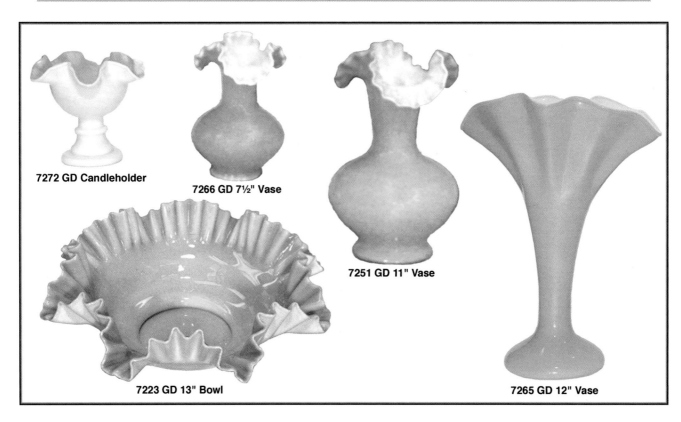

7272 GD Candleholder

7266 GD 7½" Vase

7251 GD 11" Vase

7223 GD 13" Bowl

7265 GD 12" Vase

Gold Overlay

Fenton introduced the cased Gold Overlay color in 1949 when the #711 Tiara pattern was introduced. Gold Overlay pieces have a golden amber exterior cased with an opal interior. The squat jug and six 5 oz. tumblers were combined to produce a seven-piece juice set, and the vanity set was offered with both the regular cologne bottles and the 5½" bottles. Gold Overlay was replaced by Yellow Overlay in the October 1949 price revision. This color was created by adding cadmium sulfide to the Gold Overlay formula to create a lighter, brighter yellow. For more information about the pieces available in this revised color, see the Yellow Overlay section of the chapter.

Gold Overlay	Introduced	Discontinued	Value
Basket, #711-7" handled	1949	October 1949	$65.00 – 75.00
Basket, #711-10½" handled	1949	October 1949	$125.00 – 145.00
Basket, #1924-5" handled	1949	October 1949	$55.00 – 65.00
Bottle, #711 vanity	1949	October 1949	$80.00 – 90.00
Bottle, #711-5½"	1949	October 1949	$90.00 – 110.00
Bowl, #711-7"	1949	October 1949	$30.00 – 35.00
Creamer, #711-4" handled	1949	October 1949	$35.00 – 45.00
Jar, #711 covered candy or bath powder	1949	October 1949	$80.00 – 90.00
Jug, #711 squat	1949	October 1949	$100.00 – 120.00
Jug, #711-5½" handled	1949	October 1949	$30.00 – 35.00
Jug, #711-6" handled	1949	October 1949	$35.00 – 45.00
Jug, #711-8" handled	1949	October 1949	$60.00 – 65.00
Jug, #711-9" handled	1949	October 1949	$75.00 – 85.00
Puff box, #711 covered	1949	October 1949	$50.00 – 60.00
Rose bowl, #711-4"	1949	October 1949	$35.00 – 45.00
Top hat, #1924-5"	1949	October 1949	$35.00 – 45.00

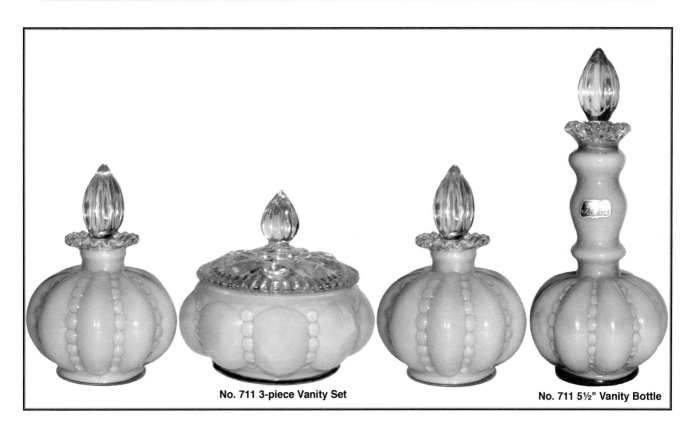

No. 711 3-piece Vanity Set   **No. 711 5½" Vanity Bottle**

Gold Overlay	Introduced	Discontinued	Value
Tumbler, #711-5 oz.	1949	October 1949	$40.00 – 45.00
Vanity set, #711	1949	October 1949	$210.00 – 240.00
Vase, #711 miniature crimped, tulip	1949	October 1949	$30.00 – 35.00
Vase, #711 miniature triangular	1949	October 1949	$30.00 – 35.00
Vase, #711-4" cupped crimped	1949	October 1949	$30.00 – 35.00
Vase, #711-4" double crimped	1949	October 1949	$27.00 – 32.00
Vase, #711-5" double crimped	1949	October 1949	$30.00 – 35.00
Vase, #711-5½" double crimped, tulip	1949	October 1949	$30.00 – 35.00
Vase, #711-5½" triangular	1949	October 1949	$30.00 – 35.00
Vase, #711-6" double crimped, tulip	1949	October 1949	$35.00 – 45.00
Vase, #711-8" double crimped, tulip	1949	October 1949	$45.00 – 55.00
Vase, #711-9" double crimped, tulip	1949	October 1949	$45.00 – 60.00
Vase, #1924-5"	1949	October 1949	$27.00 – 32.00

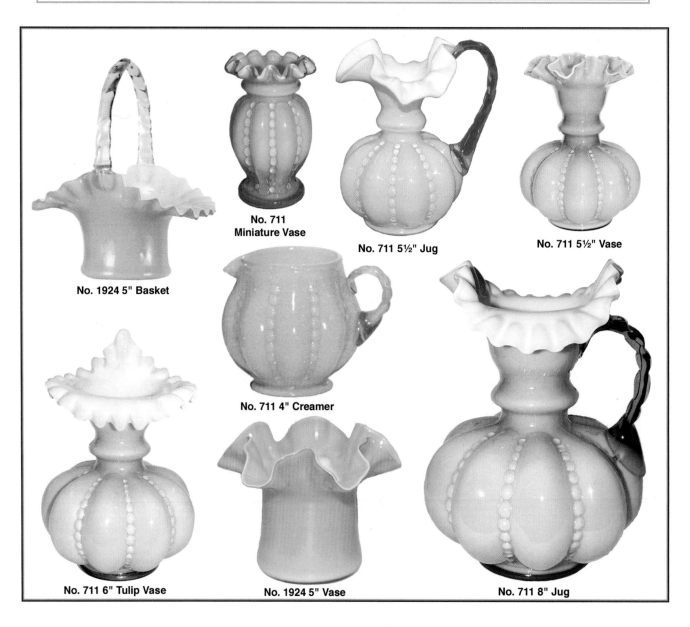

No. 711
Miniature Vase

No. 711 5½" Jug

No. 711 5½" Vase

No. 1924 5" Basket

No. 711 4" Creamer

No. 711 6" Tulip Vase

No. 1924 5" Vase

No. 711 8" Jug

Green Overlay

Green Overlay made its appearance in the Fenton line in 1949 with the introduction of the new #711 Tiara line. Green Overlay is a cased glass with an exterior emerald green layer and an interior opal layer. The color is lighter than the deep green cased Ivy color that was made in many of the Tiara shapes during the same period. Most of the Green Overlay color was discontinued by the beginning of 1952. However, the seven pieces with ware numbers included in the listing below were continued through the end of 1952.

Green Overlay	Ware No.	Introduced	Discontinued	Value
Basket, #711-7" handled		1949	1951	$50.00 – 55.00
Basket, #711-10½" handled		1949	1951	$120.00 – 130.00
Basket, #1924-5" handled	7235-GV	1949	1953	$35.00 – 40.00
Bottle, #711 vanity		1949	1950	$75.00 – 85.00
Bottle, #711-5½"		1949	1951	$80.00 – 95.00
Bowl, #711-7"	7127-GV	1949	1953	$27.00 – 32.00
Bowl, #1923-7"		1949	1950	$30.00 – 35.00
Creamer, #711-4" handled		1949	1950	$35.00 – 45.00
Jar, #711 covered candy or bath powder		1949	1950	$75.00 – 85.00
Jug, #711 squat		1949	1950	$95.00 – 110.00
Jug, #711-5½" handled		1949	1950	$30.00 – 35.00
Jug, #711-6" handled		1949	1951	$40.00 – 45.00
Jug, #711-8" handled		1949	1950	$80.00 – 90.00
Jug, #711-9" handled		1949	1950	$80.00 – 90.00
Puff box, #711 covered		1949	1951	$50.00 – 55.00
Rose bowl, #711-4"		1949	1950	$40.00 – 45.00
Top hat, #1924-5"		1949	1951	$27.00 – 32.00
Tumbler, #711-5 oz.		1949	1950	$45.00 – 50.00

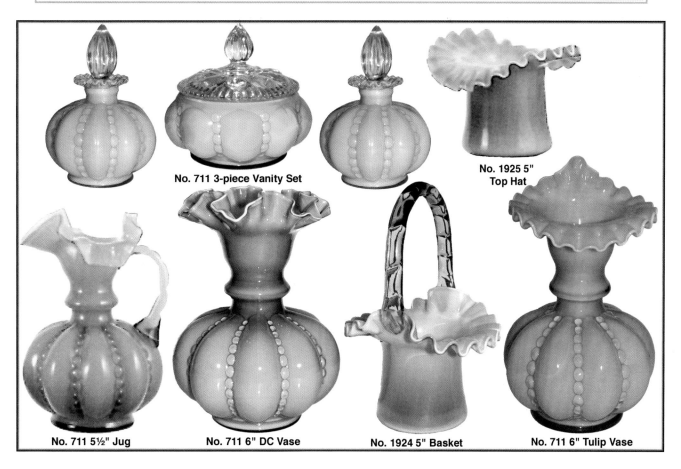

No. 711 3-piece Vanity Set

No. 1925 5"
Top Hat

No. 711 5½" Jug   No. 711 6" DC Vase   No. 1924 5" Basket   No. 711 6" Tulip Vase

Green Overlay	Ware No.	Introduced	Discontinued	Value
Vanity set, #711		1949	1950	$200.00 – 225.00
Vase, 7½"	1357-GV	July 1952	1953	$50.00 – 55.00
Vase, 8½"	1352-GV	July 1952	1954	$50.00 – 60.00
Vase, #711 miniature crimped		1949	1951	$30.00 – 32.00
Vase, #711 miniature triangular, tulip		1949	1951	$30.00 – 35.00
Vase #711-4" cupped crimped		1949	1951	$30.00 – 35.00
Vase #711-4" double crimped		1949	1951	$30.00 – 35.00
Vase, #711-5" double crimped	7155-GV	1949	1953	$35.00 – 40.00
Vase, #711-5½" crimped		1949	1950	$32.00 – 37.00
Vase, #711-5½" triangular, tulip		1949	1950	$35.00 – 40.00
Vase, #711-6" double crimped	7156-GV	1949	1953	$35.00 – 45.00
Vase, #711-6" tulip	7157-GV	1949	1953	$37.00 – 42.00
Vase, #711-8" double crimped		1949	1950	$45.00 – 50.00
Vase, #711-8" tulip		1949	1950	$50.00 – 55.00
Vase, #711-9" double crimped		1949	1950	$50.00 – 60.00
Vase, #711-9" tulip		1949	1950	$55.00 – 65.00
Vase, #1924-5"		1949	1951	$30.00 – 35.00

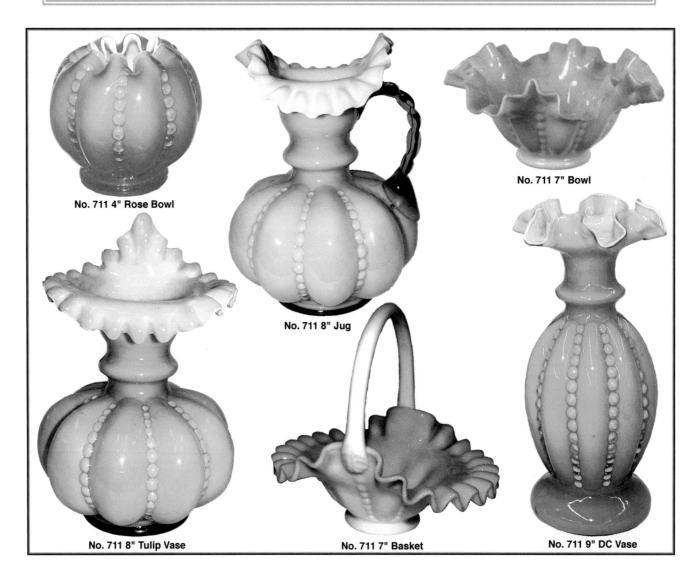

No. 711 4" Rose Bowl

No. 711 8" Jug

No. 711 7" Bowl

No. 711 8" Tulip Vase

No. 711 7" Basket

No. 711 9" DC Vase

Honey Amber

Fenton's Honey Amber color originally appeared with the Coin Dot pattern in the late 1940s. When the color re-entered the line in 1961, Colonial Amber was cased with milk glass. This color combination was used for the Wheat Sheaf vase, the No. 6080 candy box, and in the production of several different lamps in Fenton's Rose pattern. Lamp parts for use by independent lamp makers were also made in the Coin Dot pattern in Honey Amber during this era. Other patterns with Honey Amber pieces include Bubble Optic and Wild Rose with Bowknot. Several Lamps also appeared in this color again in the 1977/78 catalog. Included in this offering were two Coin Dot lamps and two lamps with a hand-painted Apple Blossom and Butterfly decoration.

Honey Amber Overlay	Ware No.	Introduced	Discontinued	Value
Candy box, Wave Crest	6080-HA	1961	1963	$80.00 – 90.00
Lamp, 20" Coin Dot	1406-HA	1977	1978	$150.00 – 175.00
Lamp, 21" Coin Dot	1401-HA	1977	1978	$225.00 – 250.00
Lamp, 21" student	7414-HB	1977	1979	$200.00 – 225.00
Lamp, 22" student	7304-HB	1977	1979	$200.00 – 225.00
Vase, 8" Wheat Sheaf	5858-HA	1961	1964	$40.00 – 50.00

7414 HB 21" Student Lamp

1406 HA 20" Coin Dot Lamp

7304 HB 22" Student Lamp

6080 HA Candy Jar

1401 HA 21" Coin Dot Lamp

5858 HA 8" Wheat Sheaf Vase

Ivy Overlay

Fenton's new cased color — Ivy — was introduced in January 1949. This was just in time for use with pieces from the newly created #711 line. Ivy pieces have a dark green exterior with an opal interior. The items marked with an asterisk in the listing below were in the original offering. Other pieces were introduced later in the year. Ivy was no longer in the Fenton line by the end of 1953. The No. 814 bottle and the No. 93 candy will usually be found with handpainted decorations. These were commonly sold as special order pieces to independent decorating companies. Another lighter green overlay color, Green Overlay, was produced during this same period.

Ivy Overlay	Ware No.	Introduced	Discontinued	Value
Basket, #1924-5" handled		1949	1952	$75.00 – 85.00
Basket, #1925-6" handled		1949	1953	$200.00 – 225.00
Bottle, #814				$200.00 – 225.00
Candy, #93				$140.00 – 160.00
Creamer, #711-4" handled		1949	1950	$45.00 – 55.00
Creamer, #1924 handled		1949	1950	$50.00 – 55.00
Jar, #711 covered candy or bath powder		1949	1951	$130.00 – 150.00
Jug, #711-6" handled		1949	1952	$50.00 – 60.00
Rose bowl, #711-4"	7124-IV	1949	1954	$40.00 – 45.00
*Rose bowl, #711-5"		1949	1952	$50.00 – 55.00
Top hat, #1924		1949	1952	$40.00 – 45.00
*Vase, #186-8" double crimp	7258-IV	1949	1953	$50.00 – 55.00
*Vase, #186-8" tulip	7250-IV	1949	1953	$50.00 – 60.00
Vase, #189-10"				$120.00 – 130.00
Vase, #194-6" double crimp		1949	1953	$30.00 – 35.00
Vase, #194-6" tulip		1949	1953	$30.00 – 40.00
Vase, #194-8" double crimp	7259-IV	1949	1954	$40.00 – 45.00
Vase, #194-8" tulip		1949	1953	$40.00 – 50.00
*Vase, #194-11" double crimp	7252-IV	1949	1953	$75.00 – 85.00
*Vase, #194-11" tulip		1949	1953	$80.00 – 90.00
Vase, #711 miniature		1949	1951	$40.00 – 45.00
Vase, #711-4"	7154-IV	1949	1954	$35.00 – 40.00
*Vase, #711-5" double crimp	5155-IV	1949	1953	$40.00 – 45.00
Vase, #711-5½" double crimp		1949	1951	$40.00 – 45.00
Vase, #711-5½" tulip		1949	1951	$40.00 – 45.00
Vase, #711-6" double crimp	7156-IV	1949	1953	$50.00 – 55.00
Vase, #711-6" tulip	7157-IV	1949	1953	$50.00 – 60.00
Vase, #711-8" double crimp		1949	1950	$65.00 – 75.00
Vase, #711-8" tulip		1949	1950	$70.00 – 80.00
*Vase, #711-9" double crimp		1949	1951	$65.00 – 75.00
*Vase, #711-9" tulip		1949	1951	$70.00 – 80.00
Vase, #1924-5"		1949	1952	$32.00 – 37.00
*Vase, #1925-6" double crimp	7256-IV	1949	1954	$50.00 – 55.00
Vase, #3001-5"	7260-IV	1950	1953	$60.00 – 7.00
Vase, #3001-7"		1950	1952	$90.00 – 110.00
Vase, #3003-6"		1950	1951	$90.00 – 110.00
Vase, #3003-7"		1950	1951	$120.00 – 140.00

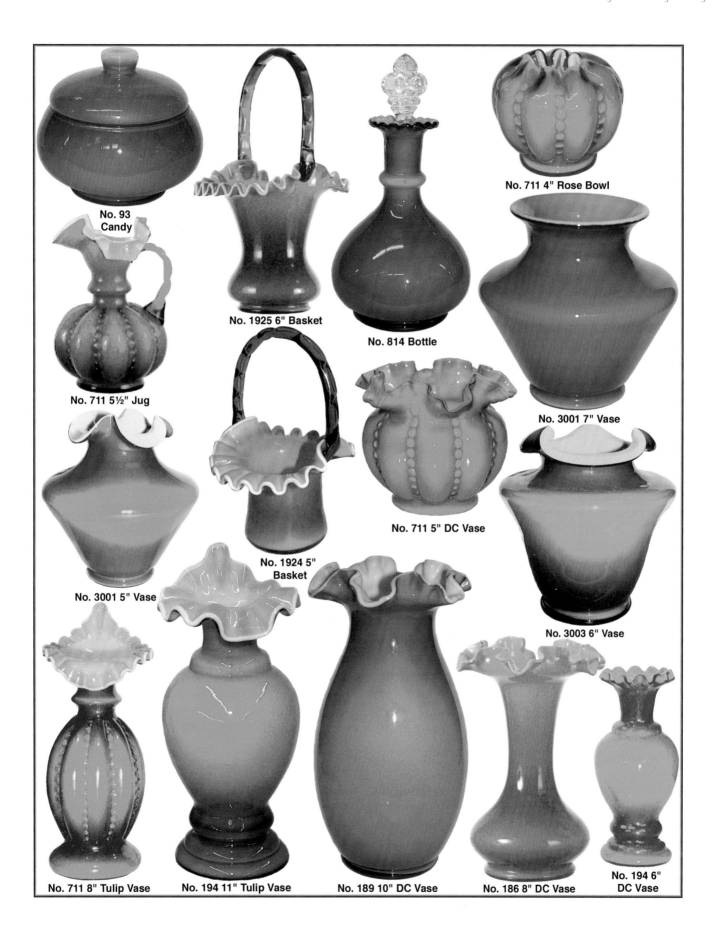

No. 93
Candy

No. 711 5½" Jug

No. 1925 6" Basket

No. 814 Bottle

No. 711 4" Rose Bowl

No. 3001 7" Vase

No. 3001 5" Vase

No. 1924 5"
Basket

No. 711 5" DC Vase

No. 3003 6" Vase

No. 711 8" Tulip Vase

No. 194 11" Tulip Vase

No. 189 10" DC Vase

No. 186 8" DC Vase

No. 194 6"
DC Vase

Jamestown Blue Overlay

The Jamestown Blue color, represented by the color code JB, is a cased color with a transparent peacock blue exterior and a milk glass interior. This color was made from January 1957 through the end of 1958. The barber bottle was only made for one year and is proving to be somewhat difficult to find on the secondary market.

A transparent version of this color was also made during the same era. For information on that color, see page 165 of this book and "Polka Dot in Jamestown Blue Transparent" is in the Supplemental Patterns and Shapes chapter of the book *Fenton Art Glass Patterns 1939 – 1980*.

Ivy Overlay	Ware No.	Introduced	Discontinued	Value
Barber bottle	7471-JB	1957	1958	$195.00 – 215.00
Bowl, 8½"	7338-JB	1957	1959	$80.00 – 90.00
Vase, 6"	7056-JB	1957	1959	$45.00 – 55.00
Vase, 6"	7456-JB	1957	1959	$35.00 – 45.00
Vase, 7½"	7457-JB	1957	1959	$60.00 – 70.00
Vase, 5"	9055-JB	1957	1959	$45.00 – 55.00

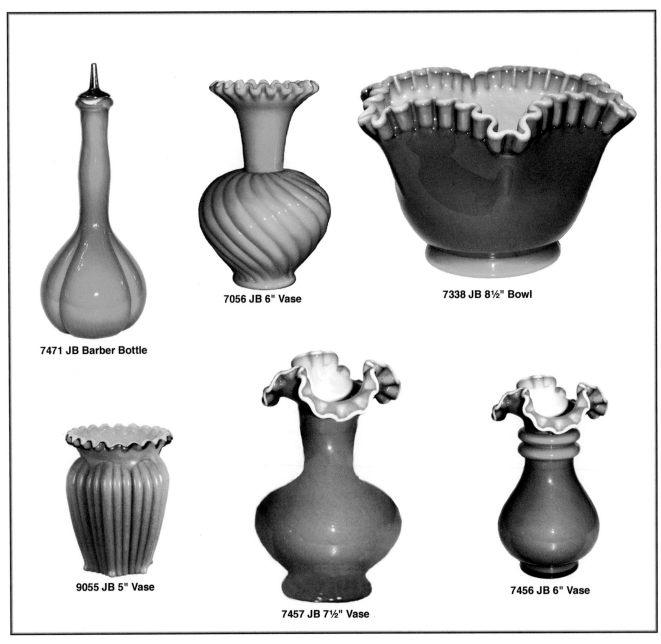

7471 JB Barber Bottle

7056 JB 6" Vase

7338 JB 8½" Bowl

9055 JB 5" Vase

7457 JB 7½" Vase

7456 JB 6" Vase

Opaque Blue Overlay

Opaque Blue Overlay is a cased color with an exterior layer of Colonial Blue and an interior layer of opal. Fenton introduced this color in 1962. With the exception of several lamps that were made later in the 1960s and 1970s, the color was discontinued at the end of 1963. Three lamps were made in Opaque Blue Overlay in 1967, but only remained in the line for one year. In 1971, two different lamps were made. These lamps were also discontinued after only one year of production. In addition to the items listed below, Opaque Blue Overlay was also used in the Bubble Optic and Hobnail lines. For examples of Opaque Blue Overlay pieces in Bubble Optic and Hobnail, see the appropriate chapters in *Fenton Art Glass Patterns 1939 – 1980*.

Opaque Blue Overlay	Ware No.	Introduced	Discontinued	Value
Basket, 7" deep	1637-OB	1962	1964	$105.00 – 115.00
Candy jar	1680-OB	1962	1964	$75.00 – 85.00
Candy jar, Wave Crest	6080-OB	1962	1963	$100.00 – 110.00
Lamp	9204-OB	1967	1968	$150.00 – 175.00
Lamp	9205-OB	1967	1968	$140.00 – 160.00
Lamp	9207-OB	1967	1968	$170.00 – 190.00
Lamp, electric courting	1691-OB	1962	1963	$100.00 – 125.00
Lamp, oil courting	1690-OB	1962	1963	$100.00 – 125.00
Lamp. 37" Rose GWTW	9202-OB	1971	1972	$240.00 – 260.00
Lamp, 38" Rose Pillar	9201-OB	1971	1972	$190.00 – 220.00
Vase, 7"	1651-OB	1962	1963	$30.00 – 40.00
Vase, 10½"	1650-OB	1962	1963	$120.00 – 140.00
Vase, 8" Wheat Sheaf	5858-OB	1962	1963	$50.00 – 60.00

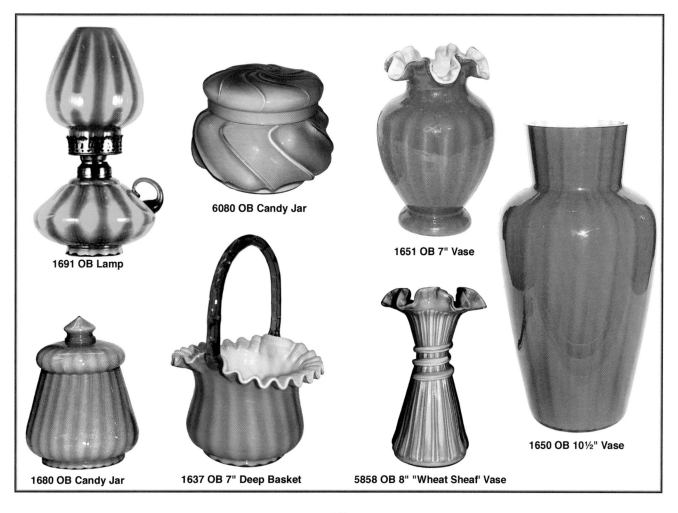

6080 OB Candy Jar

1651 OB 7" Vase

1691 OB Lamp

1650 OB 10½" Vase

1680 OB Candy Jar

1637 OB 7" Deep Basket

5858 OB 8" "Wheat Sheaf' Vase

Peach Blow

Peach Blow is a cased glass with a rich Gold Ruby interior and a milk glass exterior. This pattern was introduced in 1939. By 1940, it had been replaced by a similar pattern — Peach Crest. Pieces of Peach Crest are the same color as Peach Blow, but they have a characteristic spun crystal edge.

Although Peach Blow was discontinued in 1940, the color reappeared in several Hobnail shapes from 1952 to 1957. These pieces are listed in the Hobnail section of *Fenton Art Glass Patterns 1939 – 1980*. In addition, Fenton produced Peach Blow lamp parts for numerous companies during the 1940s. One such item is illustrated in the photo below. The No. 711-4" jug is an item that was not part of the regular Fenton line.

Fenton has made a few pieces recently which may appear to be similar to Peach Blow. In 1987, Fenton created a Dusty Rose Overlay tulip vase with a Peach Blow interior and cobalt blue crest. In mid-1990, Fenton made five pieces of Cranberry Opaline. This is also a cased glass with a deep pink interior. Included in this offering were a #7373 tulip bud vase, a #7727-14" crimped bowl, a #7371-7" vase, a #7372-13" vase, and a #8354-9" Basket Weave vase.

Peach Blow	Value
Basket, #1922-10"	$140.00 – 160.00
Bowl, #203-7" crimped, flared	$37.00 – 42.00
Bowl, #1522 -9" flared	$60.00 – 65.00
Bowl, #1522 -10" crimped, 10" oval, square, triangular	$60.00 – 70.00
Rose bowl, #201-4 crimped	$40.00 – 45.00
Rose Bowl, #201-5" crimped	$50.00 – 55.00
Rose bowl, #201-4" special	$40.00 – 50.00
Rose bowl, #201-7" special	$50.00 – 55.00
Top hat, #1922-9"	$95.00 – 110.00
Top hat, #1923-6" crimped, flared, square	$50.00 – 55.00
Top hat, #1924-4"	$30.00 – 35.00
Vase, #186-8" crimped, flared, square, triangular, tulip	$50.00 – 55.00
Vase, #187-7" crimped, flared, triangular	$45.00 – 50.00
Vase, #201-6" cupped, crimped; cupped, flared	$40.00 – 45.00
Vase, #1922-8" flared, square, triangular	$90.00 – 110.00
Vase, #1923-6" regular, square, triangular, tulip	$50.00 – 60.00
Vase, #1924-4"	$32.00 – 37.00

No. 711 4" Jug

No. 1924 4" Tulip Vase

No. 201 6" Crimped Vase

No. 201 6" Cupped Flared Vase

E. P. Paul Lamp Base

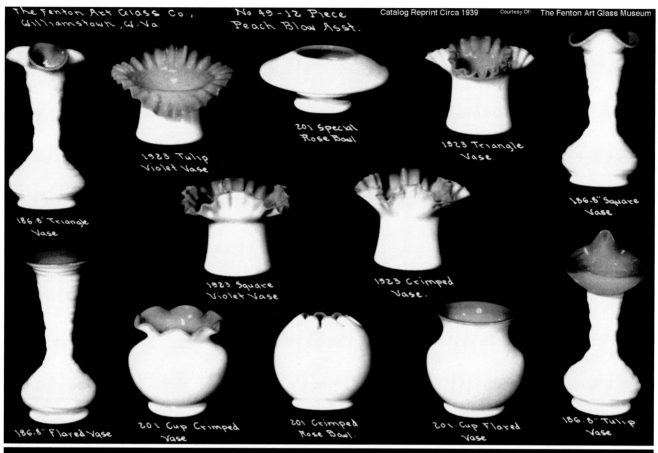

The Fenton Art Glass Co.,
Williamstown, W.Va

No 49 -12 Piece
Peach Blow Asst.

Catalog Reprint Circa 1939   Courtesy Of: The Fenton Art Glass Museum

201 Special
Rose Bowl

1923 Tulip
Violet Vase.

1923 Triangle
Vase.

186.8" Triangle
Vase

1923 Square
Violet Vase

1923 Crimped
Vase.

186.8" Square
Vase.

186.8" Flared Vase

201 Cup Crimped
Vase

201 Crimped
Rose Bowl.

201. Cup Flared
Vase

186.8" Tulip
Vase

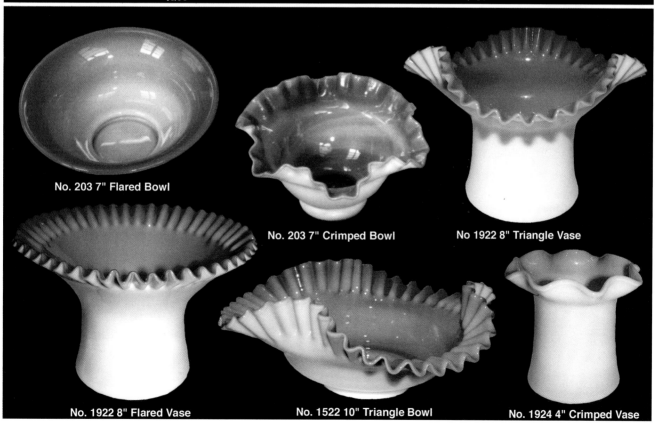

No. 203 7" Flared Bowl

No. 203 7" Crimped Bowl

No 1922 8" Triangle Vase

No. 1922 8" Flared Vase

No. 1522 10" Triangle Bowl

No. 1924 4" Crimped Vase

Plated Amberina

The name *Plated Amberina* is derived from the process by which this type of glassware is formed. Molten ruby glass is plated, or cased, over an opal interior layer. This type of glass was first produced by Edward D. Libbey. Fenton used this process to make six different Plated Amberina articles in the early 1960s. All the items in this color were introduced in January, 1962. Three of the six pieces were discontinued by December 1962, and the remainder were out of the line by the end of 1963. Some of these items were also satinized and sold through the Fenton Gift Shop.

Later, the following satin pieces in a color Fenton called Plated Amberina Velvet were made as part of the 1984 Connoisseur Collection. The top hat and cane had a production limit of 1500 and the basket was limited to 1250:

Plated Amberina	Ware No.	Plated Amberina	Ware No.
Basket, 10"	3134-PV	Top hat, 6" x 8"	3193-PV
Cane, 18"	5090-PV		

Plated Amberina	Ware No.	Introduced	Discontinued	Value
Basket, 7" deep	1637-PA	1962	1964	$120.00 – 140.00
Candy jar	1680-PA	1962	1964	$100.00 – 125.00
Lamp, electric courting	1691-PA	1962	1963	$140.00 – 160.00
Lamp, oil courting	1690-PA	1962	1963	$140.00 – 160.00
Vase, 7"	1651-PA	1962	1964	$40.00 – 45.00
Vase, 10½"	1650-PA	1962	1964	$150.00 – 170.00

1680 PA Candy Jar

1651 PA 7" Vase

1650 PA 10½" Vase

1691 PA Electric Courting Lamp

1637 PA Basket

Powder Blue Overlay

Light blue glass cased with opal was used in the production of the No. 6080 candy jar and the No. 5858 Wheat Sheaf vase. This Powder Blue Overlay color only remained in the line for one year. Notice the BV color code is the same as that for the earlier Blue Overlay color made in the 1940s and early 1950s.

Powder Blue Overlay	Ware No.	Introduced	Discontinued	Value
Candy box, Wave Crest	6080-BV	1961	1962	$110.00 – 125.00
Vase, 8" Wheat Sheaf	5858-BV	1961	1962	$65.00 – 75.00

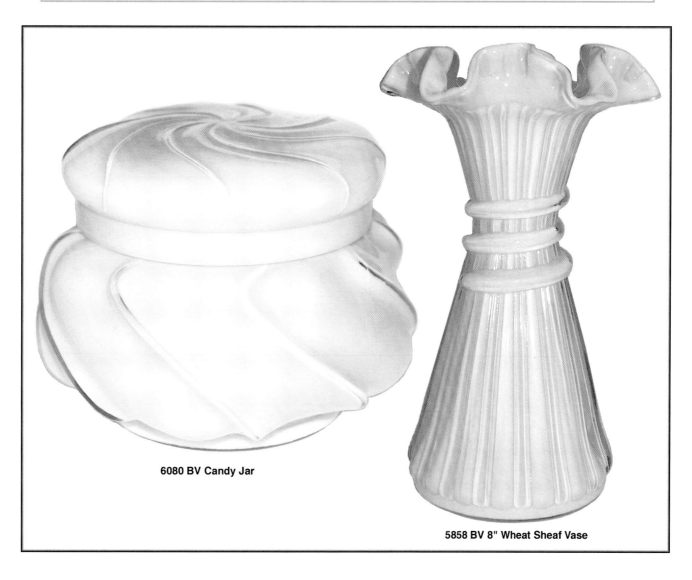

6080 BV Candy Jar

5858 BV 8" Wheat Sheaf Vase

Rose Overlay

Rose Overlay is a cased glassware that was produced by using milk glass as the interior layer and light pink or rose glass for the exterior layer. Fenton's Rose Overlay color was introduced in 1943. The color was discontinued from the regular line at the end of 1948. Many of the Rose Overlay items in the regular line were made in the Melon Rib shape. The No. 4516 jug and the No. 4517 vases were made for Weil Ceramics during the mid-1940s. The unusual 9" jug with the turned-out sides (lacking the Melon Rib pattern) may also have been made as a special order for Weil Ceramics. A 9" vase in this style has also been found. The #3917 jug is not listed in known Fenton catalogs, but catalogs from this era are not complete. This jug has also been found in Blue Overlay. The three-piece vanity set was also sold with 5½" bottles. A limited number of Rose Overlay Hobnail shapes were also produced. For more information about these shapes, see *Fenton Art Glass Patterns 1939 – 1980*.

Rose Overlay	Introduced	Discontinued	Value
Basket, #192 10½" handled	1943	1949	$100.00 – 110.00
Basket, #203-7" handled	1943	1949	$40.00 – 45.00
Basket, #1925-6"			$40.00 – 45.00
Basket, #1924-5" handled	1943	1949	$35.00 – 40.00
Bottle, #192 squat cologne	1943	1949	$55.00 – 60.00
Bottle, #192-5½"	1943	1949	$50.00 – 60.00
Bottle, #192-7"	1943	1949	$60.00 – 70.00
Bottle, #192-A cologne or vanity	1943	1949	$55.00 – 60.00
Bowl, #192-10½" double crimped	1943	1949	$50.00 – 60.00
Bowl, #203-7" double crimped	1943	1949	$20.00 – 25.00
Candleholder, #192 squat	1943	1949	$45.00 – 50.00
Creamer, #1924 handled	1943	1949	$30.00 – 35.00
Jar, #192 covered candy or bath powder	1943	1949	$45.00 – 55.00
Jug, #192 squat	1943	1946	$40.00 – 50.00
Jug, #192-5" handled	1943	1946	$20.00 – 25.00
Jug, #192-5½" handled	1943	1949	$22.00 – 27.00
Jug, #192-6" handled	1943	1949	$22.00 – 27.00
Jug, #192-8" handled	1943	1949	$50.00 – 55.00
Jug, #192-A-9" handled	1943	1949	$50.00 – 60.00
Jug, #192-A-9" turned-out body			UND
Jug, #1934-7" handled			$50.00 – 60.00
Jug, #4516-8½" handled			$55.00 – 65.00
Puff box, #192-A	1943	1949	$32.00 – 38.00
Top hat, #1924-5"	1943	1949	$22.00 – 27.00
Vanity Set, #19-A 3pc.	1943	1949	$132.00 – 147.00
Vase, #192-5" double crimped, oval, square, triangular	1943	1949	$20.00 – 22.00
Vase, #192-5½" double crimped, square	1943	1949	$20.00 – 25.00
Vase, #192-5½" triangular, tulip	1943	1949	$22.00 – 27.00
Vase, #192-6" double crimped, regular	1943	1949	$27.00 – 30.00
Vase, #192-6" square, triangular, tulip	1943	1949	$27.00 – 30.00
Vase, #192-8" double crimped, square, triangular	1943	1949	$32.00 – 37.00
Vase, #192-8" tulip	1943	1949	$35.00 – 40.00
Vase, #192-10" double crimped, square	1943	1946	$50.00 – 55.00
Vase, #192-10" triangular, tulip	1943	1946	$50.00 – 60.00
Vase, #192-A-9" double crimped, square	1943	1949	$47.00 – 52.00
Vase, #192-A-9" triangular, tulip	1943	1949	$50.00 – 55.00
Vase, #203-5" double crimped			$27.00 – 32.00
Vase, #4517-6½"			$30.00 – 35.00
Vase, #4517-11"			$50.00 – 60.00

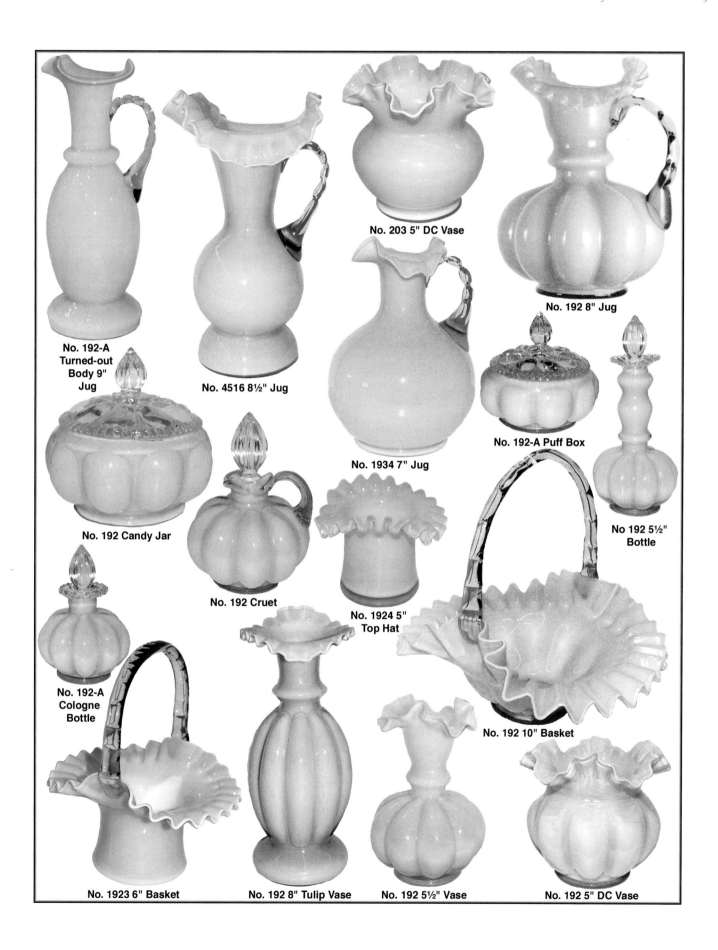

No. 203 5" DC Vase

No. 192-A
Turned-out
Body 9"
Jug

No. 4516 8½" Jug

No. 192 8" Jug

No. 1934 7" Jug

No. 192-A Puff Box

No. 192 Candy Jar

No 192 5½"
Bottle

No. 192 Cruet

No. 1924 5"
Top Hat

No. 192-A
Cologne
Bottle

No. 192 10" Basket

No. 1923 6" Basket

No. 192 8" Tulip Vase

No. 192 5½" Vase

No. 192 5" DC Vase

Ruby Overlay

Ruby Overlay (RO) is Fenton's name for its non-opalescent cranberry color that was introduced in 1942. In early catalogs, Fenton refers to this color as a "cased glass of coin gold cranberry and crystal." Ruby Overlay is a cased glass with Gold Ruby as the interior layer and crystal as the exterior layer. Most of the pieces made in the original production period from 1942 through 1948 were in the Diamond Optic line. From the mid-1950s through the 1960s, most Ruby Overlay was made in the Polka Dot pattern. For more information about these two patterns, see the book *Fenton Art Glass Patterns 1939 – 1980*. A number of lamps and miscellaneous items were made through the 1960s and 1970s. Due to the high price of gold, Fenton did not produce cranberry glass from 1978 until 1982. In 1982, Ruby Overlay entered the line once again, renamed as the more dignified Country Cranberry.

Ruby Overlay	Ware No.	Introduced	Discontinued	Value
Barber bottle, Diamond Optic	1771-RO	1957	1959	$185.00 – 225.00
Candleholder, #1523				$45.00 – 55.00
Candy box, Wave Crest	6080-RO	1956	1960	$120.00 – 140.00
Decanter, Dot Optic	2478-RO	1960	1965	$250.00 – 300.00
Epergne, 2 pc. set	7202-RO	1955	1960	$145.00 – 165.00
Ivy ball, footed	1021-MR	1955	1967	$95.00 – 115.00
Lamp, 19" mariner's	2700-RO	1969	1972	$225.00 – 250.00
Lamp, 38" Rib Optic pillar	1601-RO	1971	1972	$240.00 – 260.00
Lamp, 19½" Thumbprint student	1408-RO	1967	1975	$220.00 – 240.00
Lamp, 20" Thumbprint student	1410-RO	1967	1975	$250.00 – 290.00
Shaker, Wave Crest	6006-RO	1956	1963	$25.00 – 30.00
Vase, 12"	7361-RO	1956	1957	$200.00 – 225.00
Vase, 11½"	7364-RO	1956	1958	$200.00 – 225.00
Vase, 7½" #1720 Pinch		1952	July 1952	$40.00 – 45.00
Vase, 8½" #1721 Pinch		1952	July 1952	$65.00 – 85.00

1410 RO 20" Student Lamp

1771 RO Barber Bottle

No. 1721 8½" Pinch Vase

6080 RO Wave Crest Box

7202 RO Epergne Set

3264 RO 11½" Vase

1021 MR Footed Ivy Ball

3261 RO 12" Vase

6006 RO Salt & Pepper

1408 RO 19½" Student Lamp

Wild Rose Overlay

The dark-cranberry-over-white cased Wild Rose color was introduced into the Fenton line in 1961. The items listed below, as well as some pieces of Hobnail, Bubble Optic, Jacqueline, and Wild Rose and Bowknot, were produced in this color. All items except the lamps were out of the line by the end of 1962. The color was brought back in 1967, when several lamps in Fenton's Rose pattern were made. Production of two of the lamps was discontinued at the end of the year. The other lamp was made through the end of 1968.

Wild Rose Overlay	Ware No.	Introduced	Discontinued	Value
Candy box, Wave Crest	6080-WR	1961	1963	$100.00 – 125.00
Lamp, 22" Rose ball	9207-WR	1967	1969	$190.00 – 210.00
Lamp, 24" Rose double ball	9204-WR	1967	1968	$175.00 – 200.00
Lamp, 20½" Rose Buffet	9205-WR	1967	1968	$160.00 – 185.00
Vase, 8" Wheat Sheaf	5858-WR	1961	1963	$60.00 – 70.00

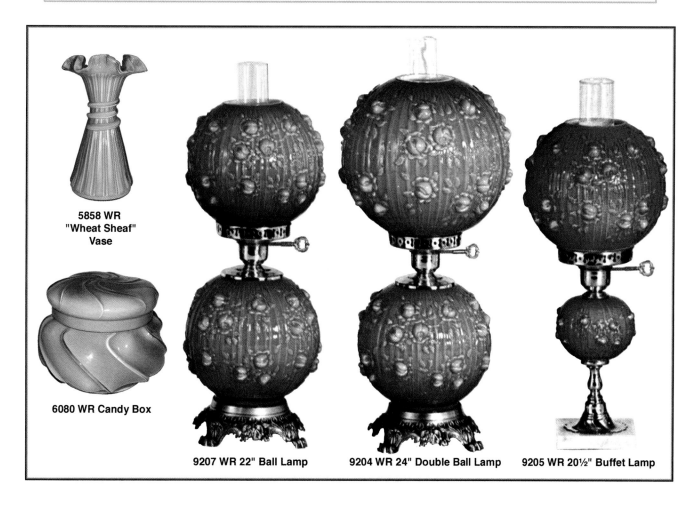

5858 WR
"Wheat Sheaf"
Vase

6080 WR Candy Box

9207 WR 22" Ball Lamp

9204 WR 24" Double Ball Lamp

9205 WR 20½" Buffet Lamp

Yellow Overlay

Yellow Overlay is a cased color that was produced in 1950. The color was produced by adding selenium sulfide (used as a lightening agent) to the Gold Overlay formula. Some of the pieces were listed on the late 1949 price list. This color was discontinued by the end of 1950. A few bowls and baskets and a number of vases were made. The color was originally intended to be made with the yellow layer on the outside. However, when the glass was made in this manner, there was a problem with cracking. When the layers were reversed, this problem disappeared. Therefore, except for some surviving early production, the yellow layer will be found on the interior surface.

Yellow Overlay	Ware No.	Introduced	Discontinued	Value
Basket, #711-7" handled		October 1949	1951	$90.00 – 100.00
Basket, #711-10½" handled		October 1949	1951	$120.00 – 140.00
Basket, #1924-5" handled		October 1949	1951	$50.00 – 60.00
Basket, #1925-6" handled		October 1949	1951	$165.00 – 185.00
Bowl, #711-7"		October 1949	1951	$35.00 – 45.00
Bowl, #1522-10"		October 1949	1951	$75.00 – 85.00
Top hat, #1924-5"		October 1949	1951	$40.00 – 45.00
Vase, #186-8" tulip		October 1949	1951	$75.00 – 85.00
Vase #711-4" double crimped		October 1949	1951	$35.00 – 45.00
Vase, #711-5" double crimped		October 1949	1951	$40.00 – 45.00
Vase, #711-5½" double crimped, tulip		October 1949	1951	$40.00 – 45.00
Vase, #711-6" double crimped, tulip		October 1949	1951	$45.00 – 50.00
Vase, #1924-5"		October 1949	1951	$35.00 – 40.00
Vase, #1925-6"		October 1949	1951	$75.00 – 85.00
Vase, #3001-5"		1950	1951	$45.00 – 55.00
Vase, #3001-7"		1950	1951	$85.00 – 95.00
Vase, #3003-6"		1950	1951	$60.00 – 65.00
Vase, #3003-7"		1950	1951	$85.00 – 95.00

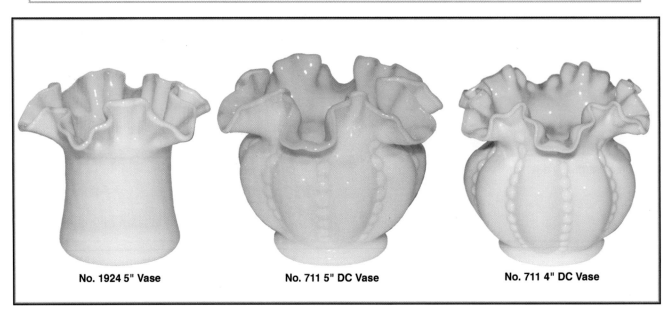

No. 1924 5" Vase   No. 711 5" DC Vase   No. 711 4" DC Vase

No. 1924 5" Basket

No. 3001 7" Vase

No. 711 7" Basket

No. 1925 6" Basket

No. 186 8" Tulip Vase

No. 3003 6" Vase

No. 1925 6" Vase

Overlay Atomizers Made for DeVilbiss

    Fenton made several cased atomizer blanks for the DeVilbiss Manufacturing Company of Toledo, Ohio, during the 1940s. The DeVilbiss Company bought glass bottles from various sources. They designed and manufactured fittings for the bottles and sold the finished product. The metal atomizer fittings shown in the photo are the same as illustrated in DeVilbiss catalogs. Balls and cords have been replaced on some bottles.

    The style of perfumizer shown to the top left of the photo is called Crest, since the atomizer top has been trimmed with an applied glass edge. Two of the three colors produced in this category — Aqua Crest and Peach Crest — are cased. The third color made was Ivory Crest. These atomizers are shown in a 1941 DeVilbiss catalog. The Aqua Crest described here is not the more familiar color with a milk glass body and blue trim. Instead, it is a Blue Overlay body ringed with a light blue edge.

    The Beaded Melon atomizers were in the DeVilbiss line in 1947. This atomizer was made in two overlay colors — Blue Overlay and Rose Overlay. It was also made in milk glass. Later, in 1991, Fenton produced this bottle for the regular line in Salem Blue (SR), Pink Pearl (HZ), Iridized Sea Mist Green (EZ), and Dusty Rose (DK). The bottle was also sampled in several other colors.

    The Backward Swirled "C" bottle was made for DeVilbiss in 1948 and 1949. This bottle was made in Blue Overlay and Rose Overlay. This bottle was sold with two different types of atomizer fittings. The version shown to the left in the photo below, is a 3 oz. bottle with a traditional squeeze ball and gold-plated atomizer top. The type shown on the right has a newly designed metal finger pump atomizer.

DeVilbiss Atomizer	Blue Overlay	Rose Overlay	Milk
Backward Swirled C	$120.00 – 140.00	$120.00 – 140.00	
Beaded Melon	$75.00 – 85.00	$5.00 – 85.00	$40.00 – 45.00
	Aqua Crest	Ivory Crest	Peach Crest
Crest	$90.00 – 110.00	$90.00 – 110.00	$120.00 – 140.00

CREST
CS750-1 IVORY CREST
CS750-2 PEACH CREST
CS750-3 AQUA CREST

BACKWARD SWIRLED C
CS750-36 ROSE OVERLAY
CS750-37 BLUE OVERLAY

S1000-36 Pastel Rose — Case Glass
S1000-37 Pastel Blue — Case Glass
Capacity ½ Dram
Retail $10.00

An exclusive new DeVilbiss development in a perfume atomizer, achieved by combination of DeVilbiss Perfumizer and bottle, as shown in sketch.

BEADED MELON
S350-22 MILK GLASS
S350-23 BLUE OVERLAY
S350-24 ROSE OVERLAY

Ivy
a new
exciting
color
in
Crests
and
Overlays

by Fenton

IVY
Fusing milk glass with a deep green overlay producing a beautiful opaque green having a gloss and brilliance that cannot be achieved any other way.

Fenton's Transparent Colors
Amber

Transparent amber was used in some of Fenton's 1930s patterns such as Georgian and Lincoln Inn. For more information about these patterns, see *Fenton Art Glass 1907 – 1939*. Upon the discontinuation of these patterns, the transparent form of the color was retired until 1952, when numerous accessory items like cigarette sets, bowls, and flower holders were made. Many of these same pieces were also made in milk glass, and most of these shapes may be found illustrated in the Milk Glass section of this book. During this time, amber was often called Antique Amber, and the color code used was AR. In the late 1950s and through the 1960s, amber was used in popular Fenton patterns like Hobnail, Thumbprint, and Valencia. For information about items made in these patterns, see the book *Fenton Art Glass Patterns 1939 – 1980*. In 1963, the color code designation for transparent amber was changed from AR to CA (*Colonial Amber*). Both these designations were used in 1963; the CA code was used exclusively starting in 1964. Colonial Amber continued in production into the 1980s. It was used extensively in the Aurora, Thumbprint, and Valencia patterns. Novelty items like the Happiness bird and the Butterfly honey jar were also made in transparent amber during this decade.

The four-piece #1952 clusterette flower set was introduced in amber in January 1952. It consisted of two round and two straight sections. The ware number of this set became No. 9002 in July 1952. The #68 console set was composed of a #66-11½" oval bowl and a pair of #67 candleholders. These pieces were only listed in the January 1952 price list. The #377 Quilted planter bookend was composed of two-pieces — the planter box and the bookend backdrop. The five-piece canasta cigarette set included the #1800 cigarette box and one each of the spade, heart, club, and diamond ashtrays. This set used ware number 5808 after July 1952. The #380 Quilted cigarette set (No. 5508) was produced by combining two #379 ashtrays with the #378 cigarette box. The Modern Swirl ashtrays were produced from moulds acquired from Rubel & Company. These ashtrays may be found in several colors in both the 9" and 5" sizes. Georgian tumblers in amber and several other colors returned to the Fenton line in the 1950s. The tumblers were available in three sizes and were also boxed in multicolor sets.

Three Polka Dot vases that are normally seen in Ruby Overlay were made in transparent amber in the first half of 1959. Since these vases were only made for a short time, they are not easily acquired by today's collectors. Later, in the 1980s when this pattern reappeared in Country Cranberry, it was called Fine Dot Optic.

Amber	Ware No.	Introduced	Discontinued	Value
Ashtray	5179-AR	1954	July 1954	$15.00 – 30.00
Ashtray, bird shape	5173-AR	1954	July 1954	$20.00 – 25.00
Ashtray, #379 Quilted		1952	1953	$6.00 – 8.00
Ashtray, #1800 Club	5875-AR	1952	July 1953	$6.00 – 8.00
Ashtray, #1800 Diamond	5876-AR	1952	July 1953	$6.00 – 8.00
Ashtray, #1800 Heart	5877-AR	1952	July 1953	$6.00 – 8.00
Ashtray, #1800 Spade	5878-AR	1952	July 1953	$6.00 – 8.00
Ashtray, 5" Modern Swirl	9175-AR/CA	1960	1971	$8.00 – 10.00
Ashtray, 9" Modern Swirl	9176-AR/CA	1960	1971	$12.00 – 14.00
Bowl, #65-6"		1952	July 1952	$9.00 – 11.00
Bowl, #66-11½" oval		1952	July 1952	$20.00 – 25.00
Canasta set, #1800-5-piece	5808-AR	1952	July 1953	$50.00 – 60.00
Candleholder, #67		1952	July 1952	$7.00 – 9.00
Cigarette box, #378 Quilted		1952	1953	$25.00 – 30.00
Cigarette box, #1800	5889-AR	1952	July 1953	$25.00 – 30.00
Cigarette set, #380 Quilted	5508-AR	1952	1953	$37.00 – 45.00
Clusterette, #1952-4 pc. set	9002-AR	1952	1954	$35.00 – 40.00
Console set, #68		1952	July 1952	$35.00 – 43.00
Honey jar	9080-AR/CA	1961	1970	$18.00 – 22.00

Amber	Ware No.	Introduced	Discontinued	Value
Ivy ball, ftd.	1021-MA	July 1952	1955	$50.00 – 60.00
Planter bookend, Quilted	5595-AR	1952	1953	$18.00 – 22.00
Relish	5174-AR	1954	1955	$25.00 – 30.00
Tumbler, 5 oz. Georgian	6545-AR	July 1953	1955	$5.00 – 7.00
Tumbler, 9 oz. Georgian	6550-AR	July 1952	1958	$5.00 – 7.00
Tumbler, 12 oz. Georgian	6547-AR	July 1953	1955	$6.00 – 8.00
Vase, 7" Polka Dot	2442-AR	1959	July 1959	$18.00 – 22.00
Vase, 8½" Polka Dot	2448-AR	1959	July 1959	$20.00 – 22.00
Vase, 10" Polka Dot	2440-AR	1959	July 1959	$27.00 – 32.00

1950's Catalog Reprint Composite Courtesy of: The Fenton Art Glass Museum

2448 AR 8½" Vase

2442 AR 7" Vase

2440 AR 10" Vase

5174 AR Relish

5179 AR Ash Tray

5173 AR Bird Ash Tray

9080 AR Honey Jar

6545 AR Georgian 5 Oz. Tumbler

9175 AR "Modern Swirl" 5" Ash Tray

6547 AR Georgian 12 Oz. Tumbler

6550 AR Georgian 9 Oz. Tumbler

1021 MA Ftd. Ivy Ball

Colonial Amber

Fenton produced transparent amber during the 1960s and 1970s using the Colonial Amber (CA) name until the color was temporarily discontinued in 1980.

Colonial Amber reappeared in the 1987/88 catalog. The following items were offered at that time:

Basket, Aurora	7638-CA	Nut dish, Valencia	8327-CA
Bell, Aurora	9667-CA	Slipper, Daisy & Button	1995-CA
Bird, Happiness	5197-CA	Vase, Aurora	7620-CA
Candy box, Butterfly	9280-CA	Vase, Hobnail	3952-CA
Hurricane candle,		Vase, Valencia bud	8356-CA
Valencia	8376-CA	Votive	8294-CA

Transparent amber was re-introduced in the 1994 catalog. The new line was called Autumn Gold and the new color code was AM. This color only appeared in the line for a single year and the following pieces were produced:

Basket, 6"	2731-AM	Cat, 3¾"	5165-AM
Basket, 8" Vulcan	9544-AM	Slipper, 6" Daisy & Button	1995-AM
Bell, 6" Barred Oval	8369-AM	Vase, 4"	7620-AM
Bird, 4"	5163-AM	Vase, 5½" Flute & Dot	9050-AM
Candy and cover, 7½"	8388-AM		

Colonial Amber	Ware No.	Introduced	Discontinued	Value
Ashtray, 5½" Swirl	7075-CA	1977	1978	$8.00 – 10.00
Ashtray, 7½" Swirl	7076-CA	1977	1978	$12.00 – 14.00
Basket, 7" Threaded Diamond Optic	8435-CA	1977	1979	$22.00 – 27.00
Bell, Threaded Diamond Optic	8465-CA	1977	1979	$20.00 – 25.00
Bird	5197-CA	1968	1977	$20.00 – 25.00
Bowl, 6½" Threaded Diamond Optic	8425-CA	1977	1979	$16.00 – 18.00
Butterfly	5170-CA	1970	1971	$12.00 – 15.00
Candy box, Colonial	8488-CA	1977	1979	$18.00 – 20.00
Candy box, Knobby Bull's Eye	9385-CA	1977	1978	$20.00 – 25.00
Candy jar, 7¼" Grape & Cable	9188-CA	1968	1970	$125.00 – 150.00
Cigarette lighter	9198-CA	1966	1969	$14.00 – 18.00
Comport, Empress	9229-CA	1962	1967	$9.00 – 11.00
Comport, Pineapple	9129-CA	1962	1967	$9.00 – 11.00
Comport, Tree of Life	9322-CA	1977	1978	$9.00 – 11.00
Fairy lamp, Heart	8406-CA	1977	1978	$20.00 – 25.00
Fairy lamp, Persian Medallion	8408-CA	1974	1976	$30.00 – 35.00
Goblet, Cactus	3445-CA	1962	1963	$10.00 – 12.00
Goblet, Empress	9245-CA	1962	1967	$10.00 – 12.00
Goblet, Flower Band	6345-CA	1962	1965	$10.00 – 12.00
Goblet, Pineapple	9045-CA	1962	1967	$10.00 – 12.00
Goblet, Stippled Scroll	9145-CA	1962	1965	$9.00 – 11.00
Lamp, 19" mariner's	2700-CA	1969	1972	$100.00 – 125.00
Lamp, 24" Poppy GWTW	9101-CA	1971	1980+	$120.00 – 140.00
Lamp, 21½" Poppy double ball	9108-CA	1966	1967	$125.00 – 150.00
Lamp, 23" Poppy double ball	9109-CA	1967	1975	$120.00 – 140.00
Lamp, 19½" Thumbprint student	1408-CA	1967	1974	$60.00 – 70.00
Lamp, 20½" Thumbprint student	1410-CA	1967	1969	$60.00 – 70.00
Pitcher, 70 oz.	3262-CA	1968	July 1968	$45.00 – 55.00
Ring tree, turtle	9199-CA	1966	1968	$10.00 – 12.00
Shoe, high button	9195-CA	1965	1966	$14.00 – 16.00
Vase, 11"	1655-CA	1968	July 1968	$27.00 – 30.00
Vase, 7" Threaded Diamond Optic	8455-CA	1977	1978	$26.00 – 28.00

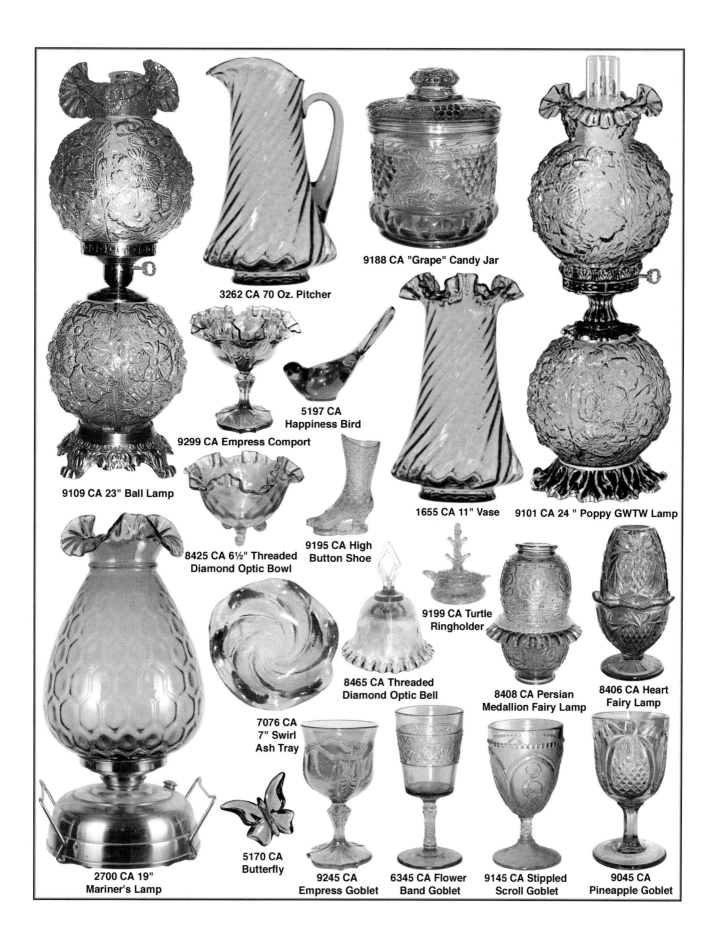

9188 CA "Grape" Candy Jar

3262 CA 70 Oz. Pitcher

5197 CA
Happiness Bird

9299 CA Empress Comport

9109 CA 23" Ball Lamp

8425 CA 6½" Threaded
Diamond Optic Bowl

9195 CA High
Button Shoe

1655 CA 11" Vase

9101 CA 24 " Poppy GWTW Lamp

9199 CA Turtle
Ringholder

8465 CA Threaded
Diamond Optic Bell

8408 CA Persian
Medallion Fairy Lamp

8406 CA Heart
Fairy Lamp

7076 CA
7" Swirl
Ash Tray

5170 CA
Butterfly

2700 CA 19"
Mariner's Lamp

9245 CA
Empress Goblet

6345 CA Flower
Band Goblet

9145 CA Stippled
Scroll Goblet

9045 CA
Pineapple Goblet

Colonial Blue and Blue Transparent

The general term *transparent blue* includes two colors in the span of forty years included in this book. Fenton's light transparent blue (BU) color was only used for a few items from its introduction in the 1950s until it was phased out in the mid-1960s. The color of the only two items still in production — the Modern Swirl ashtrays — was changed to the darker Colonial Blue in 1964. Notice the light blue decanter in the bottom right of the photo. The blue stopper and handle are unusual. Most decanters are found with a crystal stopper and handle.

The deeper blue color, Colonial Blue, first appeared in the Fenton line in 1962 and was discontinued at the end of 1979. This same Colonial Blue color was also used as an overlay to form the Opaque Blue Overlay color. Colonial Blue was used in a variety of popular patterns like Hobnail, Rose, Valencia, and Thumbprint, and for numerous pressed pattern glass styles.

Numerous other transparent blue colors have been developed in the years since Colonial Blue was discontinued. A light blue color (FB) was put into use in 1982, about the time the American Legacy line was developed. The next blue to appear in the line was cobalt blue. A medium transparent blue called Periwinkle Blue was used on a few assortments in the mid-1980s. The No. 9245 Empress goblet and the Happiness Bird were made in another blue color — Blue Royale — in the late 1980s.

Blue Transparent	Ware No.	Introduced	Discontinued	Value
Ashtray, 5" Modern Swirl	9175-BU	1960	1965	$12.00 – 14.00
Ashtray, 9" Modern Swirl	9176-BU	1960	1965	$18.00 – 20.00
Decanter, Polka Dot	2478-BU	1960	1962	$200.00 – 250.00
Tumbler. 9 oz. Georgian	6550-BU	July 1952	1954	$8.00 – 10.00
Colonial Blue	**Ware No.**	**Introduced**	**Discontinued**	**Value**
Ashtray, 5" Modern Swirl	9175-CB	July 1962	1970	$9.00 – 11.00
Ashtray, 9" Modern Swirl	9176-CB	July 1962	1970	$18.00 – 20.00
Ashtray, 5½" Swirl	7075-CB	1977	1978	$9.00 – 11.00
Ashtray, 7½" Swirl	7076-CB	1977	1978	$18.00 – 20.00
Basket, 7" Threaded Diamond Optic	8435-CB	1977	1979	$30.00 – 35.00
Bell, Threaded Diamond Optic	8465-CB	1977	1979	$25.00 – 30.00
Bird, Happiness	5197-CB	1969	1979	$25.00 – 30.00
Bowl, 6½" Threaded Diamond Optic	8425-CB	1977	1978	$18.00 – 22.00
Butterfly	5170-CB	1970	1971	$18.00 – 22.00
Candy box, Colonial	8488-CB	1977	1979	$30.00 – 35.00
Candy box, Knobby Bull's Eye	9385-CB	1977	1978	$35.00 – 40.00
Cigarette lighter	9198-CB	1966	1969	$20.00 – 25.00
Comport, Empress	9229-CB	1962	1967	$12.00 – 15.00
Comport, Pineapple	9129-CB	1962	1967	$12.00 – 15.00
Comport, Tree of Life	9322-CB	1977	1978	$12.00 – 15.00
Fairy light, Heart	8406-CB	1977	July 1977	$30.00 – 35.00
Fairy light, Persian Medallion	8408-CB	1974	1976	$40.00 – 45.00
Goblet, Cactus	3445-CB	1962	1963	$14.00 – 16.00
Goblet, Empress	9245-CB	1962	1967	$14.00 – 16.00
Goblet, Flower Band	6345-CB	1962	1965	$14.00 – 16.00
Goblet, Pineapple	9045-CB	1962	1967	$14.00 – 16.00
Goblet, Stippled Scroll	9145-CB	1962	1965	$14.00 – 16.00
Ring tree, turtle	9199-CB	1966	1968	$16.00 – 18.00
Shoe, high button	9195-CB	1965	1966	$20.00 – 25.00
Vase, 7" Threaded Diamond Optic	8455-CB	1977	1978	$35.00 – 40.00

9229 CB Empress Comport

6345 CB Flower Band Goblet

9045 CB Pineapple Goblet

9145 CB Stippled Scroll Goblet

9245 CB Empress Goblet

9129 CB Pineapple Comport

5197 CB Happiness Bird

9385 CB Knobby Bulls Eye Candy Box

8408 CB Persian Medallion Fairy Lamp

8406 CB Heart Fairy Lamp

9199 CB Turtle Ring Tree

8425 CB 6½" Threaded Diamond Optic Bowl

8488 CB Colonial Candy Box

8455 CB 7" Threaded Diamond Optic Vase

8465 CB Threaded Diamond Optic Bell

2478 BU Polka Dot Decanter

Colonial Green

Fenton changed transparent green from an emerald color to an olive shade in 1963. The new green was used for the major patterns of the time such as Hobnail, Rose, Thumbprint, and Valencia. In addition, the color was used for numerous lamps and decorative accessories. The two Modern Swirl ashtrays continued in production through this color transformation and will be found in both emerald green and Colonial Green.

The No. 9188 Grape candy was fashioned from an old Northwood tobacco jar mould. This was a popular item that was made in various transparent and opaque colors. It is still a popular item that makes a reappearance in a new color on occasion. The Modern Swirl ashtrays were discontinued at the end of 1970. The shape re-entered the a few years later with new Ware numbers. The replacement 5" Swirl ashtray had the new ware number 7075 and the 7" size was listed as number 7076.

Colonial Green was also used to produce the overlay color Shelley Green Overlay. This cased Colonial Green over milk combination was used to produce lamps.

Yellow Overlay	Ware No.	Introduced	Discontinued	Value
Ashtray, 5" Modern Swirl	9175-CG	1965	1971	$8.00 – 10.00
Ashtray, 9" Modern Swirl	9176-CG	1965	1971	$12.00 – 14.00
Butterfly	5170-CG	1970	1971	$12.00 – 15.00
Candy jar, 7¼" Grape & Cable	9188-CG	1968	1970	$125.00 – 150.00
Cigarette lighter	9198-CG	1966	1969	$14.00 – 18.00
Comport, Empress	9229-CG	1965	1967	$9.00 – 11.00
Comport, Pineapple	9129-CG	1965	1967	$9.00 – 11.00
Fairy lamp, Persian Medallion	8408-CG	1974	1976	$30.00 – 35.00
Goblet, Empress	9245-CG	1965	1967	$10.00 – 12.00
Goblet, Pineapple	9045-CG	1965	1967	$10.00 – 12.00
Lamp. 24" Poppy GWTW	9101-CG	1971	1977	$120.00 – 140.00
Lamp, 21½" Poppy double ball	9108-CG	1966	1967	$130.00 – 155.00
Lamp, 23" Poppy double ball	9109-CG	1967	1973	$120.00 – 140.00
Lamp, 19½" Thumbprint student	1408-CG	1967	1970	$60.00 – 70.00
Lamp, 20" Thumbprint student	1410-CG	1967	1969	$60.00 – 70.00
Pitcher, 70 oz.	3262-CG	1968	July 1968	$45.00 – 55.00
Ring tree, turtle	9199-CG	1966	1968	$10.00 – 12.00
Shoe, high button	9195-CG	1965	1966	$14.00 – 16.00
Vase, 11"	1655-CG	1968	July 1968	$27.00 – 32.00

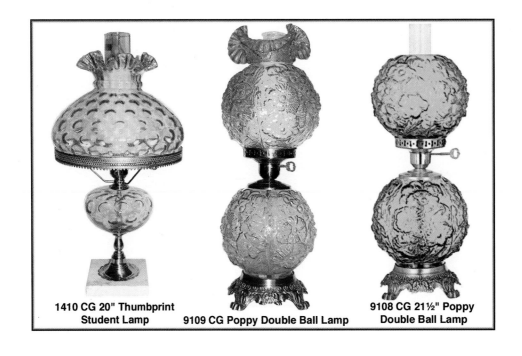

1410 CG 20" Thumbprint Student Lamp

9109 CG Poppy Double Ball Lamp

9108 CG 21½" Poppy Double Ball Lamp

9188 Grape
Candy Jar

9045 CG
Pineapple Goblet

9245 CG
Empress Goblet

3262 CG 70 Oz. Pitcher

9129 CG Pineapple
Comport

5170 CG Butterfly

9199 CG Turtle
Ringtree

1655 CG 11" Vase

9195 CG High
Button Shoe

9198 CG Cigarette Lighter

8408 CG Persian Medallion
Fairy Lamp

9229 CG Empress Comport

9175 CG 5" Ash Tray

1408 CG 19½"
Thumbprint Student Lamp

Green Transparent

Fenton used several color codes after July 1952 to designate transparent green. Through the 1950s dark and light green were distinguished by using the respective codes DG and LG. In the early 1960s, the Modern Swirl ashtrays were produced in a deep emerald green that was given the color code GN. In July 1961, this color code was changed to GR. Another shade of transparent green was made by Fenton during the 1960s. An olive green (CG) was introduced in 1963 and was used extensively in the Hobnail and Thumbprint patterns. Later, in 1978, a deeper emerald green, called Springtime Green (GT), appeared in the Fenton line.

During the early 1950s, two dark green (No. 9078-DG) ashtrays were packaged with two milk glass (No. 9078 -MI) ashtrays in an attractive gift box. The gift set was marketed as the No. 9009 ashtray set. The #752 console set was sold as both a three-piece and five-piece set. The three-piece set consisted of a planter bowl and a pair of candleholders; the larger set added another pair of candleholders.

The four-piece #1952 clusterette flower set was introduced in light green (LG) in January 1952. It consisted of two round and two straight sections. The ware number of this set became #9002 in July 1952. The #68 console set was composed of a #66-11½" oval bowl and a pair of #67 candleholders. These pieces were only listed in the January 1952 price list. The #377 Quilted planter bookend was composed of two pieces — the planter box and the bookend backdrop. The five-piece canasta cigarette set included the #1800 cigarette box and one each of the spade, heart, club, and diamond ashtrays. This set used ware #5808 after July 1952. The #380 Quilted cigarette set (No. 5508) was produced by combining two #379 ashtrays with the #378 cigarette box. This set was only listed during 1952. For more information about many of these shapes, see the Milk Glass section of this book.

Green Transparent	Ware No.	Introduced	Discontinued	Value
Ashtray, 5" Modern Swirl	9175-GN	1960	1963	$8.00 – 10.00
Ashtray, 9" Modern Swirl	9176-GN	1960	1963	$12.00 – 14.00
Ashtray, #379 Quilted		1952	1953	$6.00 – 8.00
Ashtray, #1728 square	9078-DG	1952	1954	$10.00 – 12.00
Ashtray, #1800 Club	5875-LG	1952	July 1953	$6.00 – 8.00
Ashtray, #1800 Diamond	5876-LG	1952	July 1953	$6.00 – 8.00
Ashtray, #1800 Heart	5877-LG	1952	July 1953	$6.00 – 8.00
Ashtray, #1800 Spade	5878-LG	1952	July 1953	$6.00 – 8.00
Bowl, #65-6"		1952	July 1952	$9.00 – 11.00
Bowl, #66-11½" oval		1952	July 1952	$20.00 – 25.00
Bowl, #752-13" rect. planter		1951	July 1952	$35.00 – 45.00
Bowl, #1562-13" oval	9023-DG	1952	1953	$25.00 – 30.00
Canasta set, #1800 5-pc.	5808-LG	1952	July 1953	$50.00 – 62.00
Candleholder, #67		1952	July 1952	$7.00 – 9.00
Candleholder, #752		1951	July 1952	$8.00 – 10.00
Cigarette box, #378 Quilted		1952	1953	$25.00 – 30.00
Cigarette box, #1800	5889-LG	1952	July 1953	$25.00 – 30.00
Cigarette set, #380 Quilted	5508-LG	1952	1953	$37.00 – 43.00
Clusterette, #1952 4 pc. set	9002-DG	1952	July 1953	$35.00 – 45.00
Console set, #68		1952	July 1952	$34.00 – 43.00
Ivy ball, milk foot	1021-MG	July 1952	1957	$75.00 – 85.00
Ivy ball and base, #705	7322-DG	1952	1953	$55.00 – 65.00
Planter, Quilted bookend	5595-LG	1952	1953	$35.00 – 40.00
Pot and saucer, #400	7299 -DG	1952	1954	$35.00 – 40.00
Tumbler, 5 oz. Georgian	6545-DG	July 1953	1954	$5.00 – 7.00
Tumbler, 5 oz. Georgian	6545-LG	July 1953	1954	$5.00 – 7.00
Tumbler, 9 oz. Georgian	6550-DG	July 1952	1955	$5.00 – 7.00
Tumbler, 12 oz. Georgian	6547-DG	July 1953	1954	$7.00 – 9.00

Green Transparent	Ware No.	Introduced	Discontinued	Value
Vase, #182-9½"	7358-DG	1952	July 1953	$30.00 – 35.00
Vase, #182-9½" 2-handled	7359-DG	1952	1954	$85.00 – 95.00
Vase, #183-6½"	7253-DG	1952	1953	$12.00 – 14.00
Vase, #894-9"		1952	July 1952	$30.00 – 35.00
Vase, #1720-7½" pinch		1952	July 1952	$16.00 – 18.00
Vase, #1721-8½"		1952	July 1952	$30.00 – 35.00
Tumbler, 9 oz. Georgian	6550-LG	July 1952	1958	$5.00 – 7.00
Tumbler, 12 oz. Georgian	6547-LG	July 1953	1954	$7.00 – 9.00

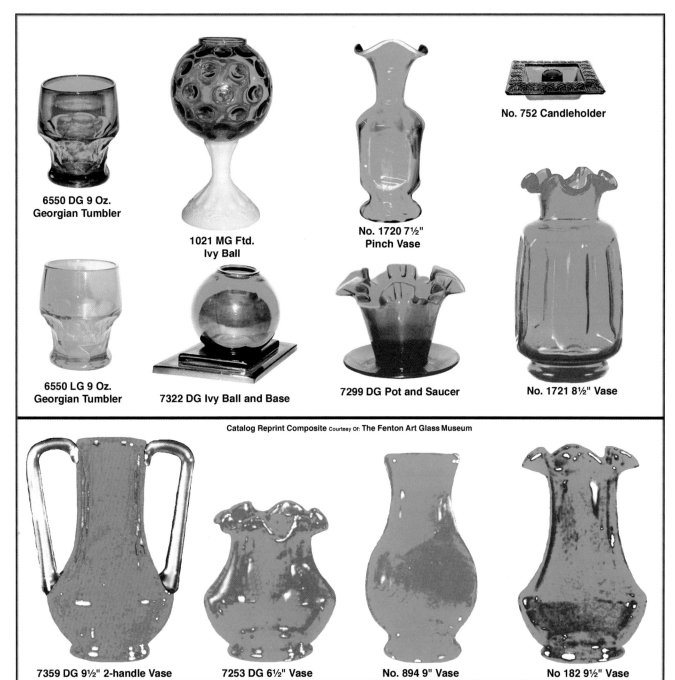

No. 752 Candleholder

6550 DG 9 Oz.
Georgian Tumbler

1021 MG Ftd.
Ivy Ball

No. 1720 7½"
Pinch Vase

6550 LG 9 Oz.
Georgian Tumbler

7322 DG Ivy Ball and Base

7299 DG Pot and Saucer

No. 1721 8½" Vase

Catalog Reprint Composite Courtesy Of: The Fenton Art Glass Museum

7359 DG 9½" 2-handle Vase

7253 DG 6½" Vase

No. 894 9" Vase

No 182 9½" Vase

163

Springtime Green

Transparent Springtime Green is a deep, bright emerald green color. It is essentially the same color as earlier items in the Fenton line with the GN and GR codes. The ten shapes listed below were produced in this color with the code GT from January 1977 until December 1978.

For other items in the Springtime Green color, see the Hobnail pattern in the book *Fenton Art Glass Patterns 1939 – 1980*.

Eight items in a transparent teal green appeared in the Fenton line in 1987. The new color was called Teal Royale (OC). In the decade of the nineties, Fenton returned to producing a line of items in a transparent medium green color called Sea Mist Green (LE).

Springtime Green	Ware No.	Introduced	Discontinued	Value
Ashtray, 5½" Swirl	7075-GT	1977	1978	$8.00 – 10.00
Ashtray, 7½" Swirl	7076-GT	1977	1978	$12.00 – 14.00
Basket, 7" Threaded Diamond Optic	8435-GT	1977	1979	$25.00 – 30.00
Bell, Threaded Diamond Optic	8465-GT	1977	1979	$25.00 – 30.00
Bowl, 6½" Threaded Diamond Optic	8425-GT	1977	1979	$16.00 – 18.00
Candy box, Colonial	8488-GT	1977	1979	$22.00 – 27.00
Candy box, Knobby Bull's Eye	9385-GT	1977	1978	$25.00 – 30.00
Comport, Tree of Life	9322-GT	1977	1979	$11.00 – 13.00
Fairy lamp, Heart	8406-GT	1977	1979	$25.00 – 30.00
Vase, 7" Threaded Diamond Optic	8455-GT	1977	1978	$27.00 – 32.00

8435 GT 7"
Threaded Diamond
Optic Basket

8455 GT 7"
Threaded Diamond Optic Vase

8406 GT Heart
Fairy Lamp

9322 GT
Tree Of Life Comport

8488 GT
Colonial Candy Box

8425 GT 6½" Threaded
Diamond Optic Bowl

8465 Gt Threaded Diamond Optic Bell

9385 GT Knobby Bulls Eye Candy Box

7075 GT 5½" Swirl Ash Tray

Jamestown Blue Transparent

Fenton's transparent teal color is called Jamestown Blue Transparent (JT) to distinguish it from a cased teal color that Fenton made at the same time. The cased color is called Jamestown Blue Overlay (JB). Fenton's catalogs from the period referred to the Jamestown Blue color as a replica of early Peacock Blue. Transparent Jamestown Blue was introduced in January 1957 and remained in production through December 1959, although most of the pieces were discontinued by the middle of that year. Pieces in the regular line include those listed below and another eleven items in the Polka Dot pattern. For more information about Polka Dot in Jamestown Blue Transparent, see the book *Fenton Art Glass Patterns 1939 – 1980.*

An ivy vase within a transparent Coin Dot teal-colored ball was made in combination with an attached milk glass base. The color code for this combination was JM.

The No. 6209-MI (milk glass) tray with a chrome handle was combined with three transparent Jamestown Blue pieces — two No. 6206 shakers and one No. 6289 mustard — to form a condiment set. However, this item was not sold in the regular line, but could be bought through the Fenton Gift Shop.

For information about the overlay color Jamestown Blue (JB) see "Jamestown Blue" in the Overlay section of this book.

Jamestown Blue Transparent	Ware No.	Introduced	Discontinued	Value
Candy box	6080-JT	1958	July 1959	$110.00 – 125.00
Ivy ball, milk foot	1021-JM	1957	1960	$95.00 – 110.00
Shaker	6206-JT	1958	July 1959	$9.00 – 11.00

1021 JM Ftd. Ivy Ball

6206 JT Shakers

6080 JT Candy Box

Orange

The heat-sensitive chemicals used to produce Fenton's orange resulted in more of an amberina color than a true orange. Orange was introduced into the Fenton line in 1963. Six items in the Diamond Optic pattern and a Thumbprint swung vase were in the 1963/64 catalog. Later, other items were added to the line. Orange also became an important color in Fenton's Daisy and Button, Hobnail, Roses, and Valencia patterns. For more information about these patterns, see the book *Fenton Art Glass Patterns 1939 – 1980*. Fenton's Old Virginia Glass division also marketed pieces in the Fine Cut pattern in orange.

Although the orange items listed below were made primarily in the 1960s, orange was not discontinued until the end of 1977. Two vases from Fenton's Verly's moulds were made in orange satin for a brief time during the last half of 1968.

Orange	Ware No.	Introduced	Discontinued	Value
Ashtray, 5" Modern Swirl	9175-OR	1965	1970	$8.00 – 10.00
Ashtray, 9" Modern Swirl	9176-OR	1965	1970	$14.00 – 16.00
Butterfly	5170-OR	1970	1971	$18.00 – 22.00
Candy jar, 7¼" Grape & Cable	9188-OR	1968	1970	$150.00 – 170.00
Cigarette lighter	9198-OR	1966	1969	$14.00 – 18.00
Ring tree, turtle	9199-OR	1966	1968	$14.00 – 16.00
Shoe, high button	9195-OR	1965	1966	$15.00 – 18.00
Vase, Empress	8252-OR	1968	July 1968	$90.00 – 100.00
Vase, Mandarin	8251-OR	1968	July 1968	$100.00 – 125.00
Vase, Vessel of Gems	8253-OR	1968	1969	$50.00 – 60.00

Orange Satin	Ware No.	Introduced	Discontinued	Value
Vase, Empress	8252-OE	1968	July 1968	$100.00 – 125.00
Vase, Mandarin	8251-OE	1968	July 1968	$120.00 – 140.00

8252 OR Empress Vase

8253 OR Vessel of Gems Vase

8251 OR Mandarin Vase

9175 OR 5" Swirl Ash Tray

9188 OR Grape Candy Jar

9195 OR High Button Shoe

Ruby

Fenton's ruby color was used in several popular patterns such as Georgian, Lincoln Inn, and Dancing Ladies during the 1930s. Opalescent glassware became the focus of production during the 1940s, and transparent ruby items did not reappear in the general line until the 1950s. Later, the Hobnail and Thumbprint patterns and several Poppy lamps were also made in ruby.

Ruby colored glassware was also used in special Valentine's Day assortments offered in the the early part of the year. These pieces were often hand decorated, and the offer for these items usually expired in early February. Beginning in the 1970s, hand-decorated ruby items were often included as part of the Christmas assortments that were available from July through December each year.

Orange	Ware No.	Introduced	Discontinued	Value
Ashtray, 5" Modern Swirl	9175-RU	1966	1969	$9.00 – 11.00
Ashtray, 9" Modern Swirl	9176-RU	1966	1969	$18.00 – 20.00
Bird	5197-RU	1977	1980+	$30.00 – 35.00
Cigarette lighter	9198-RU	1966	1969	$20.00 – 22.00
Ivy ball and base, #705	7322-RU	1952	1953	$85.00 – 95.00
Lamp, 24" GWTW	9101-RU	1971	1980+	$190.00 – 210.00
Lamp, 20" Poppy student	9107-RU	1972	1979	$125.00 – 150.00
*Santa candle light	5106-RU	July 1969	1980	$35.00 – 45.00
Tumbler, 5 oz. Georgian	6545-RU	July 1953	1954	$6.00 – 8.00
Tumbler. 9 oz. Georgian	6550-RU	July 1952	July 1954	$6.00 – 8.00
Tumbler, 12 oz. Georgian	6547-RU	July 1953	July 1954	$8.00 – 10.00
Vase, #182-9½"	7358-RU	1952	1953	$35.00 – 45.00
Vase, #182-9½" 2-handle	7359-RU	1952	1953	$120.00 – 140.00
Vase, #183-6½"	7253-RU	1952	1953	$18.00 – 20.00
Vase, #894-9"		1952	July 1952	$35.00 – 45.00

*Only in the line from July to Dec. after 1972.

9107 RU Poppy 20" Student Lamp

9176 RU 9" Modern Swirl Ash Tray

5197 RU Happiness Bird

7322 RU Ivy Ball with Milk Base

6550 RU Georgian 9 Oz. Tumbler

5106 RU Santa Candle Light

Wisteria

Production of the pale orchid color that Fenton named Wisteria was very limited. The color is much lighter than Mulberry or Plum, but is very similar to Fenton's Lilac of the early nineties. With the exception of a few special items that were made later, only the ten shapes listed below were produced in this color, and production was limited to the span of the 1977/78 catalog. The same shapes were also made in Colonial Amber, Colonial Blue, and Springtime Green during the same period.

Wisteria	Ware No.	Introduced	Discontinued	Value
Ashtray, 5½" Swirl	7075-WT	1977	1978	$12.00 – 14.00
Ashtray, 7½" Swirl	7076-WT	1977	1978	$18.00 – 22.00
Basket, 7" Threaded Diamond Optic	8435-WT	1977	1979	$35.00 – 45.00
Bell, Threaded Diamond Optic	8465-WT	1977	1979	$30.00 – 35.00
Bowl, 6½" Threaded Diamond Optic	8425-WT	1977	1979	$18.00 – 22.00
Candy box, Colonial	8488-WT	1977	1979	$30.00 – 35.00
Candy box, Knobby Bulls Eye	9385-WT	1977	June 1977	$35.00 – 40.00
Comport, Tree of Life	9322-WT	1977	1979	$12.00 – 15.00
Fairy lamp, Heart	8406-WT	1977	1979	$35.00 – 40.00
Vase, 7" Threaded Diamond Optic	8455-WT	1977	1978	$35.00 – 45.00

Catalog Reprint Composite Circa 1977
Courtesy Of:
The Fenton Art Glass Museum

Wisteria

A rich "new-old" color achieved with a rare earth element, neodymium. Wisteria's slightly higher price results from the use of neodymium, which makes this glass almost as costly to make as our gold base glasses. A dichroic color, it is best displayed under incandescent or living warm fluorescent lighting.

8435 WT
7" THREADED
DIAMOND OPTIC BASKET

9385 WT
KNOBBY BULLS EYE CANDY BOX

8455 WT
7" THREADED
DIAMOND OPTIC VASE

8406 WT
HEART
FAIRY LIGHT

9322 WT
TREE OF LIFE COMPORT

8488 WT
COLONIAL CANDY BOX

Miscellaneous Transparent Colors

Fenton's Amethyst is a deep transparent purple color. This color was used to for producing Georgian tumblers reissued in the 1950s. Colonial Pink was used extensively with a few of the 1960s tableware lines such as Thumbprint and Rose. Not many other accessory items were made in this color. After the 1930s, crystal was used sparingly. A few of the tableware lines such as Hobnail, Priscilla, and Valencia were made in crystal for short periods. Most other crystal items made during this time were satinized. Numerous crystal items came back into the Fenton line again during the 1980s. Smoke was another color that was used very sparingly. A number of items were made in this color for Rubel & Co. during the early 1950s. Two ashtrays and a relish from Rubel moulds were placed in the regular line during 1954.

Zodiac medallions and paperweights were introduced in the July 1969 supplement. Both series featured a figure for each Zodiac sign. The medallions were made in different colors and made colorful displays or attractive mobiles. The color of each medallion is shown in the catalog reprints on the following pages. The paperweights were crystal with frosted highlights.

Amethyst	Ware No.	Introduced	Discontinued	Value
Ivy ball, ftd.	1021-MY	July 1952	1955	$75.00 – 85.00
Tumbler, 9 oz. Georgian	6550-AY	July 1952	1955	$5.00 – 7.00
Colonial Pink				
Ashtray, 5" Modern Swirl	9175-CP	July 1962	1966	$7.00 – 9.00
Ashtray, 9" Modern Swirl	9176-CP	July 1962	1966	$14.00 – 16.00
Comport, Empress	9229-CP	1962	1965	$11.00 – 13.00
Comport, Pineapple	9129-CP	1962	1965	$11.00 – 13.00
Goblet, Cactus	3445-CP	1962	1963	$10.00 – 12.00
Goblet, Empress	9245-CP	1962	1965	$10.00 – 12.00
Goblet, Flower Band	6345-CP	1962	1965	$10.00 – 12.00
Goblet, Pineapple	9045-CP	1962	1965	$10.00 – 12.00
Goblet, Stippled Scroll	9145-CP	1962	1965	$10.00 – 12.00
Crystal				
Arranger, mini	9193-CY	1971	1974	$4.00 – 5.00
Ashtray, 5" Modern Swirl	9175-CY	1960	July 1962	$6.00 – 8.00
Ashtray, 9" Modern Swirl	9176-CY	1960	July 1962	$9.00 – 11.00
Bird	5197-CY	1968	1974	$14.00 – 18.00
Epergne, petite	6674-CY	1958	1960	$4.00 – 5.00
Flower block	9093-CY	1956	1958	$4.00 – 5.00
Ladle, mayonnaise	R9523-CY	1960	1964	$4.00 – 5.00
Ladle, punch	9527-CY	1952	1958	$18.00 – 20.00
Ladle, punch	9522-CY	1956	1964	$18.00 – 20.00
Tumbler, 9 oz. Georgian	6550-CY	July 1952	1954	$3.00 – 5.00
Smoke				
Ashtray	5179-SK	1954	July 1954	UND
Ashtray, bird	5173-SK	1954	1955	UND
Relish	5174-SK	1954	1955	UND
Zodiac Item				
Medallion				$15.00 – 18.00
Paperweight				$9.00 – 11.00

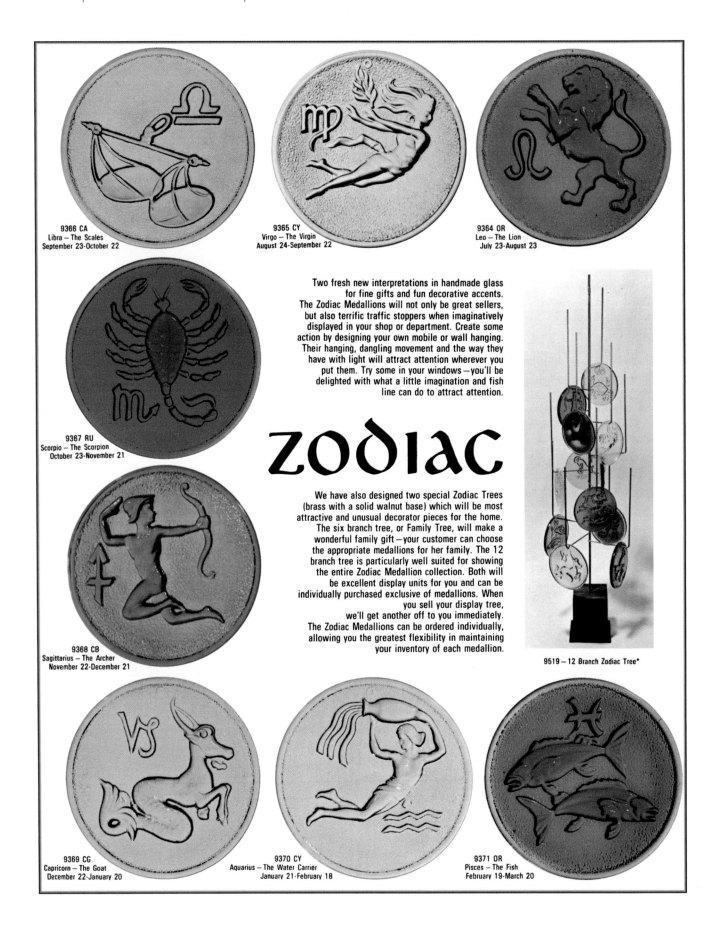

9366 CA
Libra — The Scales
September 23-October 22

9365 CY
Virgo — The Virgin
August 24-September 22

9364 OR
Leo — The Lion
July 23-August 23

9367 RU
Scorpio — The Scorpion
October 23-November 21

Two fresh new interpretations in handmade glass for fine gifts and fun decorative accents. The Zodiac Medallions will not only be great sellers, but also terrific traffic stoppers when imaginatively displayed in your shop or department. Create some action by designing your own mobile or wall hanging. Their hanging, dangling movement and the way they have with light will attract attention wherever you put them. Try some in your windows—you'll be delighted with what a little imagination and fish line can do to attract attention.

ZODIAC

We have also designed two special Zodiac Trees (brass with a solid walnut base) which will be most attractive and unusual decorator pieces for the home. The six branch tree, or Family Tree, will make a wonderful family gift—your customer can choose the appropriate medallions for her family. The 12 branch tree is particularly well suited for showing the entire Zodiac Medallion collection. Both will be excellent display units for you and can be individually purchased exclusive of medallions. When you sell your display tree, we'll get another off to you immediately. The Zodiac Medallions can be ordered individually, allowing you the greatest flexibility in maintaining your inventory of each medallion.

9519 – 12 Branch Zodiac Tree*

9368 CB
Sagittarius — The Archer
November 22-December 21

9369 CG
Capricorn — The Goat
December 22-January 20

9370 CY
Aquarius — The Water Carrier
January 21-February 18

9371 OR
Pisces — The Fish
February 19-March 20

9363 CG
Cancer – The Crab
June 22-July 22

9362 CB
Gemini – The Twins
May 21 – June 21

9361 RU
Taurus – The Bull
April 21-May 20

Fenton

THE COLLECTOR SERIES OF PAPERWEIGHTS will make an excellent gift addition to your year-round sales. Each is frosted to subtly highlight the beautifully carved figure. The Collector Series is attractively packaged in a gold foil gift box with a flocked insert as illustrated. (The figure for each Zodiac sign is illustrated on the Medallions which encircle the page.)

9360 CA
Aries – The Ram
March 21-April 20

Attention Getting
Display Mobiles
are easy to create.

*9518 and 9519
Zodiac Trees are
priced and shipped
without Medallions.
Order Medallions
separately.

9518 – 6 Branch Zodiac Tree*

9340 CY – Aries Paperweight	9344 CY – Leo Paperweight	9348 CY – Sagittarius Paperweight
9341 CY – Taurus Paperweight	9345 CY – Virgo Paperweight	9349 CY – Capricorn Paperweight
9342 CY – Gemini Paperweight	9346 CY – Libra Paperweight	9350 CY – Aquarius Paperweight
9343 CY – Cancer Paperweight	9347 CY – Scorpio Paperweight	9351 CY – Pisces Paperweight

Zodiac Catalog Reprints Courtesy Of: **The Fenton Art Glass Museum**

171

Fenton's Hand-Decorated Patterns

During the late 1960s, Fenton began to address the feasibility of getting back into the hand-decorating business. The company began as a hand-decorating shop, and a hand-decorating shop had been maintained until the constraints of the Depression years forced severe cutbacks. The search for a decorating department head culminated in the hiring of Louise Piper. She had received her training painting glassware for some of the factories in the Jeannette, Pennsylvania, area. As the head decorator for Fenton, some of her responsibilities in addition to painting were training other decorators and designing new decorations.

Fenton's first hand-painted decoration was Decorated Violets, which later became known as Violets in the Snow. The pattern was introduced into the line in July 1968 and was a huge success. The initial assortment featured 16 pieces from the Silver Crest pattern adorned with hand-painted purple violets. Later, other milk glass pieces, especially small animal figures, were decorated with this pattern. The pattern continued to be popular through the 1970s as numerous other shapes were added. The line was discontinued at the end of 1984. For more information about the Violets in the Snow pattern and other hand-painted decorations on Crest or Hobnail backgrounds, see the book *Fenton Art Glass Patterns 1939 – 1980*.

Two new hand-painted decorations were added to the general line in mid-1969. The new Yellow Rose and Apple Blossom decorations were also set against a Silver Crest background. The same nine shapes of Silver Crest were decorated with each pattern. Both decorations were discontinued at the end of 1970.

Fenton's new Burmese color was introduced in the January 1970 catalog supplement. The six shapes made in this color were also sold with a transfer leaf decoration. Production of this pattern was discontinued at the end of 1972.

Hand-painted Bluebells set against a milk Hobnail background graced the 1971 catalog. This pattern was out of the line by the end of 1972.

The first pieces of hand-painted Burmese also entered the Fenton line in 1971. This pattern of pink roses set against a Burmese background was designed by Louise Piper. New items were added to this pattern and old pieces were discontinued throughout the 1970s. Production of some of the vases and the 21" student lamp was continued into the 1980s. Also, numerous pieces with this decoration have been made for QVC and other special-order interests.

The July 1971, supplement introduced customers to five specially decorated milk Hobnail pieces. These were hand painted with sprigs of holly, to add color to the Christmas season. The decoration was expanded in the ensuing years to include items other than Hobnail. This was the start of a tradition of producing specially decorated items for Christmas that continues even now.

In July, 1972, the first three pieces of the Pink Anemone pattern on a Custard Satin background were introduced. Many people had trouble with this name, so in about 1977, Fenton began referring to the pattern as simply Pink Blossom. Numerous items were added to the line through the years, and some of the original pieces were produced into the 1980s. The pattern was finally discontinued at the end of 1985. Custard Satin was also chosen as the background for a new Christmas Holly decorated series. The first two items, a happiness bird and a two-piece fairy light, were displayed in the July catalog. More items were added to this series in later years. A ruby fairy light with a white hand painted Christmas Holly decoration was the first of a series of holly-decorated items to be introduced. New pieces of this series were introduced in the late 1970s, and most items continued into the 1980s.

In 1973, a lamp in a new Burmese hand-painted pattern called Scenic Decorated Burmese was introduced. This was followed during the next few years with six more pieces of hand-painted Burmese with a scenic tree set against a mountainous background. All of these pieces were discontinued by 1980, with the exception of the student lamp, which remained in production into the early 1980s.

Starting in the mid-1970s, numerous decorations were set against satin backgrounds. In 1975, Daisies on Custard Satin was introduced. This was also the first year that decorators began including their signatures on their work.

The first pieces of Log Cabin on Custard appeared in 1976. Bluebirds on Custard was introduced in 1977. Two new decorations on milk glass also were produced. The Butterflies pattern was hand painted on popular novelty items and a few pieces from the Silver Crest line. Cardinals in Winter, introduced in July 1977, featured a brightly colored red cardinal sitting on a pine bough against a milk glass background. The decade ended with a few more decorations on satin glass. Blue Roses on blue satin, Daisies on Cameo, and Christmas Morn were introduced in 1978. Chocolate Roses on Cameo and Old Mill were placed in production in 1979.

Decoration Codes and Descriptions

Fenton used a two-letter decoration code that was used in combination with ware numbers to identify each item in the line. With a few exceptions, each hand-decorated pattern is identified by a unique two-letter combination. Most of the decoration codes used between 1969 and 1980 are identified on the following pages. The dates of manufacture are only pertinent to the scope of time covered by this book, 1939 – 1980.

Decoration	Code	Years of Manufacture	Description
Apple Blossom	AB	July 1969 – 1971	Apple Blossom is a pink floral decoration on Silver Crest.
Blue Bell Decorated	BB	1971 – 1973	This blue floral-decorated pattern was developed by Louise Piper for use on milk glass Hobnail pieces.
Bluebirds on Custard	BC	1977 – 1980	Eight items were produced with hand-painted bluebirds against a Custard Satin background.
Blue Roses	WB	July 1972 – 1973	This code was used for a Blue Roses on Custard Satin egg.
Blue Roses on Blue Satin	BL	1978 – 1980+	Hand-painted blue roses were placed against a light blue satin background.
Blue Satin on White (Hand Rubbed)	TB	July 1969 – 1970	This decoration code was used on two blue hand-rubbed candy jars made for the last six months of 1969.
Brown Rose	BN	1973	This code was used for a Brown Roses on Custard Satin egg.
Brown Satin on Custard (Hand Rubbed)	TS	July 1969 – 1970	This decoration code was used on two brown hand-rubbed candy jars made for the last six months of 1969.
Butterflies	BY	1977 – 1979	A combination of Silver Crest and other milk glass pieces were used with this butterfly and floral decoration.
Butterfly with Blossom on Honey Amber	HB	1977 – 1979	Hand-painted lamps were made in this overlay color.
Cardinals in Winter	CW	July 1977 – 1980	A bright red cardinal was depicted against a milk glass background.
Chocolate Roses on Cameo Satin	DR	1979 – 1980+	Brown roses were painted on satin beige glass ware.
Christmas Holly on Custard	CH	July 1972 – 1979	Sprigs of holly with red berries were painted on Custard Satin.
Christmas Holly on Ruby	RH	July 1972 – 1980+	A white enamel holly decoration was depicted on transparent ruby glass.
Christmas Morn	CV	July 1978 – 1979	Christmas Morn was the first in a series of annual, very limited production, special Christmas offerings that featured classic Christmas scenes.

Decoration	Code	Years of Manufacture	Description
Daisies on Cameo Satin	CD	1978 – 1980+	Orange Daisies were painted on a beige satin glassware.
Daisies on Custard	DC	1975 – 1980+	White brown-eyed daisies were painted on Custard Satin glass.
Decorated Holly on Milk	DH	July 1971 – 1976	Green holly sprigs were hand painted on milk Hobnail.
Green Rose	GR	1973	This code was used for a Green Rose on Custard Satin egg.
Green Satin on Custard (Hand Rubbed)	TG	July 1969 – 1970	This decoration code was used on two green hand-rubbed candy jars made for the last six months of 1969.
Leaf Decorated Burmese	BD	1970 – 7971	This was a transfer-type decoration featuring an Autumn-colored leaf.
Log Cabin on Custard Satin	LC	1976 – 1980+	A log cabin scene was painted on Custard Satin glassware.
Love Rose on Ruby	LR	1979 – 1981	A white rose and "Love" were painted on transparent ruby.
Love Rose on White	LW	1979 – 1981	A pink rose and "Love" were painted on milk glass pieces.
Nature's Christmas	NC	1979	Nature's Christmas was the second in a series of annual, limited production, special Christmas offering that featured classic Christmas scenes. This years production had a deer scene.
Old Mill	OM	1979 – 1980+	An old mill on a river was painted on Custard Satin.
Pink Anemone (Pink Blossom)	PY	July 1972 – 1980+	A pink iced floral decoration was applied to Custard Satin.
Purple Rose	PR	1973	A purple rose and trim decorated a Custard Satin egg.
Rose Burmese	RB	1971 – 1980+	This decoration features pink roses on Burmese glass.
Roses on Custard	RC	1977 – 1980+	Pink roses were painted on Custard Satin Glass.
Roses on Ruby	RH	1978 – 1980+	Enameled white roses were painted on transparent ruby.
Roses on White	RW	1974 – 1976	Pink roses were used to decorate milk glass Hobnail.
Scenic Decorated Burmese	DB	1973 – 1980+	A colorful tree and mountain scene were painted on several shapes of Burmese.
Violets on Custard	VC	1973	Violets were painted on a Custard Satin egg.
Yellow Rose	YR	July 1969 – 1971	This yellow floral-decorated pattern was developed by Louise Piper for use on Silver Crest pieces.

Bluebirds on Custard Satin

Eight items with the hand-painted Bluebirds on Custard decoration debuted in January 1977. Fenton catalogs portray the decoration as "happy little birds hand painted on delicate stem and leaf backdrops depicting the pleasant feel of a summertime meadow." All of the pieces in this line were discontinued by December 1979. The No. 7437 basket was discontinued at the end of 1978. It was replaced by the No. 7237 basket the next year.

Bluebirds on Custard Satin	Ware No.	Introduced	Discontinued	Value
Basket	7437-BC	1977	1979	$75.00 – 85.00
Basket, 7"	7237-BC	1979	1980	$75.00 – 85.00
Bell, Medallion	8267-BC	1977	1980	$32.00 – 37.00
Bird	5197-BC	1977	1980	$40.00 – 45.00
Fairy light	7300-BC	1977	1980	$40.00 – 50.00
Lamp, 19½" student	9308-BC	1977	1980	$250.00 – 290.00
Vase, 4½"	7254-BC	1977	1980	$30.00 – 35.00
Vase, 10"	7257-BC	1977	1980	$75.00 – 85.00
Vase, bud	9056-BC	1977	1980	$30.00 – 35.00

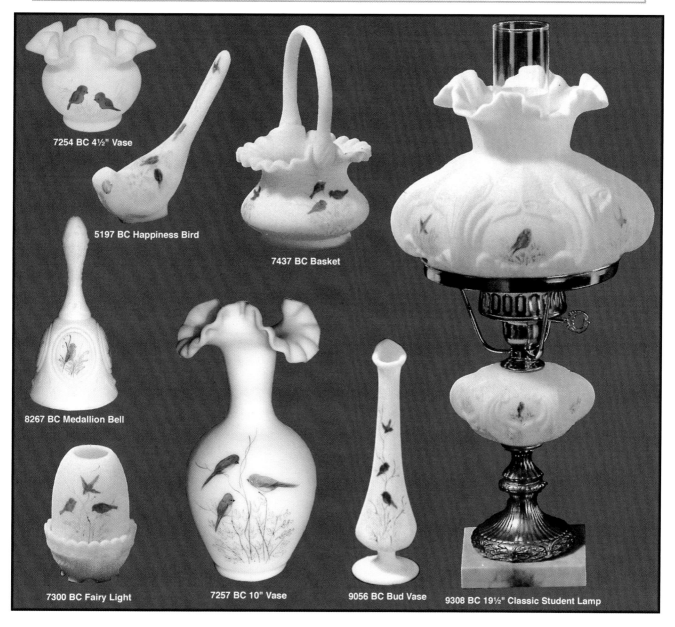

7254 BC 4½" Vase

5197 BC Happiness Bird

7437 BC Basket

8267 BC Medallion Bell

7300 BC Fairy Light

7257 BC 10" Vase

9056 BC Bud Vase

9308 BC 19½" Classic Student Lamp

Blue Roses on Blue Satin

Fenton introduced the Blue Roses on blue satin pattern in January 1978. Ads proclaimed the decoration as "dainty blue roses hand painted on Fenton's new 'barely blue' glass." Many of these decorated pieces will be found on a lighter shade of blue satin than was used for the regular undecorated ware. Fifteen pieces of this pattern were offered initially. New pieces were added over the next few years as the pattern continued into the early 1980s. The Blue Roses decoration was discontinued at the end of 1982.

Blue Roses on Custard (BQ) was a hand-painted decoration used on seven shapes of custard glass miniature items made during 1981. These pieces were included in a special Valentine's Day offer:

Blue Roses on Custard	Ware No.	Blue Roses on Custard	Ware No.
Basket	9536-BQ	Toothpick	9592-BQ
Boot	9590-BQ	Vase, 5"	7554-BQ
Jewel box	9589-BQ	Vase, bud 8½"	9556-BQ
Slipper	9591-BQ		

Blue Roses on Blue Satin	Ware No.	Introduced	Discontinued	Value
Basket, 7"	7237-BL	1978	1980+	$45.00 – 55.00
Bell, Medallion	8267-BL	1978	1980+	$30.00 – 35.00
Bird, Happiness	5197-BL	1978	1980+	$30.00 – 35.00
Bird, small	5163-BL	1978	1980+	$30.00 – 35.00
Bunny	5162-BL	1978	1980+	$37.00 – 42.00
Candy box	7484-BL	1979	1980+	$50.00 – 55.00
Cat	5165-BL	1979	1980+	$32.00 – 37.00
Comport, ftd.	7249-BL	1978	1980+	$50.00 – 60.00
Fairy light, 2-pc.	7300-BL	1978	1980+	$37.00 – 42.00
Frog	5166-BL	1979	1980+	$32.00 – 37.00
Ginger jar, 3-pc.	7288-BL	1978	1980+	$130.00 – 150.00
Hurricane lamp, 11"	7311-BL	1979	1980+	$145.00 – 185.00
Lamp, 20" Classic	9309-BL	1978	1980+	$250.00 – 300.00
Lamp, 16" hammered Colonial	7205-BL	1978	1980+	$175.00 – 225.00
Lamp, 21" student	7209-BL	1978	1980+	$300.00 – 350.00
Swan	5161-BL	1978	1980+	$18.00 – 22.00
Vase, 4½"	7254-BL	1978	1980+	$30.00 – 35.00
Vase, 7"	7252-BL	1978	1980+	$60.00 – 65.00
Vase, bud	9056-BL	1978	1980+	$27.00 – 32.00
Vase, 11" tulip	7255-BL	1979	1980+	$90.00 – 120.00

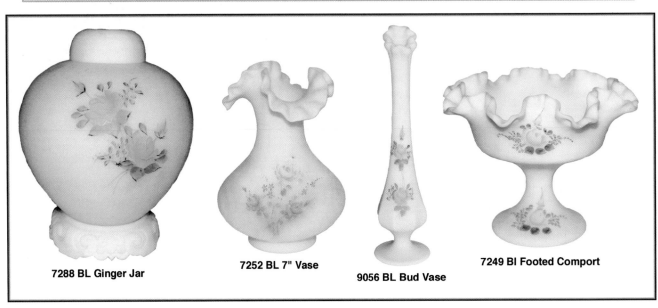

7288 BL Ginger Jar   **7252 BL 7" Vase**   **9056 BL Bud Vase**   **7249 Bl Footed Comport**

5161 BL Swan

5165 BL Cat

5162 Bl Bunny

7484 Candy Box

7209 BL 21" Student Lamp

9309 BL 20" Classic Lamp

5163 BL Small Bird

8267 Medallion Bell

7300 BL Fairy Light

7254 BL 4½" Vase

7205 BL 16" Hammered Colonial Lamp

7255 BL Tulip Vase

Butterflies

A total of eight different pieces composed Fenton's Butterflies pattern. The pattern was hand-painted on popular novelty items and a few selected pieces from the Silver Crest line. Blue and yellow butterflies with ice frosted bodies and wing tips are featured fluttering over hand-painted dainty blue and yellow flowers. Each piece is artist signed. The pattern was introduced in January 1977 and all pieces were discontinued by December 1978.

Butterflies	Ware No.	Introduced	Discontinued	Value
Basket, 7"	7237-BY	1977	1979	$60.00 – 65.00
Bell, Medallion	8267-BY	1977	1979	$27.00 – 32.00
Candy box, Medallion	8288-BY	1977	1979	$75.00 – 85.00
Fairy lamp	7300-BY	1977	1979	$60.00 – 70.00
Lamp, 19½" student	9308-BY	1977	1979	$300.00 – 350.00
Vase, 4½"	7254-BY	1977	1979	$20.00 – 25.00
Vase, 7"	7252-BY	1977	1979	$40.00 – 45.00
Vase, bud	9056-BY	1977	1979	$22.00 – 27.00

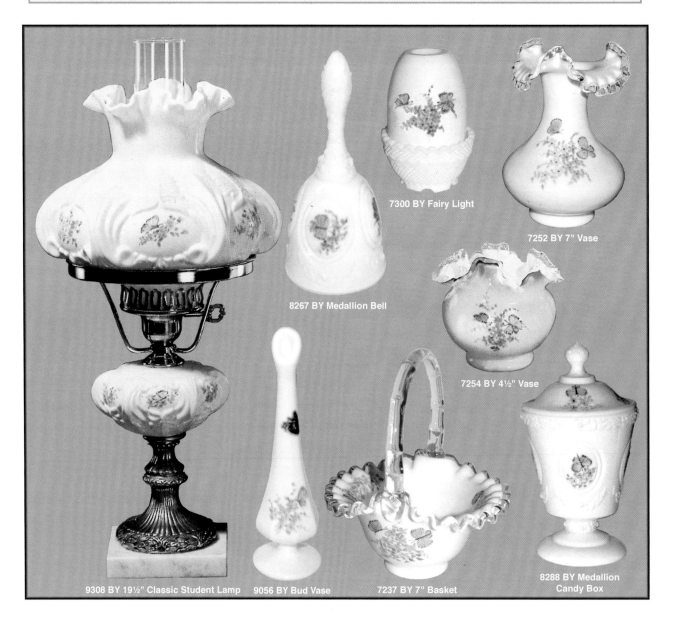

7300 BY Fairy Light

7252 BY 7" Vase

8267 BY Medallion Bell

7254 BY 4½" Vase

9308 BY 19½" Classic Student Lamp   9056 BY Bud Vase   7237 BY 7" Basket   8288 BY Medallion Candy Box

Cardinals in Winter

The Cardinals in Winter series debuted in Fenton's July 1977 catalog supplement. This hand-painted decoration depicted a brightly colored red cardinal sitting on a pine bough against a milk glass background. The pattern was only in the line for three years. The square planter and the 16" hammered Colonial lamp were only in the line for a short time and are especially hard to find.

Cardinals in Winter	Ware No.	Introduced	Discontinued	Value
Basket, 7"	7237-CW	July 1977	1980	$75.00 – 85.00
Bell, Medallion	8267-CW	July 1977	1980	$30.00 – 35.00
Bird, Happiness	5197-CW	July 1977	1980	$32.00 – 37.00
Fairy light	7300-CW	July 1977	1980	$40.00 – 45.00
Lamp, 16" hammered Colonial	7206-CW	1978	July 1979	$175.00 – 200.00
Lamp, 19½" student	9308-CW	July 1977	1980	$250.00 – 275.00
Planter, square	8494-CW	1978	1979	$65.00 – 75.00
Vase, 4½"	7254-CW	1978	1980	$30.00 – 35.00
Vase, 7"	7252-CW	1978	July 1979	$45.00 – 55.00
Vase, bud	9056-CW	July 1977	1980	$22.00 – 27.00

5197 CW Happiness Bird

7300 CW Fairy Light

7254 CW Vase

8494 CW Square Planter

7252 CW 7" Vase

9056 CW Bud Vase

9308 CW Classic Student Lamp

7237 CW 7" Basket

8267 CW Medallion Bell

7206 CW 15" Hammered Colonial Lamp

Chocolate Roses on Cameo Satin

Fenton's hand-painted Chocolate Roses decoration was introduced in January 1979. The painting featured brown roses on Cameo Satin glassware. Numerous lamps and novelty items were produced during the four years this pattern remained in the line. During the early 1980s, new shapes such as the No. 9054 tall bud vase, the No. 8056 Wave Crest vase, the No. 5140 egg on stand, the No. 5169 duckling, and several Basket Weave–style shapes were added. Chocolate Roses was discontinued at the end of 1982. A similar decoration, Chocolate Roses on Custard, was produced as a special order for the Hershey Chocolate Company of Hershey, Pennsylvania, during the late 1970s.

Chocolate Roses on Cameo Satin	Ware No.	Introduced	Discontinued	Value
Basket, 7"	7237-DR	1979	1980+	$35.00 – 40.00
Bell, Medallion	8267-DR	1979	1980+	$25.00 – 30.00
Bird, Happiness	5197-DR	1979	1980+	$27.00 – 32.00
Bird, small	5163-DR	1979	1980+	$25.00 – 30.00
Bunny	5162-DR	1979	1980+	$25.00 – 30.00
Candy box	7484-DR	1979	1980+	$40.00 – 45.00
Cat	5165-DR	1979	1980+	$25.00 – 30.00
Comport, ftd.	7429-DR	1979	1980+	$40.00 – 45.00
Fairy light, 2-pc.	7300-DR	1979	1980+	$3200 – 37.00
Frog	5166-DR	1979	1980+	$22.00 – 25.00
Hurricane lamp, 11"	7311-DR	1979	1980+	$145.00 – 175.00
Lamp, 20½" hammered Colonial	7215-DR	1979	1980+	$225.00 – 250.00
Lamp, 21½" student	7309-DR	1979	1980+	$225.00 – 275.00
Swan	5161-DR	1979	1980+	$22.00 – 25.00
Temple jar	7488-DR	1979	1980+	$40.00 – 50.00
Vase, 4½"	7254-DR	1979	1980+	$20.00 – 22.00
Vase, 7"	7252-DR	1979	1980+	$40.00 – 45.00
Vase, bud	9056-DR	1979	1980+	$18.00 – 20.00

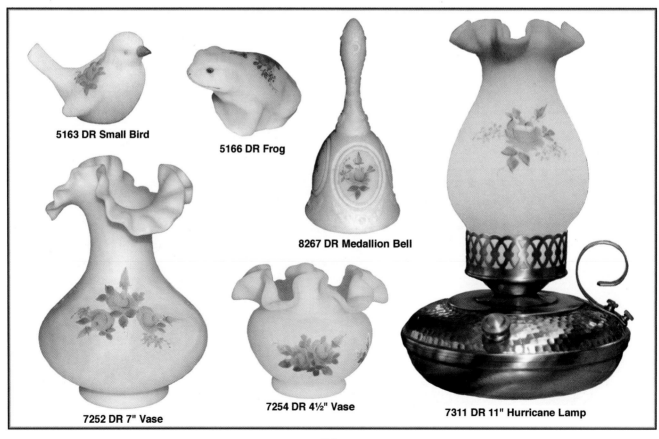

5163 DR Small Bird

5166 DR Frog

8267 DR Medallion Bell

7252 DR 7" Vase

7254 DR 4½" Vase

7311 DR 11" Hurricane Lamp

7484 DR Candy Box

7429 DR Footed Comport

5162 DR Bunny

7237 DR 7" Basket

5197 DR Happiness Bird

5165 DR Cat

9056 DR Bud Vase

7488 DR Temple Jar

7309 DR 21½" Student Lamp

5161 DR Swan

**7300 DR
Fairy Light**

7215 DR 20½" Hammered Colonial Lamp

Christmas Morn

The Limited Edition hand-painted decoration Christmas Morn was featured on the front cover of Fenton's July 1978 catalog supplement. This pattern was heralded as the first in a special series of forthcoming annual presentations depicting the theme Christmas Classics. Each hand-decorated piece was artist signed, dated, gift boxed, and packed with a descriptive minibooklet. Sales to resellers of the three items in this first edition were limited as follows:

Bell — eight per store.
Fairy light — six per store.
Lamp — two per store.

Christmas Morn	Ware No.	Introduced	Discontinued	Value
Bell	7466-CV	July 1978	1979	$40.00 – 45.00
Fairy light	7300-CV	July 1978	1979	$50.00 – 60.00
Lamp, 16" hammered Colonial	7204-CV	July 1978	1979	$250.00 – 290.00

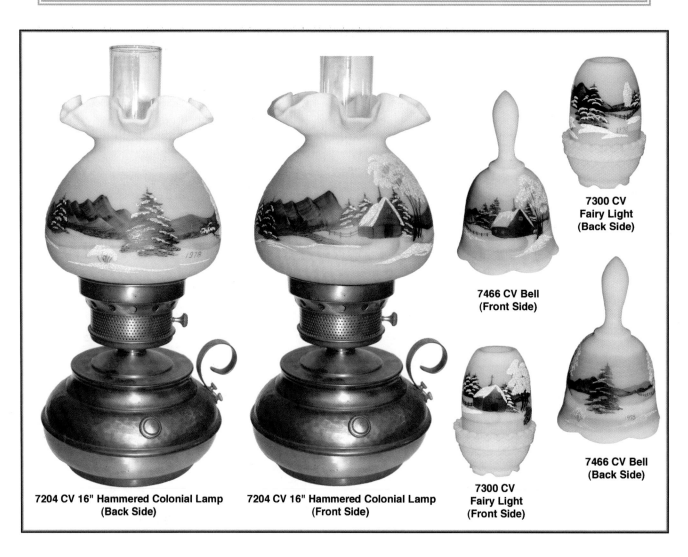

7204 CV 16" Hammered Colonial Lamp
(Back Side)

7204 CV 16" Hammered Colonial Lamp
(Front Side)

7466 CV Bell
(Front Side)

7300 CV
Fairy Light
(Back Side)

7300 CV
Fairy Light
(Front Side)

7466 CV Bell
(Back Side)

Custard Holly

Fenton's Christmas Holly on Custard Satin decoration was offered during the months of July through December, beginning in 1972. Since the 4½" vase and basket were only made in 1978, they will be more difficult to acquire. Most pieces were discontinued by the end of 1978, but the bell and fairy light continued to be made into the early 1980s. The decoration varied slightly through the years. Some variation in the pattern is illustrated on the fairy lights in the photo below.

Custard Holly	Ware No.	Introduced	Discontinued	Value
Basket, 7"	7237-CH	July 1978	1979	$60.00 – 70.00
Bell, Medallion	8267-CH	July 1975	1980+	$27.00 – 32.00
Bird, Happiness	5197-CH	July 1972	1979	$30.00 – 35.00
Candy box, Medallion	8288-CH	July 1976	1979	$60.00 – 70.00
Egg	5140-CH	July 1973	1974	$30.00 – 35.00
Fairy light	7300-CH	July 1972	1980+	$40.00 – 50.00
Vase, 4½"	7254-CH	July 1978	1979	$20.00 – 25.00
Vase, bud	9056-CH	July 1976	1979	$18.00 – 22.00

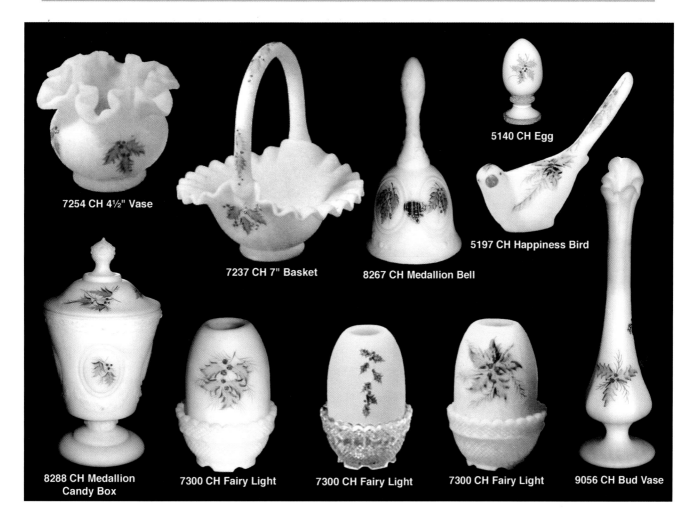

7254 CH 4½" Vase

7237 CH 7" Basket

8267 CH Medallion Bell

5140 CH Egg

5197 CH Happiness Bird

8288 CH Medallion Candy Box

7300 CH Fairy Light

7300 CH Fairy Light

7300 CH Fairy Light

9056 CH Bud Vase

Daisies on Cameo Satin

Fenton's hand-painted Daisies on Cameo decoration was composed of sprays of autumn-colored floral daisies on a beige satin glass background. New items during the early 1980s included the No. 9054 tall bud vase, the No. 6056 Wave Crest vase, the No. 5169 duckling, and the No. 7506 hanging swag lamp. Additional Basket Weave pattern items with this decoration added in 1981 included the No. 9462 bell, the No. 9304 fairy light, the No. 9305 20" student lamp, and the No. 9356 bud vase. This pattern was produced from January 1978 through December 1983.

Daisies on Cameo Satin	Ware No.	Introduced	Discontinued	Value
Basket, 7"	7237-CD	1978	1980+	$35.00 – 40.00
Bell, Medallion	8267-CD	1978	1980+	$25.00 – 30.00
Bird, Happiness	5197-CD	1978	1980+	$27.00 – 32.00
Bird, small	5163-CD	1978	1980+	$25.00 – 30.00
Bunny	5162-CD	1978	1980+	$25.00 – 30.00
Candy box	7484-CD	1979	1980+	$40.00 – 45.00
Cat	5165-CD	1979	1980+	$25.00 – 30.00
Comport, ftd.	7429-CD	1978	1980+	$40.00 – 45.00
Fairy light	7300-CD	1978	1980+	$32.00 – 37.00
Frog	5166-CD	1979	1980+	$22.00 – 25.00
Lamp, 16" hammered Colonial	7204-CD	1978	1980+	$150.00 – 175.00
Lamp, 20½" hammered Colonial	7215-CD	1979	1980+	$225.00 – 250.00
Lamp, 11" hurricane	7311-CD	1979	1980+	$150.00 – 175.00
Lamp, 21" student	7209-CD	1978	1980+	$225.00 – 250.00
Swan	5161-CD	1978	1980+	$20.00 – 25.00
Temple jar	7488-CD	1979	1980+	$40.00 – 50.00
Vase, 4½"	7254-CD	1978	1980+	$20.00 – 22.00
Vase, 7"	7252-CD	1978	1980+	$40.00 – 45.00
Vase, bud	9056-CD	1978	1980+	$19.00 – 22.00
Vase, tulip	7255-CD	1979	1980+	$80.00 – 95.00

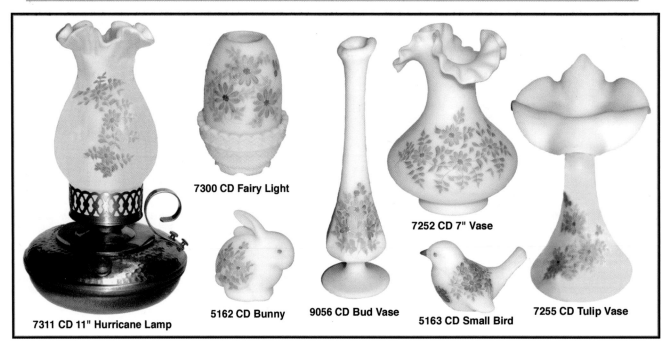

7311 CD 11" Hurricane Lamp

7300 CD Fairy Light

5162 CD Bunny

9056 CD Bud Vase

7252 CD 7" Vase

5163 CD Small Bird

7255 CD Tulip Vase

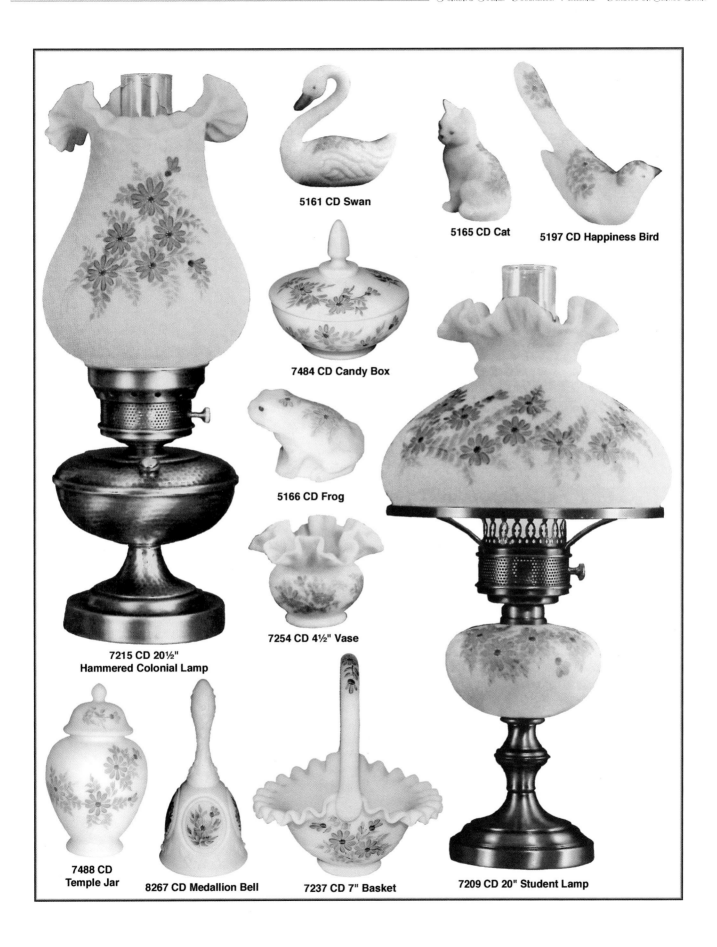

5161 CD Swan

5165 CD Cat

5197 CD Happiness Bird

7484 CD Candy Box

5166 CD Frog

7254 CD 4½" Vase

7215 CD 20½"
Hammered Colonial Lamp

7488 CD
Temple Jar

8267 CD Medallion Bell

7237 CD 7" Basket

7209 CD 20" Student Lamp

Daisies on Custard Satin

Fenton introduced a hand-painted brown-eyed white daisy spray decoration on Custard Satin glass in 1975. Many of the pieces were produced until the pattern was discontinued in 1982. However, a few items, such as the Classic lamp, 11" vase, and the square planter, were only made for a short time. Acquiring examples of these Daisies on Custard Satin pieces will be especially difficult for collectors today.

Daisies on Custard Satin	Ware No.	Introduced	Discontinued	Value
Basket	7437-DC	1975	1980	$35.00 – 42.00
Basket, 7"	7237-DC	1975	1980+	$35.00 – 40.00
Bell, Medallion	8267-DC	1976	1980+	$25.00 – 30.00
Bird, Happiness	5197-DC	1975	1980+	$25.00 – 30.00
Bird, small	5163-DC	1978	1980+	$25.00 – 30.00
Bunny	5162-DC	1978	1980+	$30.00 – 35.00
Candy box	7380-DC	1975	1978	$35.00 – 45.00
Candy box	7484-DC	1979	1980+	$25.00 – 30.00
Candy box, Medallion	8288-DC	1976	1980+	$47.00 – 50.00
Candy or puff box	7480-DC	1976	1978	$60.00 – 70.00
Cat	5165-DC	1979	1980+	$25.00 – 32.00
Comport, ftd.	7429-DC	1975	1980+	$25.00 – 35.00
Donkey	5125-DC	1978	1980+	$45.00 – 50.00
Fairy light	7300-DC	1975	1980+	$30.00 – 35.00
Frog	5166-DC	1979	1980+	$25.00 – 32.00
Hurricane lamp (electric)	7408-DC	1975	1978	$80.00 – 90.00
Lamp, 21" Classic	9307-DC	1978	1979	$225.00 – 265.00
Lamp, 16" hammered Colonial	7204-DC	1978	1980+	$190.00 – 210.00
Lamp, 19½" student	9308-DC	1976	1980+	$225.00 – 265.00

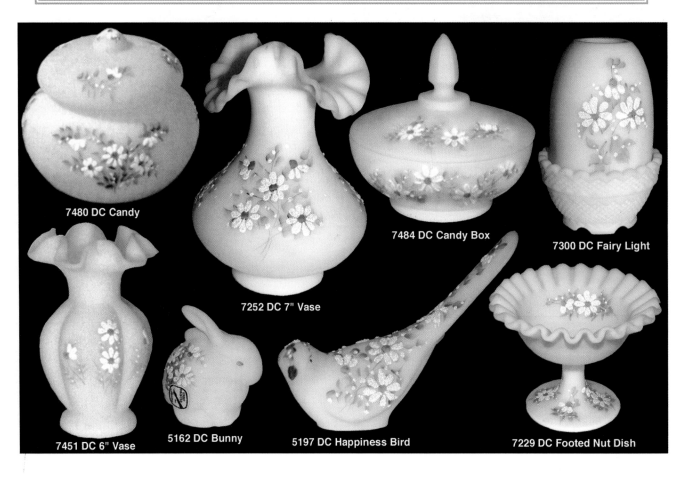

7480 DC Candy

7484 DC Candy Box

7300 DC Fairy Light

7252 DC 7" Vase

7451 DC 6" Vase

5162 DC Bunny

5197 DC Happiness Bird

7229 DC Footed Nut Dish

Daisies on Custard Satin	Ware No.	Introduced	Discontinued	Value
Lamp, 21" student	7410-DC	1975	1980+	$250.00 – 285.00
Nut dish, ftd.	7229-DC	1975	1980+	$17.00 – 19.00
Planter, square	8494-DC	1978	1979	$25.00 – 30.00
Swan	5161-DC	1978	1980+	$20.00 – 22.00
Vase, 6"	7256-DC	1976	1979	$25.00 – 30.00
Vase, 6"	7451-DC	1978	1980+	$18.00 – 20.00
Vase, 7"	7252-DC	1975	1980+	$25.00 – 30.00
Vase, 10"	7257-DC	1979	1980+	$40.00 – 50.00
Vase, 11"	7251-DC	1975	1978	$50.00 – 55.00
Vase, 11"	7458-DC	1978	1979	$50.00 – 60.00
Vase, bud	9056-DC	1976	1980+	$18.00 – 20.00

9056 DC
Bud Vase

7429 DC Footed
Comport

5125 DC Donkey

5163 DC Small Bird

5165 DC Cat

8288 DC Medallion
Candy Box

7127 DC
10" Vase

8267 DC Medallion Bell

7204 DC 16"
Hammered Colonial Lamp

5166 DC Frog

7410 DC 21"
Student Lamp

7408 DC Hurricane Lamp

7458 DC 11" Vase

7237 DC Basket

9308 DC 19½"
Student Lamp

Decorated Holly

Fenton's Decorated Holly pattern was offered in the July catalog supplements for a few years during the early to mid-1970s. The Holly decoration was painted on various milk glass pieces. Items included novelties such as the Happiness bird, the small egg paperweight, and selected pieces from the Hobnail and Silver Crest patterns.

Decorated Holly	Ware No.	Introduced	Discontinued	Value
Basket, 7" Hobnail	3837-DH	July 1973	1975	$45.00 – 55.00
Basket, 8½" Hobnail	3638-DH	July 1972	1973	$55.00 – 65.00
Basket, small SC Posey	7436-DH	July 1972	1973	$35.00 – 40.00
Bell, Hobnail	3667-DH	July 1971	1976	$35.00 – 40.00
Bird, Happiness	5197-DH	July 1975	1976	$32.00 – 37.00
Bowl, 10½" Hobnail	3624-DH	July 1971	1972	$45.00 – 55.00
Candleholder, Hobnail	3974-DH	July 1971	1972	$15.00 – 20.00
Candleholder, 6" Hobnail	3674-DH	July 1971	1972	$25.00 – 30.00
Candy box, Hobnail	3886-DH	July 1973	1974	$45.00 – 55.00
Comport, 6" ftd. Hobnail	3628-DH	July 1973	1974	$35.00 – 38.00
Egg	5140-DH	July 1972	1973	$27.00 – 32.00
Fairy lamp, Hobnail	3608-DH	July 1973	1976	$45.00 – 50.00
Nut dish, ftd. SC	7229-DH	July 1972	1973	$22.00 – 25.00
Vase, 10" Hobnail bud	3950-DH	July 1974	1975	$30.00 – 35.00
Vase, Hobnail handkerchief	3951-DH	July 1973	1974	$45.00 – 50.00
Vase, 6" SC	7451-DH	July 1972	1973	$27.00 – 30.00

Hand Decorated Holly
A new treatment of "Frosted" Glass fired onto the Holly Design

7436 DH Posey Basket

3638 DH 8 1/2" Basket

5140 DH Egg

3608 DH Fairy Light

7229 DH Nut Dish

Catalog Reprint July, 1972
Courtesy Of:
The Fenton Art Glass Museum

3608 DH Fairy Light

7451 DH 6" Vase

3674 DH 6" Candleholder

3624 DH 9 1/2" Bowl

5197 DH Happiness Bird

3974 DH Candleholder

Hand-Rubbed Decorations

Fenton's July 1969 supplement introduced three new hand-rubbed finishes on two popular covered jars. These finishes really accented the patterns of the jars. The colors were as follows: hand-rubbed blue satin on milk (TB), hand-rubbed green satin on a cream-colored base over opaque milk glass (TG), and hand-rubbed Brown Satin on a cream-colored base over opaque milk glass (TS). All of the decorated jars were out of the line by the end of December 1969. In 1981, the TB code was used for the Antique Blue color of the Currier & Ives items in the general line.

Hand Rubbed Decorations	Ware No.	Introduced	Discontinued	Value
Candy jar, ftd.	9088-TB	July 1969	1970	$55.00 – 65.00
Candy jar, ftd.	9088-TG	July 1969	1970	$50.00 – 55.00
Candy jar, ftd.	9088-TS	July 1969	1970	$40.00 – 50.00
Tobacco or candy jar	9188-TB	July 1969	1970	$100.00 – 125.00
Tobacco or candy jar	9188-TG	July 1969	1970	$100.00 – 125.00
Tobacco or candy jar	9188-TS	July 1969	1970	$80.00 – 90.00

9188 TG Tobacco Jar   **9088 TB Candy Box**   **9188 TG Tobacco Jar**

Holly on Ruby

Fenton's Christmas Holly on ruby design consisted of sprays of hand-painted white enamel holly on ruby glassware. Holly-decorated ruby was a special Christmas pattern. Therefore, the pattern was only offered in the July catalog supplements from 1972 through 1982. The longest running item in this series was the fairy light, which was the first item introduced in July 1972; it remained in production until the pattern was discontinued in December 1982. Other items in Fenton's Christmas Holly series included pieces of holly-decorated milk glass, Custard glass, and milk glass Hobnail. Pieces in other colors of Christmas Holly glassware may be found under the corresponding colors in this chapter. More information about holly-decorated Hobnail may also be found in the book *Fenton Art Glass Patterns 1939 – 1980*.

Holly on Ruby	Ware No.	Introduced	Discontinued	Value
Basket, 7"	7237-RH	July 1977	1980	$45.00 – 55.00
Bell, Medallion	8267-RH	July 1975	1980+	$27.00 – 32.00
Bird, Happiness	5197-RH	1979	1980	$32.00 – 37.00
Candy box, Medallion	8288-RH	July 1976	1980	$85.00 – 95.00
Fairy light	1700-RH	July 1972	1980+	$40.00 – 45.00
Vase, 4½"	7254-RH	July 1978	1980	$18.00 – 22.00
Vase, 10" bud	9056-RH	July 1976	1978	$22.00 – 27.00

9056 RH 10" Bud Vase

8288 RH Medallion Candy Box

7237 RH 7" Basket

5197 RH Happiness Bird

1700 RH Fairy Light

8267 RH Medallion Bell

7254 RH 4½" Vase

Leaf Decorated Burmese

Leaf Decorated Burmese (BD) was introduced in 1970. The decoration consisted of a leaf decal that was applied on a Burmese background by hand. The pieces were then refired to permanently adhere the decals. Notice that the cruet with the stopper was only in the line for a single year. Production of this pattern was discontinued at the end of 1972.

Leaf Decorated Burmese	Ware No.	Introduced	Discontinued	Value
Basket	7437-BD	1970	1973	$95.00 – 110.00
Bowl, 8"	7422-BD	1970	1973	$95.00 – 110.00
Cruet vase	7462-BD	1971	1973	$80.00 – 90.00
Cruet w/stopper	7468-BD	1972	1973	$185.00 – 200.00
Fairy lamp	7392-BD	1970	1972	$175.00 – 225.00
Fairy lamp, 2-pc.	7492-BD	1971	1973	$85.00 – 95.00
Rose bowl	7424-BD	1970	1973	$35.00 – 40.00
Vase, 7"	7252-BD	1970	1973	$75.00 – 85.00
Pitcher	7461-BD	1970	1973	$65.00 – 75.00

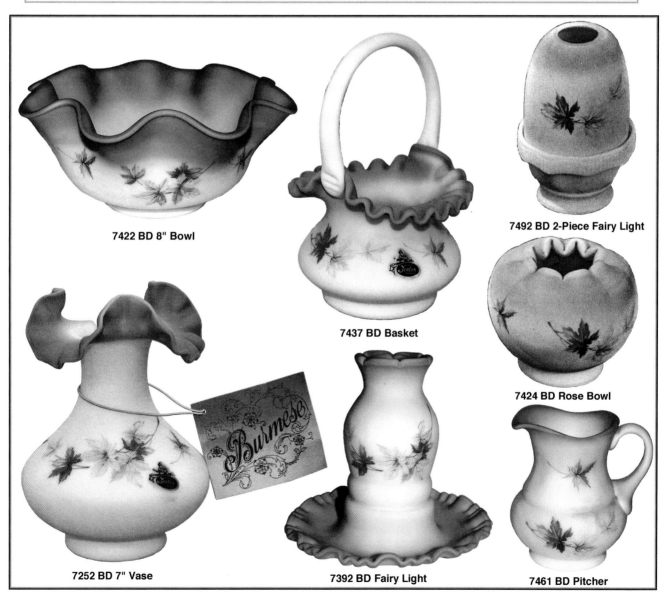

7422 BD 8" Bowl

7492 BD 2-Piece Fairy Light

7437 BD Basket

7424 BD Rose Bowl

7252 BD 7" Vase

7392 BD Fairy Light

7461 BD Pitcher

Log Cabin on Custard Satin

Fenton's popular Log Cabin on Custard Satin pattern was introduced in 1976. The pattern highlights a log cabin in a wooded area. All of the original items continued to be made into the 1980s and new shapes were added through the years. The Log Cabin scene on a Custard Satin background was finally discontinued at the end of 1989. However, the Log Cabin scene continued in the regular line with the introduction of two Log Cabin on Ivory Satin (LH) lamps in January 1990.

Log Cabin on Custard Satin	Ware No.	Introduced	Discontinued	Value
Basket	7437-LC	1976	1980+	$70.00 – 80.00
Bell	7362-LC	1979	1980+	$40.00 – 45.00
Fairy light	7300-LC	1976	1980+	$45.00 – 55.00
Ginger jar, 3-pc.	7288-LC	1978	1980+	$175.00 – 200.00
Hurricane lamp, 11"	7311-LC	1979	1980+	$175.00 – 200.00
Lamp, 16" hammered Colonial	7204-LC	1978	1980+	$200.00 – 225.00
Lamp, 20½" hammered Colonial	7215-LC	1979	1980+	$225.00 – 250.00
Lamp, 21" student	7412-LC	1976	1980+	$450.00 – 525.00
Temple jar	7488-LC	1979	1980+	$75.00 – 85.00
Vase, 7"	7252-LC	1976	1980+	$55.00 – 65.00

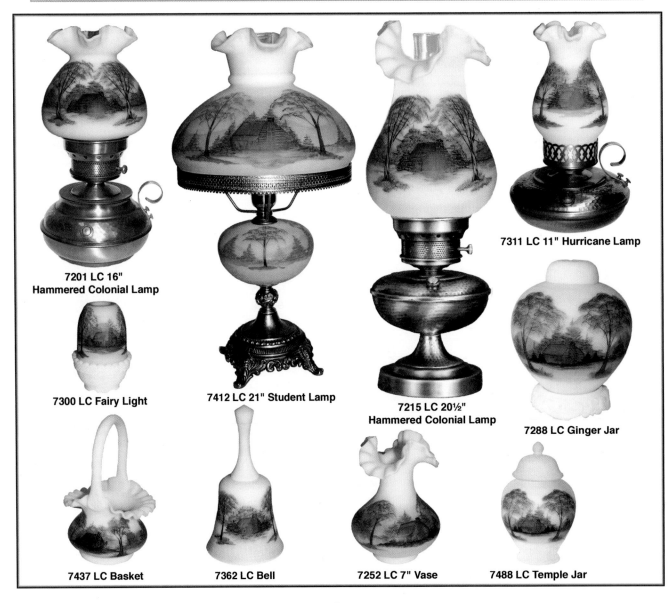

7201 LC 16"
Hammered Colonial Lamp

7300 LC Fairy Light

7412 LC 21" Student Lamp

7215 LC 20½"
Hammered Colonial Lamp

7311 LC 11" Hurricane Lamp

7288 LC Ginger Jar

7437 LC Basket

7362 LC Bell

7252 LC 7" Vase

7488 LC Temple Jar

Love Rose

Two variations of this six-item pattern were produced. One style featured a single pink rose with the word *Love* against a milk glass background. The other variation used a single white rose with the word *Love* on a transparent ruby background. These pieces were promoted as being especially appropriate anniversary gifts, or as Christmas or Valentine's Day gifts. Pieces with this pattern were in the regular line for two years.

Love Rose	Ware No.	Introduced	Discontinued	Value
Bell	7362-LR	1979	1981	$25.00 – 30.00
Bell	7362-LW	1979	1981	$22.00 – 27.00
Fairy light	1700-LR	1979	1981	$37.00 – 42.00
Fairy light	1700-LW	1979	1981	$45.00 – 55.00
Vase, bud	9056-LR	1979	1981	$20.00 – 22.00
Vase, bud	9056-LW	1979	1981	$20.00 – 22.00

7362 LR Bell

9056 LR Bud Vase

9056 LW Bud Vase

7300 LW Fairy Light

Nature's Christmas

There were four items in this special Christmas pattern that featured a wooded scene with deer. This assortment followed Christmas Morn as the second deign in the Christmas Classics series. All pieces were artist signed, dated, limited in number, and attractively gift boxed. An 8" collector's plate with a wooden easel was added to this offering.

Nature's Christmas	Ware No.	Introduced	Discontinued	Value
Bell	7466-NC	July 1979	1980	$40.00 – 45.00
Fairy light, 2-pc.	7300-NC	July 1979	1980	$50.00 – 55.00
Lamp, 16" hammered Colonial	7204-NC	July 1979	1980	$240.00 – 260.00
Plate, 8"	7418-NC	July 1979	1980	$25.00 – 30.00

7466 NC Bell
(Front Side)

7466 NC Bell
(Back Side)

7300 NC
Fairy Light

7418 NC 8" Plate

7204 NC 16" Hammered Colonial Lamp

Old Mill Scene

Only four items were produced in this colorful hand-painted pattern on a Custard Satin background. The subject is a scenic old mill with a waterwheel, along a stream that is surrounded by trees and with mountains rising in the distance. All of the items entered the line in January 1979, and the pattern was discontinued at the end of 1980.

Old Mill Scene	Ware No.	Introduced	Discontinued	Value
Bell	7362-OM	1979	1981	$42.00 – 47.00
Fairy light	7300-OM	1979	1981	$50.00 – 60.00
Lamp, 21" student	7410-OM	1979	1981	$400.00 – 450.00
Vase, 10"	7257-OM	1979	1981	$85.00 – 95.00

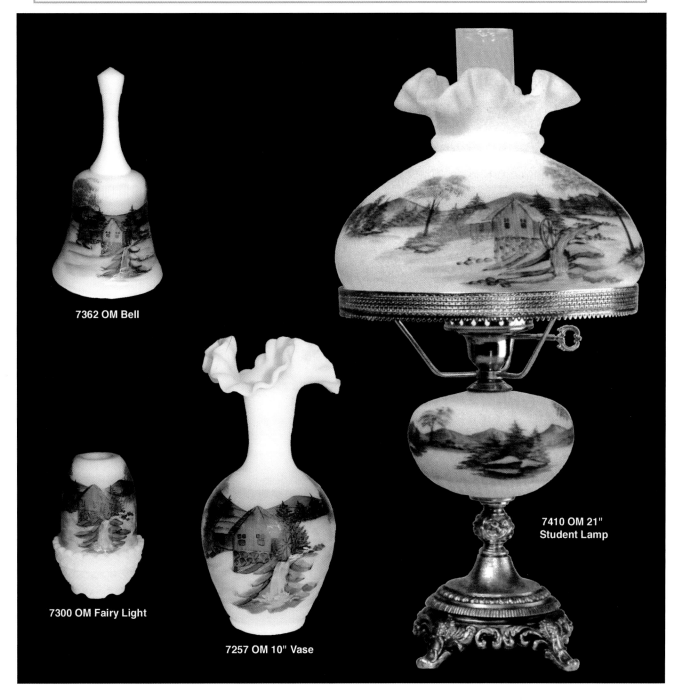

7362 OM Bell

7300 OM Fairy Light

7257 OM 10" Vase

7410 OM 21" Student Lamp

Pink Blossom

This dainty pink floral hand-painted decoration on Custard Satin was introduced as Pink Anemone in July 1972. Later, about 1977, Fenton began referring to the pattern as Pink Blossom. Numerous items were added to the line through the years, and some of the original pieces were made into the 1980s. The number of different pieces produced began to decline during the early 1980s, but the remaining pieces continued to sell well, and the final items were not discontinued until the end of 1985.

After the designs were painted, small particles of glass were applied to the petals. These added to the attractiveness of the hand-painted decoration. The pieces were then refired to produce an effect Fenton called *icing*.

Beginning in 1981, the Pink Blossom decoration was also used on a seven-piece line of miniatures. The following items were part of this series:

Miniature	Ware No.	Miniature	Ware No.
Basket	9536-PY	Toothpick/Votive	9592-PY
Boot	9590-PY	Vase, 5" blown	7554-PY
Jewel box, oval	9589-PY	Vase, bud	9556-PY
Slipper	9591-PY		

New items in 1982 included three different sizes of picture frames. New animal figures were a popular addition to the pattern in 1984. These new figures included a bear cub, an elephant, and a whale.

Notice that the square planter and the 11" vase were only made during 1978. These pieces and several other items (including the egg and the hurricane lamp) that were only made for a short time are proving to be elusive for collectors.

Pink Blossom	Ware No.	Introduced	Discontinued	Value
Basket	7437-PY	1973	1980+	$32.00 – 35.00
Basket, 7"	7237-PY	1976	1980+	$40.00 – 45.00
Bell, Medallion	8267-PY	1976	1980+	$27.00 – 32.00
Bird, Happiness	5197-PY	July 1972	1980+	$30.00 – 35.00
Bird, small	5163-PY	1978	1980+	$30.00 – 35.00
Bunny	5162-PY	1978	1980+	$30.00 – 35.00
Candy box	7380-PY	1973	1976	$60.00 – 65.00
Candy box	7484-PY	1979	1980+	$32.00 – 37.00
Candy box, Medallion	8288-PY	1976	1980+	$70.00 – 80.00
Cat	5165-PY	1979	1980+	$35.00 – 40.00
Comport, ftd.	7429-PY	1974	1980+	$35.00 – 40.00
Egg	5143-PY	July 1972	1975	$32.00 – 35.00
Fairy lamp	7300-PY	July 1972	1980+	$35.00 – 40.00
Frog	5166-PY	1979	1980+	$30.00 – 35.00
Hurricane lamp	7409-PY	1973	1976	$100.00 – 125.00
Lamp, 19½" student	9308-PY	1976	1980+	$250.00 – 275.00
Lamp, 21" student	7410-PY	1974	1978	$300.00 – 325.00
Nut dish, ftd.	7229-PY	1974	1980+	$18.00 – 20.00
Pitcher	7461-PY	1974	1978	$27.00 – 32.00
Planter, square	8294-PY	1978	1979	$40.00 – 45.00
Swan	5161-PY	1978	1980+	$25.00 – 30.00
Temple jar	7488-PY	1979	1980+	$35.00 – 45.00
Vase, 4½"	7254-PY	1975	1980+	$20.00 – 25.00
Vase, 6"	7256-PY	1976	1978	$40.00 – 45.00
Vase, 6	7451-PY	1978	1980+	$22.00 – 27.00
Vase, 7"	7252-PY	1973	1980+	$40.00 – 45.00
Vase, 11"	7458-PY	1978	1979	$80.00 – 85.00
Vase, bud	9056-PY	1976	1980+	$20.00 – 25.00

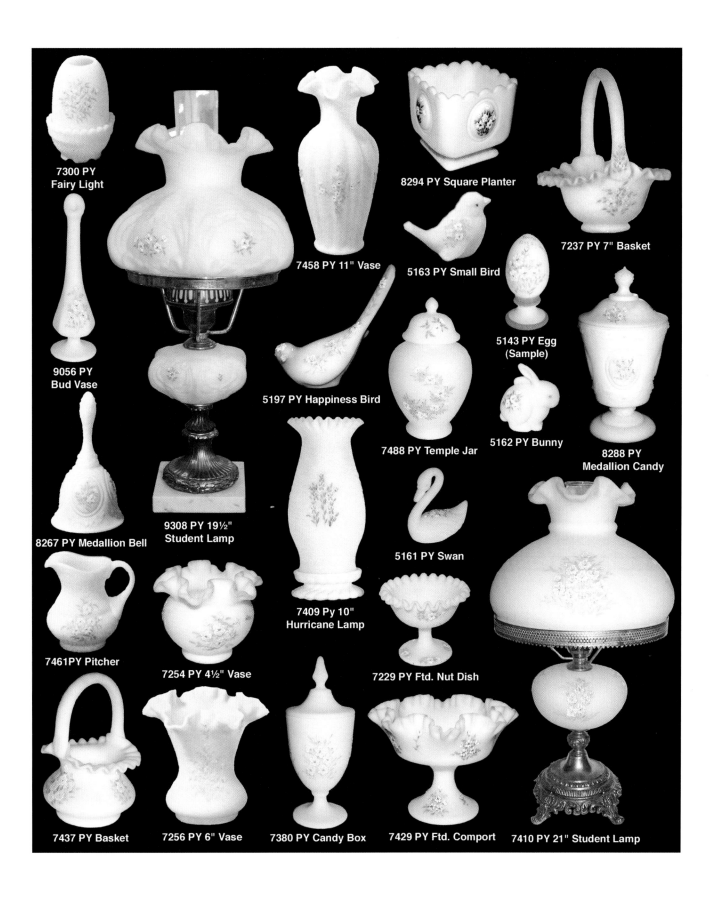

7300 PY
Fairy Light

7458 PY 11" Vase

8294 PY Square Planter

5163 PY Small Bird

7237 PY 7" Basket

9056 PY
Bud Vase

5197 PY Happiness Bird

7488 PY Temple Jar

5143 PY Egg
(Sample)

5162 PY Bunny

8288 PY
Medallion Candy

8267 PY Medallion Bell

9308 PY 19½"
Student Lamp

5161 PY Swan

7461PY Pitcher

7254 PY 4½" Vase

7409 Py 10"
Hurricane Lamp

7229 PY Ftd. Nut Dish

7437 PY Basket

7256 PY 6" Vase

7380 PY Candy Box

7429 PY Ftd. Comport

7410 PY 21" Student Lamp

Rose Burmese

Rose Burmese (RB), which was introduced in 1971, was the first hand-painted decoration on Burmese. This pattern was designed by Louise Piper. New items were added to this pattern and old pieces were discontinued to keep the line interesting throughout the 1970s. Production of some of the vases and the 21" student lamp was continued into the 1980s. Several pieces, such as the No. 7392 fairy lamp, No. 7284 candy box, and the No. 7202 epergne set, were only made for a short time. Collectors will have some difficulty finding these items today.

Rose Burmese	Ware No.	Introduced	Discontinued	Value
Basket	7437-RB	1971	1980+	$120.00 – 135.00
Basket, 7" deep	7238-RB	1973	1976	$180.00 – 215.00
Bowl, 8"	7422-RB	1971	1976	$90.00 – 110.00
Candy box	7284-RB	1973	1975	$250.00 – 275.00
Cruet vase	7462-RB	1971	1975	$90.00 – 100.00
Cruet w/stopper	7468-RB	1972	1978	$190.00 – 210.00
Epergne set, 2-pc.	7202-RB	1975	1977	$270.00 – 295.00
Fairy lamp	7392-RB	1971	1972	$200.00 – 275.00
Fairy lamp, 2 pc.	7492-RB	1971	1978	$100.00 – 115.00
Lamp, 20"	9306-RB	1977	1979	$500.00 – 650.00
Lamp, 21" student	7410-RB	1971	1980+	$500.00 – 600.00
Lamp, 36" table	7405-RB	1971	1973	$400.00 – 600.00
Pitcher	7461-RB	1971	1977	$90.00 – 110.00
Rose bowl	7424-RB	1971	1979	$50.00 – 60.00
Vase, 5"	7457-RB	1975	1980+	$55.00 – 65.00
Vase, 6½"	7460-RB	1979	1980+	$75.00 – 85.00
Vase, 7"	7252-RB	1971	1980+	$90.00 – 110.00
Vase, 7"	7253-RB	1971	1976	$85.00 – 95.00
Vase, 8"	7459-RB	1973	1976	$80.00 – 90.00
Vase, 10"	7257-RB	1977	1980+	$130.00 – 145.00
Vase, 11"	7251-RB	1973	1977	$180.00 – 195.00
Vase, bud	7348-RB	1979	1980+	$55.00 – 65.00
Vase, 7" pinch	7359-RB	1971	1980+	$75.00 – 85.00
Vase, tulip	7255-RB	1977	1980+	$130.00 – 150.00

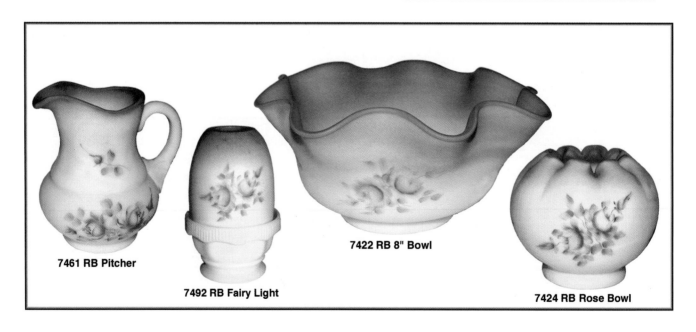

7461 RB Pitcher

7492 RB Fairy Light

7422 RB 8" Bowl

7424 RB Rose Bowl

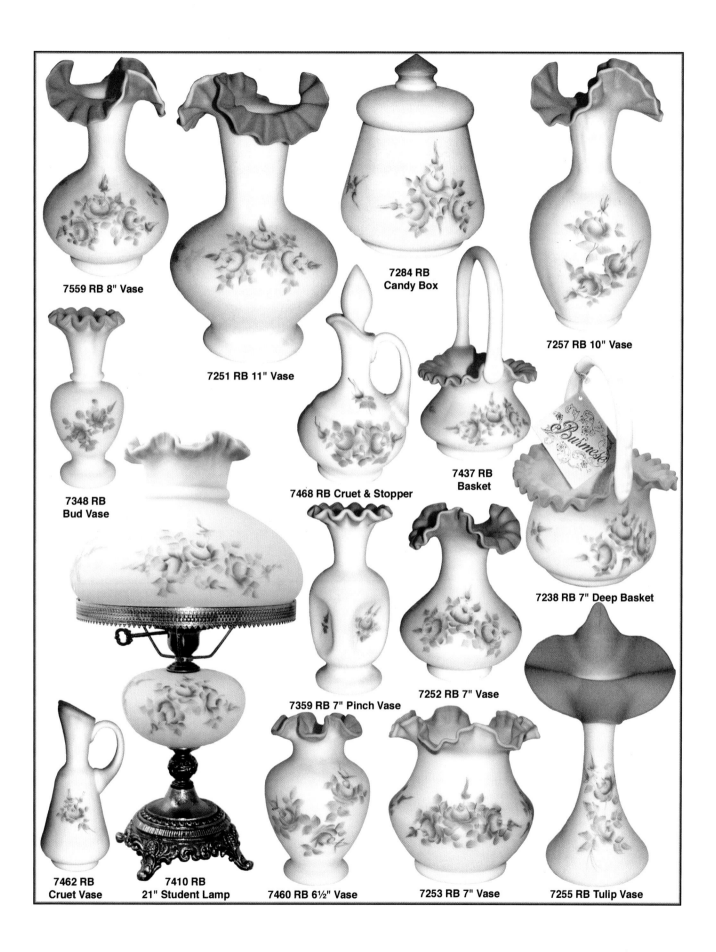

7559 RB 8" Vase

7251 RB 11" Vase

7284 RB Candy Box

7257 RB 10" Vase

7348 RB Bud Vase

7468 RB Cruet & Stopper

7437 RB Basket

7238 RB 7" Deep Basket

7359 RB 7" Pinch Vase

7252 RB 7" Vase

7462 RB Cruet Vase

7410 RB 21" Student Lamp

7460 RB 6½" Vase

7253 RB 7" Vase

7255 RB Tulip Vase

Roses on Custard Satin

Fenton's Roses on Custard Satin pattern was introduced into the line in 1976, with the No. 5197 Happiness Bird. Fenton catalogs described this decoration as "orangish colored roses hand painted on custard satin glass." Two years later, eight more items were added to this line. More items were added to this pattern again in 1979, and all of the items continued to be produced into the early 1980s.

The No. 9054 tall bud vase with this decoration entered the line in January 1980. Additions to this pattern in January 1981 included the No. 5169 duckling figure, the No. 5140 egg on stand, and the No. 7507-25½" French Provincial lamp. New items in 1983 were the No. 9504 Basket Weave candlelight and the No. 5160 fawn figure. The decoration was discontinued at the end of 1983.

Roses on Custard Satin	Ware No.	Introduced	Discontinued	Value
Basket, 7"	7237-RC	1978	1980+	$40.00 – 50.00
Bell, Medallion	8267-RC	1978	1980+	$27.00 – 32.00
Bird, Happiness	5197-RC	1976	1980+	$32.00 – 37.00
Bird, small	5163-RC	1978	1980+	$30.00 – 35.00
Bunny	5162-RC	1978	1980+	$30.00 – 35.00
Candy box	7484-RC	1979	1980+	$50.00 – 60.00
Cat	5165-RC	1979	1980+	$50.00 – 55.00
Comport, ftd.	7429-RC	1979	1980+	$50.00 – 55.00
Fairy light, 2-pc.	7300-RC	1978	1980+	$40.00 – 50.00
Frog	5166-RC	1979	1980+	$30.00 – 35.00
Hurricane lamp, 11"	7311-RC	1979	1980+	$165.00 – 180.00
Lamp, 16" hammered Colonial	7204-RC	1978	1980+	$275.00 – 300.00
Swan	5161-RC	1978	1980+	$30.00 – 35.00
Vase, 6"	7451-RC	1978	1980+	$27.00 – 32.00
Vase, bud	9056-RC	1978	1980+	$25.00 – 30.00

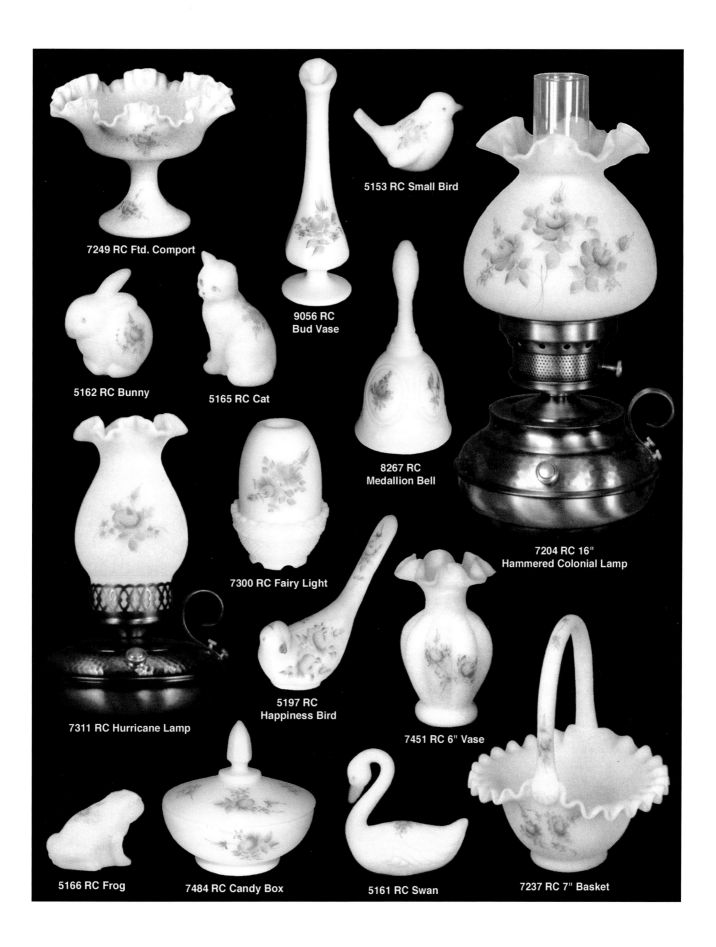

7249 RC Ftd. Comport

5153 RC Small Bird

9056 RC
Bud Vase

5162 RC Bunny

5165 RC Cat

8267 RC
Medallion Bell

7204 RC 16"
Hammered Colonial Lamp

7300 RC Fairy Light

7311 RC Hurricane Lamp

5197 RC
Happiness Bird

7451 RC 6" Vase

5166 RC Frog

7484 RC Candy Box

5161 RC Swan

7237 RC 7" Basket

Roses on Ruby

This late 1970s and early 1980s Fenton pattern features white enamel hand-painted roses on ruby glassware. Pieces of this pattern made perfect Christmas or Valentine's Day gifts. Because it remained popular in the line, several new items were added to this pattern during the early 1980s. The No. 9054 tall bud vase, No. 7564 bell, and No. 7229 nut dish were new pieces in this pattern in January 1980.

Roses on Ruby	Ware No.	Introduced	Discontinued	Value
Basket, 7"	7237-RD	1978	1980+	$40.00 – 45.00
Bell	8267-RD	1978	1980+	$30.00 – 35.00
Bird, Happiness	5197-RD	1978	1980+	$30.00 – 35.00
Candy box	7484-RD	1979	1980+	$40.00 – 45.00
Fairy light	1700-RD	1978	1980+	$30.00 – 35.00
Lamp, 16" hammered Colonial	7204-RD	1979	1980+	$225.00 – 250.00
Vase, 4½"	7254-RD	1978	1980+	$18.00 – 20.00
Vase, bud	9056-RD	1978	1980+	$18.00 – 22.00

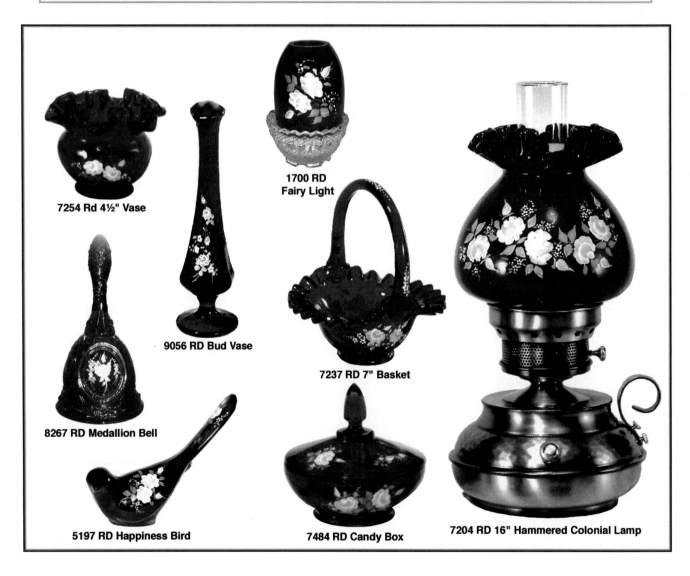

7254 Rd 4½" Vase

9056 RD Bud Vase

1700 RD Fairy Light

7237 RD 7" Basket

8267 RD Medallion Bell

5197 RD Happiness Bird

7484 RD Candy Box

7204 RD 16" Hammered Colonial Lamp

Scenic Decorated Burmese

Scenic Decorated Burmese pieces depict various hand-painted outdoor scenes that have a tree in the foreground and mountains in the background. The first piece of the pattern to be introduced — the 21" student lamp — made its appearance in January 1973. Several other items were added over the next two years. All of the pieces were discontinued by 1980, with the exception of the student lamp, which remained in production into the early 1980s.

Scenic Decorated Burmese	Ware No.	Introduced	Discontinued	Value
Basket	7437-DB	1974	1980	$85.00 – 95.00
Fairy lamp, 2-pc.	7492-DB	1974	1978	$50.00 – 60.00
Lamp, 21" student	7411-DB	1973	1980+	$350.00 – 450.00
Rose bowl	7424-DB	1974	1979	$40.00 – 45.00
Vase, 5"	7457-DB	1975	1980	$60.00 – 70.00
Vase, 7"	7252-DB	1974	1980	$80.00 – 95.00

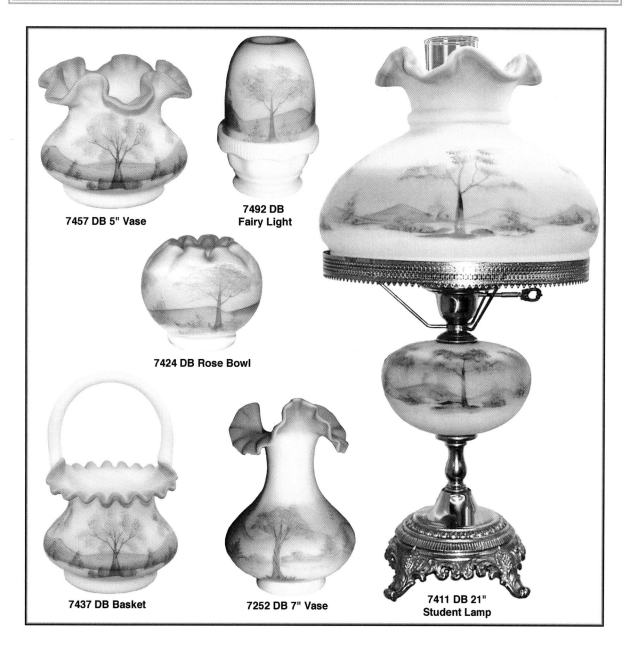

7457 DB 5" Vase

7492 DB
Fairy Light

7424 DB Rose Bowl

7437 DB Basket

7252 DB 7" Vase

7411 DB 21"
Student Lamp

Special Items
The Barber Influence

The Barber Collection of Vases

Robert Barber was a glass craftsman who became the artist in residence at Fenton Art Glass in 1975. Barber was allowed to experiment freely, and in April 1975, four of his special hand-crafted art glass pieces were selected and offered as limited edition collectibles to Fenton customers. These creations were favorably received by Fenton dealers; therefore, another six shapes were commissioned in a second limited edition offering. However, this series did not sell as well as anticipated, and dealers began to exercise their return privileges for these special items. As a result, the experiment with offhand glassware was discontinued, and Robert Barber's energies were focused in other directions. Later creations included a collection of art glass eggs available in the July 1976 supplement. However, Fenton could not successfully implement the Barber ideas and designs into creations that produced effective sales results, and the company was forced to let him go in 1977.

Production of the Barber Collection pieces was limited in number, and each piece was numbered sequentially.

Barber Collection Vases	Ware No.	Limit	Value
Vase, 12½" Hyacinth Feather	0001-HF	450	$500.00 – 600.00
Vase, 11" Turquoise Iridescent Hanging Heart	0002-TH	600	$300.00 – 350.00
Vase, 7½" Bittersweet Hanging Heart	0003-BH	750	$275.00 – 300.00
Vase, 7½" Blue Feather	0004-BF	1000	$300.00 – 320.00
Vase, 11" Summer Tapestry	0005-ST	550	$295.00 – 320.00
Vase, 7½" Cascade	0006-CV	700	$300.00 – 350.00
Vase, 10" Custard Iridescent Hanging Heart	0007-CI	600	$250.00 – 275.00
Vase, 10" Turquoise Iridescent Hanging Heart	0008-TH	600	$250.00 – 300.00
Vase, 9" Amethyst and white Labyrinth	0009-LA	700	$250.00 – 275.00
Vase, 9" blue and white Labyrinth	0010-LB	700	$275.00 – 300.00

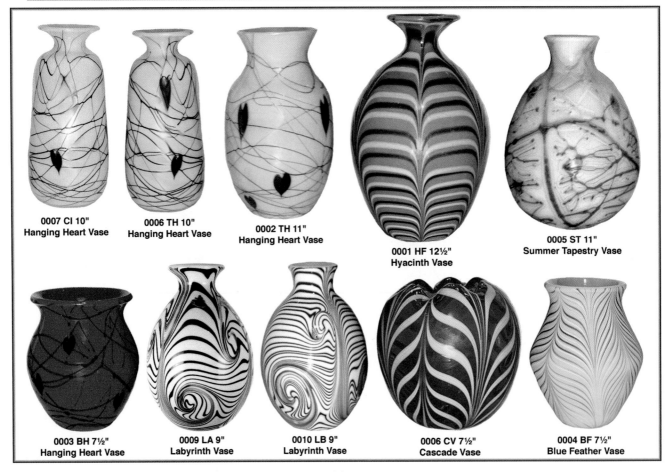

0007 CI 10"
Hanging Heart Vase

0006 TH 10"
Hanging Heart Vase

0002 TH 11"
Hanging Heart Vase

0001 HF 12½"
Hyacinth Vase

0005 ST 11"
Summer Tapestry Vase

0003 BH 7½"
Hanging Heart Vase

0009 LA 9"
Labyrinth Vase

0010 LB 9"
Labyrinth Vase

0006 CV 7½"
Cascade Vase

0004 BF 7½"
Blue Feather Vase

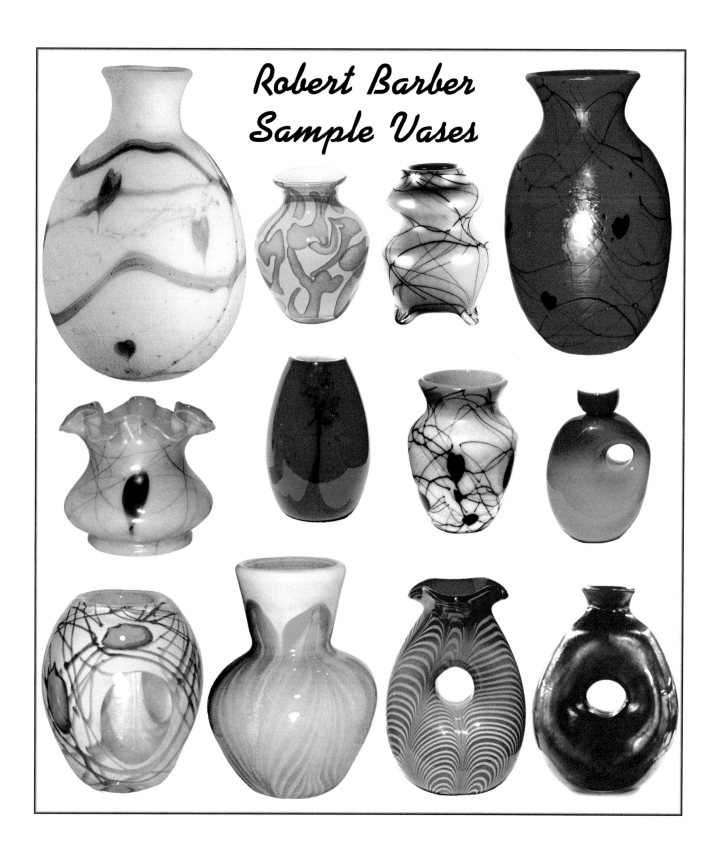

Robert Barber
Sample Vases

The Barber Collection of Egg Paperweights

A collection of six colorful egg paperweights created by Robert Barber appeared in the July 1976 catalog supplement. Each egg was marked with the Fenton logo and dated. Ads touted the desirability of these eggs and hinted at the possibility of a forthcoming series, but these paperweights were only available in the Fenton price lists through December 1976. An annual series of egg paperweights never developed. Colors listed below offer a general guideline to what was offered. Each egg had individual characteristics, with the basic colors interlaced in a unique and distinctive swirl pattern.

Barber Egg Paperweight	Ware No.	Value
Egg, pink	5001-EG	$225.00 – 250.00
Egg, dark blue	5002-EG	$225.00 – 250.00
Egg, light blue	5004-EG	$225.00 – 250.00
Egg, reddish-orange	5005-EG	$225.00 – 250.00
Egg, green	5007-EG	$225.00 – 250.00
Egg, multi-color	5008-EG	$225.00 – 250.00

Catalog Reprint Courtesy Of: The Fenton Art Glass Museum

Egg Paperweights

5008 EG · 5002 EG · 5005 EG · 5007 EG · 5001 EG · 5004 EG

Fascinating colors, intriguing patterns, exquisite craftsmanship. Designed for the "glass-collector" as well as the "glass-giver". For a "present with a future", show your customer a Fenton Egg Paperweight. Each piece is marked with the Fenton name and dated.

Fenton's Olde Virginia Glass Line

During the mid-1950s, the Fenton Art Glass Company began selling to catalog wholesalers such as Bennett Brothers and the General Merchandise Company. These companies acted as wholesalers to retail outlets such as gift shops and department stores. In an attempt to protect its regular Fenton accounts from unwanted competition, Fenton did not sell identical items from the current regular line to these catalog distributors. In the beginning, the items grouped in these listings had no specific name. However, in about 1959, "Olde Virginia Glass" began to appear in company ads. Later, in 1971, "OVG" began to appear on some individual glass items. By 1973, the OVG logo was being used on all items in the Olde Virginia Glass line.

New patterns were added and old ones were discontinued through the years. Colors and individual items in patterns also varied from year to year. Eventually, as marketing tactics changed, the need for catalog wholesalers diminished and the niche the Olde Virginia Glass line had filled began to erode. By 1980, Fenton determined that other ventures were more lucrative, and the entire Olde Virginia Glass line was abandoned.

Among the first items included in this selection were pieces of Thumbprint in milk. This pattern was later added to the regular line in other colors. Early offerings in milk Hobnail were an epergne set and a beverage set consisting of an 80 oz. pitcher and eight 12 oz. tumblers. Other items in the mid-1950s listings were plates and compotes with the Laced Edge design.

In the late 1960s, when this pattern was incorporated into the Olde Virginia line, Cactus was sold in milk and Colonial Amber under the name Desert Tree. In the 1970s, Daisy and Button and Fine Cut and Block were important Olde Virginia Line patterns. Pieces from these patterns were also included in the regular Fenton catalog, but identical colors for the regular line items and the catalog house runs were not produced at the same time.

In a 1967 letter to its representatives, Fenton explained the policy of selling glass to catalog houses and other non-traditional outlets. The letter stated "Olde Virginia Glass will be sold to discount stores, accounts that we have sent sufficient outlet letters and other accounts that do not handle our regular line. It will not be offered to junk shops and service stations." Representatives were given the opportunity to service many of these accounts, but some of the orders would also be handled directly by the factory. Representatives received a commission on sales from their contacts, part of which could be rebated to the customer as a discount. Representatives did not receive a commission from factory direct sales in their territory, and sales from the Olde Virginia line could not be used to satisfy sales quotas.

The following pages illustrate items made for the Olde Virginia line with the use of Fenton catalog reprints. The first ads illustrate the milk Thumbprint that was part of the line in the mid-1950s. The progression of changes is followed through the years with other reprints.

1956 Fenton's plan to serve the needs of catalog resellers and discount stores included the production of pieces that were not associated with the regular catalog offering. Selected items were made available in milk Hobnail, Lacey Edge, and Thumbprint. The Thumbprint covered compote was also called a wedding compote.

1958 The Lacey Edge compote was still available, but the banana bowl and planter plate were no longer listed.

Hobnail		Milk
Epergne		$45.00 – 50.00
Jug, 80 oz.		$85.00 – 110.00
Tumbler, 12 oz.		$12.00 – 14.00
Lacey Edge	**Ware No.**	**Milk**
Banana bowl	9024	$40.00 – 50.00
Comport	9029	$25.00 – 35.00
Planter plate	9099	$15.00 – 18.00
Thumbprint	**Ware No.**	**Milk**
Cakeplate, ftd.	4413	$22.00 – 27.00
Chip 'n dip	4404	$30.00 – 35.00
Compote and cover	4484	$40.00 – 50.00
Lamp, hurricane	4498	$45.00 – 55.00
Lavabo	4467	$65.00 – 75.00
Nut dish, ftd.	4428	$8.00 – 10.00

Thumbprint proved to be a popular design, and additional pieces were added. The salt and pepper and the creamer, sugar, and lid were combined to produce a five-piece breakfast set. The 15-piece punch set included the large bowl and base, with 12 cups and a crystal ladle. The two-tier tidbit consisted of a 13" ruffled plate and a 9" ruffled plate.

Thumbprint	Ware No.	Milk
Candy and cover	4480	$20.00 – 25.00
Creamer		$7.00 – 9.00
Punch bowl and stand		$120.00 – 150.00
Punch cup		$6.00 – 8.00
Salt and pepper	4408	$14.00 – 16.00
Sugar and lid		$14.00 – 16.00
Tidbit, 2-tier	4494	$30.00 – 40.00

1959 The Hobnail beverage set and epergne were discontinued. The Hobnail epergne was replaced by the No. 4401 Thumbprint epergne. Discontinued Thumbprint pieces included the hurricane candle, the punch set, and the two-tier tidbit. The Lacey Edge footed compote was also discontinued. New pieces added in Thumbprint included:

Thumbprint	Ware No.	Milk
Basket, 7"	4437	$18.00 – 22.00
Basket, 8½"	4438	$22.00 – 27.00
Basket, 6½" oval	4430	$12.00 – 14.00
Bowl, 12" round	4427	$25.00 – 30.00
Candleholder, tall	4473	$14.00 – 16.00
Candy box, oval	4486	$18.00 – 20.00
Epergne set	4401	$60.00 – 70.00
Planter, hanging	4405	$45.00 – 55.00
Planter, 10" rectangular	4490	$18.00 – 22.00
Vase, bud	4456	$10.00 – 12.00

1961 New items added to the Olde Virginia line in milk Thumbprint included:

Thumbprint	Ware No.	Milk
Candleholder, low	4474	$10.00 – 12.00
Comport, ftd	4429	$8.00 – 10.00
Goblet	4445	$7.00 – 9.00

1962 The bud vase, epergne set, and 8½" basket in Thumbprint were made in Topaz Opalescent. A Colonial Blue and Colonial Amber 11" vase and courting lamps — oil and electric — were new, in a polka-dot optic pattern that was different than on the regular line Iitems.

Thumbprint	Ware No.	Milk	Topaz Opalescent
Basket, 8½"	4438	$22.00 – 27.00	$45.00 – 55.00
Epergne set	4401	$60.00 – 70.00	$145.00 – 185.00
Planter, 4½" square	4497	$14.00 – 18.00	
Vase, bud	4456	$10.00 – 12.00	$12.00 – 18.00
Miscellaneous	Ware No.	Colonial Amber	Colonial Blue
Lamp, electric	2491	$20.00 – 25.00	$30.00 – 35.00
Lamp, oil	2490	$20.00 – 25.00	$30.00 – 35.00
Vase, 11"	2462	$22.00 – 27.00	$27.00 – 32.00

OLDE VIRGINIA GLASS
WILLIAMSTOWN, WEST VIRGINIA

4438 MI
8½" Basket

4486 MI
Oval Candy Box

4484 MI
Covered Compote

4467 MI
Lavabo

4490 MI
10" Planter

4405 MI
Hanging Planter

4456 MI
Bud Vase
(Packed 1 pair

4428 MI
Footed Nut Dish

4413 MI
Footed Cakeplate

4404 MI
Chip 'n Dip

4430 MI
6½" Oval Basket

4408 MI
Salt and
Pepper Set

4427 MI
Round bowl

4473 MI
Candleholder
(Packed 1 pair)

4401 MI
4-pc. Epergne Set

4437 MI
Handled Basket

EARLY AMERICAN
REPRODUCTIONS
IN HANDMADE MILK GLASS

Olde
Virginia
Glass
HAND MADE

209

1967 The Cactus pattern was in the regular Fenton line during the early 1960s in milk and topaz opalescent. When the pattern was revived for the OVG line it was called Desert Tree. The following pieces were made for the OVG line in milk and Colonial Amber.

Desert Tree	Ware No.	Colonial Amber	Milk
Basket, 7" handled	3437	$18.00 – 22.00	$25.00 – 35.00
Basket, 10" handled	3430	$20.00 – 30.00	$25.00 – 35.00
Bonbon, handled	3435	$7.00 – 9.00	$8.00 – 10.00
Bowl, 10"	3420	$20.00 – 25.00	$20.00 – 30.00
Butter, ¼ lb. covered	3477	$20.00 – 25.00	$20.00 – 30.00
Candleholder	3474	$10.00 – 12.00	$18.00 – 22.00
Candy jar	3480	$25.00 – 30.00	$30.00 – 40.00
Compote	3429	$12.00 – 14.00	$12.00 – 14.00
Creamer	3468	$10.00 – 12.00	$12.00 – 14.00
Salt and pepper	3406	$16.00 – 18.00	$20.00 – 25.00
Sugar, covered or candy bowl	3488	$18.00 – 22.00	$25.00 – 30.00
Vase, ftd.	3460	$18.00 – 20.00	$18.00 – 20.00
Vase, bud	3450	$8.00 – 10.00	$8.00 – 10.00

1969 Daisy and Button and Fine Cut and Block became the major patterns in the OVG line during the 1970s. The No. 1933 sugar and the No. 1963 creamer were combined to produce the No. 1903 sugar and creamer set. The No. 5175 ashtray was called a pelican, but has at times been referred to as a duck. This is a design Fenton acquired from a former Verly's mould. The No. 1050-7" vase was not made in milk.

Daisy & Button	Ware No.	Colonial Amber	Colonial Blue	Colonial Green	Colonial Orange/Milk
Basket, 5" handled	1935	$18.00 – 22.00	$25.00 – 27.00	$18.00 – 22.00	$20.00 – 25.00
Basket, 6" handled	1936	$20.00 – 25.00	$27.00 – 32.00	$20.00 – 25.00	$25.00 – 30.00
Bootee	1994	$18.00 – 20.00	$25.00 – 30.00	$18.00 – 20.00	$25.00 – 30.00
Bowl, 7" cupped	1927	$16.00 – 18.00	$20.00 – 25.00	$16.00 – 18.00	$20.00 – 25.00
Bowl, oval	1921	$18.00 – 22.00	$25.00 – 30.00	$18.00 – 22.00	$25.00 – 30.00
Bowl, 9" oval	1929	$18.00 – 22.00	$25.00 – 30.00	$18.00 – 22.00	$25.00 – 30.00
Creamer	1963	$9.00 – 11.00	$11.00 – 13.00	$9.00 – 11.00	$10.00 – 12.00
Hat	1992	$9.00 – 11.00	$12.00 – 14.00	$9.00 – 11.00	$12.00 – 14.00
Slipper	1995	$11.00 – 13.00	$16.00 – 18.00	$11.00 – 13.00	$12.00 – 14.00
Sugar	1933	$9.00 – 11.00	$11.00 – 13.00	$9.00 – 11.00	$10.00 – 12.00
Vase, 8"	1958	$22.00 – 27.00	$30.00 – 35.00	$22.00 – 27.00	$25.00 – 30.00
Vase, 8" fan	1959	$22.00 – 27.00	$30.00 – 35.00	$22.00 – 27.00	$28.00 – 30.00

Fine Cut & Block	Ware No.	Colonial Amber	Colonial Blue	Colonial Green	Colonial Orange/Milk
Bonbon, ftd.	9121	$12.00 – 14.00	$18.00 – 22.00	$12.00 – 14.00	$14.00 – 16.00
Candy box	9180	$18.00 – 22.00	$25.00 – 30.00	$18.00 – 22.00	$20.00 – 25.00
Compote	9120	$10.00 – 12.00	$14.00 – 16.00	$10.00 – 12.00	$12.00 – 14.00

Miscellaneous	Ware No.	Colonial Amber	Colonial Blue	Colonial Green	Colonial Orange/Milk
Ashtray, bird	5173	$18.00 – 22.00	$20.00 – 25.00	$18.00 – 22.00	$18.00 – 22.00
Ashtray, pelican	5175	$20.00 – 25.00	$25.00 – 30.00	$20.00 – 25.00	$20.00 – 25.00
Candy box, triang.	9084	$18.00 – 22.00	$25.00 – 27.00	$18.00 – 22.00	$20.00 – 25.00
Vase, 7"	1050	$13.00 – 15.00	$16.00 – 18.00	$13.00 – 15.00	$14.00 – 16.00

Olde Virginia Glass

Catalog Reprint Composite
Courtesy Of:
The Fenton Art Glass Museum

1927 CA
7" Bowl

1929 CA
9" Oval Bowl

1921 CA
Oval Bowl

1958 CA
8" Vase

1959 CA
8" Fan Vase

1936 CA
6" Basket

1992 CA
Hat

1995 CA
Slipper

1994 CA
Bootee

1903 CA
Sugar and Cream Set

1935 CA
5" Basket

9180 CB
Candy Box

9120 CB
Compote

9121 CB
Fld. Bonbon

5175 CG
Duck Ash Tray

1050 CG
7" Vase

9084 CG
Candy Box

5173 CG
Bird Ash Tray

1970 The No. 5173 bird ashtray, No. 5175 pelican ashtray, No. 9084 candy box and the No. 1050 vase were discontinued. The following items were added in the Daisy and Button and Fine Cut and Block patterns.

Daisy & Button	Ware No.	Colonial Amber	Colonial Blue	Colonial Green	Colonial Orange/Milk
Bell	1967	$20.00 – 22.00	$25.00 – 27.00	$20.00 – 22.00	$20.00 – 22.00
Candleholder	1970	$9.00 – 11.00	$12.00 – 14.00	$9.00 – 11.00	$10.00 – 12.00
Salt and pepper	1906	$14.00 – 16.00	$18.00 – 22.00	$14.00 – 16.00	$16.00 – 18.00
Fine Cut & Block	**Ware No.**	**Colonial Amber**	**Colonial Blue**	**Colonial Green**	**Colonial Orange/Milk**
Fairy light	9102	$20.00 – 25.00	$27.00 – 32.00	$20.00 – 25.00	$22.00 – 27.00
Vase, swung	9158	$18.00 – 22.00	$22.00 – 27.00	$18.00 – 22.00	$20.00 – 22.00

1971 The No. 1925-10½" bowl, No. 1930-10½" basket, No. 9137-7" basket, No. 9151 footed nut dish, and No. 9152 swung vase were added in all colors. The No. 9172 candle bowl was added in Colonial Amber, Colonial Green, and milk. The No. 9180 candy was added in Carnival. The No. 1929-9" bowl, No. 1935-5" basket, No. 1936-6" basket, No. 1959-8" fan vase, and No. 1992 hat were discontinued in Colonial Blue and Colonial Orange. The No. 1927-7" bowl was discontinued. The No. 1994 bootee was discontinued in Colonial Orange and the No. 1958 vase was discontinued in all colors except milk.

Daisy & Button	Ware No.	Colonial Amber	Colonial Blue	Colonial Green	Colonial Orange/Milk	
Basket, 10½"	1930	$25.00 – 30.00	$35.00 – 40.00	$25.00 – 30.00	$30.00 – 35.00	
Bowl, 10½"	1925	$20.00 – 22.00	$27.00 – 32.00	$20.00 – 22.00	$25.00 – 30.00	
Fine Cut & Block	**Ware No.**	**Colonial Amber**	**Colonial Blue**	**Colonial Green**	**Colonial Orange/Milk**	**Carnival**
Basket, 7"	9137	$18.00 – 22.00	$25.00 – 27.00	$18.00 – 22.00	$22.00 – 25.00	
Candle bowl	9172	$12.00 – 14.00	$14.00 – 18.00	$12.00 – 14.00	$14.00 – 16.00	
Candy	9180	$22.00 – 27.00	$27.00 – 32.00	$22.00 – 27.00	$27.00 – 30.00	$35.00 – 45.00
Nut dish, ftd.	9151	$14.00 – 16.00	$18.00 – 20.00	$14.00 – 16.00	$16.00 – 18.00	
Vase, swung	9152	$18.00 – 22.00	$22.00 – 27.00	$18.00 – 22.00	$20.00 – 22.00	

NEW FOR 1970

Olde Virginia Glass
Williamstown, W. Va. 26187

9158 MI Swung Vase

1970 MI Candleholder

9102 MI Fairy Light w/Candle

9137 MI 7" Basket

1967 MI Bell

1906 MI Salt and Pepper

Olde Virginia Glass

Williamstown, W. Va.

NEW for 1971

9172 MI
Candle Bowl

9152 MI
Swung Vase

1930 MI
10½" Basket

9151 MI
Ftd. Nut Dish

1925 MI
10½" Bowl

1970 MI
Candleholder

1972 The No. 1903 creamer and sugar set and the No. 1906 salt and pepper were discontinued in all colors except milk. The No. 1936-6" basket was discontinued, and the No. 1921 oval bowl was discontinued in Colonial Orange. The No. 1992 hat, 1994 bootee, 1995 slipper, No. 9151 footed nut dish, 9158 swung vase, and 9120 compote were added in Carnival.

Daisy & Button	Ware No.	Carnival
Bootee	1994	$20.00 – 25.00
Hat	1992	$18.00 – 22.00
Slipper	1995	$20.00 – 25.00
Fine Cut & Block	Ware No.	Carnival
Compote	9120	$27.00 – 32.00
Nut dish, ftd.	9151	$25.00 – 30.00
Vase, swung	9158	$40.00 – 45.00

1973 The No. 1921 oval bowl was added in Custard and discontinued in all other colors except milk. The No. 1925-10½" bowl and No. 1970 candleholder were discontinued in Colonial Orange. The No. 1929-9" oval bowl and the No. 1959-8" fan vase were discontinued in all colors except milk. The No. 1930-10½" basket was discontinued in Colonial Amber and Colonial Orange. The No. 1930-5" basket was discontinued in Colonial Blue and Colonial Orange. The No. 9151 footed nut dish was discontinued in all colors except Carnival. The No. 9158 swung vase was discontinued in Carnival and Colonial Orange and the No. 9152 swung vase was discontinued in Colonial Orange. The No. 1921 oval bowl, No. 1967 bell, No. 1970 candlholder, No. 1992 hat, No. 1995 slipper, No. 9102 fairy light, No. 9120 compote, No. 9137-7" basket, No. 9158 swung vase, No. 9172 candle bowl, and No. 9180 candy box were added to the line in Custard. Three different candle bowl floral arrangements were offered in milk — No. 9140 Spring, No. 9141 Fall, and No. 9142 for the Christmas season. These arrangements consisted of a display carton with a 3" x 9" candle, a flower ring, and the candle bowl. Production of items listed for 1973 continued during 1974 and 1975.

CANDLE BOWL ARRANGEMENTS

Attractively packaged in the display gift box, these combinations of the popular Candle Bowl and Candle and Flower Ring will add plus sales and profits. Packed 4 assorted arrangements to a master carton for each season.

THE CANDLE BOWL

9140 MI (Spring)

9141 MI (Fall)

9142 MI (Christmas)

Catalog Reprint Courtesy of: The Fenton Art Glass Museum

ORIGINAL FORMULA CARNIVAL GLASS

These collector's pieces of "Carnival Glass" were created from the original formula used in 1907 when we introduced this unique hand glass treatment to the American public.

In recent years antique Carnival Glass has become extremely valuable as one of the most collectible types of Early American glassware.

Carnival Glass authorities have acclaimed our reproduction of this treatment as the closest thing to the antique Iridescent formula ever produced.

9120 CN
Compote

9158 CN
Swung Vase

9180 CN
Candy Box

9151 CN
Ftd. Nut Dish

1995 CN
Slipper

1992 CN
Hat

1994 CN
Bootee

Daisy & Button	Ware No.	Custard
Bell	1967	$18.00 – 22.00
Bowl, oval	1921	$18.00 – 20.00
Candleholder	1970	$12.00 – 14.00
Hat	1992	$10.00 – 12.00
Slipper	1995	$18.00 – 22.00

Fine Cut & Block	Ware No.	Custard
Basket, 7"	9137	$25.00 – 30.00
Candle bowl	9172	$12.00 – 14.00
Candy box	9180	$25.00 – 30.00
Compote	9120	$16.00 – 18.00
Fairy light	9102	$25.00 – 30.00
Vase, swung	9158	$27.00 – 32.00

1976 The folowing items were discontinued: the No. 1906 salt and pepper, No. 1933 sugar, No. 1963 creamer, No. 1935-5" basket, No. 1958-8" vase, No. 1959-8" fan vase, and the No. 1922 hat, in all colors; the No. 9152 swung vase in Colonial Amber and Colonial Blue, the No. 1970 candleholder in Colonial Blue, the No. 9180 candy box in Colonial Green, and the No. 1994 bootee and No. 9120 compote in Carnival. The No. 9140, No. 9141, and No. 9142 candle block arrangements were also discontinued.

1977 The No. 1925-10½" bowl, No. 1929-9" oval bowl, No. 1930-10½" basket, No. 1994 bootee, No. 9152 swung vase, and No. 9172 candle bowl were discontinued. Also, any items previously in the line were discontinued in all colors except Custard and Milk. New items introduced in blue opaque are listed below. Notice that the new No. 2807-20" Wild Rose and Bowknot student lamp was made in blue opaque, Custard, and Milk.

Daisy & Button	Ware No.	Blue Opaque		
Bell	1967	$22.00 – 27.00		
Bowl, oval	1921	$25.00 – 28.00		
Candleholder	1970	$16.00 – 18.00		
Slipper	1995	$22.00 – 25.00		

Fine Cut & Block	Ware No.	Blue Opaque	Custard	Milk
Basket, 7"	9137	$30.00 – 35.00	$25.00 – 30.00	$20.00 – 25.00
Bowl, 7"	9127	$22.00 – 27.00	$18.00 – 22.00	$16.00 – 18.00
Bowl, ftd.	9122	$30.00 – 35.00	$28.00 – 30.00	$25.00 – 27.00
Candy box	9180	$35.00 – 40.00	$25.00 – 30.00	$22.00 – 27.00
Compote	9120	$18.00 – 20.00	$14.00 – 16.00	$14.00 – 16.00
Creamer, sugar & lid	9103			$20.00 – 25.00
Fairy light	9102	$30.00 – 35.00	$25.00 – 30.00	$18.00 – 22.00
Salt and pepper, ftd.	9106			$20.00 – 22.00
Vase, 4½"	9157	$18.00 – 22.00	$14.00 – 16.00	$12.00 – 14.00
Vase, swung	9158	$35.00 – 40.00	$27.00 – 32.00	$22.00 – 27.00

Wild Rose & Bowknot	Ware No.	Blue Opaque	Custard	Milk
Lamp, 20" student	2807	$185.00 – 2.00.00	$150.00 – 175.00	$160.00 – 180.00

Olde Virginia Glass

Handmade "in the age old manner" in three popular early American patterns (Wild Rose and Bow Knot, Daisy & Button and Fine Cut & Block) and three early American colors (Opaque Blue-BG, Custard-CT and Milk Glass-MI).

9158 BG, CT, MI
Swung Vase

1970 BG, CT, MI
Candleholder

9120 BG, CT, MI
Compote

2807 BG, CT, MI
Student Lamp

9180 BG, CT, MI
Candy Box

9137 BG, CT, MI
7" Basket

9122 BG, CT, MI
Ftd. Bowl

9102 BG, CT, MI
Fairy Light w/Candle

1921 BG, CT, MI
Oval Bowl

1967 BG, CT, MI
Bell

9157 BG, CT, MI
4½" Vase

1995 BG, CT, MI
Slipper

9127 BG, CT, MI
7" Bowl

9106 MI Only
Salt & Pepper Set

9103 MI Only
Cov'd. Sugar & Cream Set

1979 Toward the end of the 1970s, the catalog houses were losing their following, and orders for glassware from the Olde Virginia Glass line were decreasing. All items in the opaque blue, milk, and Custard colors were discontinued. This also included the Wild Rose and Bowknot lamp. The lamp and items in the blue opaque color are not easily found today, since they were only in production for a short time.

The following items were made in Cameo Opalescent and crystal.

Daisy and Button	Ware No.	Cameo Opalescent	Crystal
Bell	1967	$25.00 – 30.00	$11.00 – 13.00
Bowl, 10½"	1925	$35.00 – 40.00	$16.00 – 18.00
Bowl, oval	1921	$27.00 – 32.00	$12.00 – 15.00
Candleholder	1970	$16.00 – 18.00	$10.00 – 12.00
Slipper	1995	$18.00 – 22.00	$11.00 – 13.00
Fine Cut and Block	**Ware No.**	**Cameo Opalescent**	**Crystal**
Basket, 7" handled	9137	$30.00 – 35.00	$18.00 – 20.00
Bowl, 7"	9120	$22.00 – 27.00	$10.00 – 12.00
Candle bowl	9172	$16.00 – 18.00	$11.00 – 13.00
Candy box	9180	$35.00 – 40.00	$18.00 – 22.00
Compote	9120	$18.00 – 22.00	$12.00 – 14.00
Creamer		$12.00 – 14.00	$7.00 – 9.00
Fairy light	9102	$27.00 – 32.00	$12.00 – 14.00
Salt and pepper	9106	$25.00 – 30.00	$12.00 – 14.00
Sugar and lid		$20.00 – 25.00	$10.00 – 12.00
Vase, 4½"	9157	$20.00 – 22.00	$9.00 – 11.00
Vase, swung	9158	$30.00 – 35.00	$16.00 – 18.00

The Ware Number for the Fine Cut and Block covered sugar and creamer set is 9103. The Olde Virginia line was discontinued at the end of 1979. Some pieces of the Fine Cut and Block pattern in crystal entered the regular Fenton line in 1980.

Catalog Reprint Courtesy Of: **The Fenton Art Glass Museum**

9102 CB

9102 OR

9102 CG

9102 CA

9102 MI

9102 CT

FAIRY LIGHTS W/CANDLE

Excellent sales, and popular in all colors, these little lights will lead your "Impulse Buying".

Olde Virginia Glass CAMEO OPALESCENT

Cameo Opalescent in antique Daisy & Button and Fine Cut & Block patterns. Each Functional piece carefully handmade, beautifully polished and authentic in every detail. Sensibly priced for special appeal in the gift market.

9120 CO
Compote

9180 CO
Candy Box

9172 CO
Candle Bowl

9137 CO
7" Basket

9158 CO
Medium Swung Vase

1995 CO
Slipper

1921 CO
Oval Bowl

1967 CO
Bell

9102 CO
Fairy Light

9106 CO
Salt & Pepper Set

9127 CO
7" Bowl

1925 CO
10 1/2" Bowl

9157 CO
4 1/2" Vase

9103 CO
Cov'd. Sugar & Cream Set

1970 CO
Candleholder

Catalog Reprint Composite Courtesy Of: The Fenton Art Glass Museum

Desert Tree by OLDE VIRGINIA GLASS

Catalog Reprint Circa 1967
Courtesy Of:
The Fenton Art Glass Museum

3430 MI
10" Basket

3474 MI
Candleholder

3437 MI
7" Basket

3406 MI
Salt & Pepper

3450 MI
Bud Vase

3429 MI
Compote

3460 MI
Ftd. Vase

3480 MI
Candy Jar

3477 MI
1/4 lb. Cov'd. Butter

3435 MI
Bon Bon

3488 MI
Sugar or Candy Bowl

3468 MI
Creamer

3420 MI
10" Bowl

3430 CA
10" Basket

3474 CA
Candleholder

3437 CA
7" Basket

3406 CA
Salt & Pepper

3450 CA
Bud Vase

3429 CA
Compote

3460 CA
Ftd. Vase

3480 CA
Candy Jar

3477 CA
1/4 lb. Cov'd. Butter

3435 CA
Bon Bon

3488 CA
Sugar or Candy Bowl

3468 CA
Creamer

3420 CA
10" Bowl

Red-Cliff Goblets

The catalog page shown below illustrates goblets made by Fenton for the Red-Cliff Company of Chicago. The catalog is from 1965. Later, when Red-Cliff went out of business, Fenton acquired these moulds. The moulds were modified to produce the Collectibells illustrated on page 48.

Item	Amber	Blue	Crystal	Green
Goblet	$10.00 – 14.00	$14.00 – 20.00	$6.00 – 10.00	$10.00 – 14.00

Early American Pattern Glass
IN SPARKLING COLORS AND CRYSTAL
HAND MOLDED REPRODUCTIONS BY SKILLED ARTISANS
(Each Genuine Red-Cliff Piece is Stamped with our Seal for Identification.)

GRAPE PATTERN
No. G-9045 $3.00
GOBLET

KNOBBY BULL'S EYE PATTERN
No. K-9045 $3.00
GOBLET

SABLE' ARCHE PATTERN
No. A-9045 $3.50
GOBLET

SYDENHAM PATTERN
No. S-9045 $3.00
GOBLET

WHITTON PATTERN
No. W-9045 $3.00
GOBLET

AVAILABLE COLORS:
C L — CRYSTAL OR CLEAR
O C — OLD COLONY AMBER
A Q — ANTIQUE AMBER
J B — JAMESTOWN BLUE (LIGHT)
B B — BEDFORD BLUE (DARK)
S G — SHENANDOAH GREEN (MEDIUM)

(TRADEMARK)
RED-CLIFF RC HAND MOLDED
Fine Glass Reproductions

RETAIL PRICES:
#9045—GOBLETS . . . .(as illustrated)
*#9044—WINES . . . .$2.50 EA.
#9028—SCALLOPED NUT DISH . . . .$3.00 EA.
#9029—BUTTERFLY CRIMP COMPORT . .$3.00 EA.
#9129—GARLAND EDGE COMPORT . . .$3.00 EA.
#9145—SWEETMEAT DISH . . . .$3.00 EA.

(In All Colors and All Patterns)
*Wine glasses available in Knobby Bull's Eye pattern only at present

221

Milk Thumbprint OVG No. 4498-10" hurricane lamp made about 1958. $45.00 – 55.00.

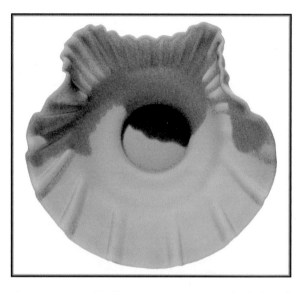

Green satin (GA) No. 9020-12" shell bowl made from 1952 to 1954. $110.00 – 125.00.

Peach Satin (PA) No. 9020-12" shell bowl made from 1952 to 1954. $90.00 – 110.00.

Roses on Milk No. 7257-6" two-handled vase hand painted by Louise Piper, December 1968. Presented to Frank Fenton upon Ms. Piper's retirement in 1981. UND.

Green cased No. 1921-10" top hat made about 1940. $175.00 – 200.00.

Bibliography

Books

Ezell, Elaine and George Newhouse. *Cruets, Cruets, Cruets*, volume I. Marietta, Ohio: Antique Publications, 1991.

Heacock, William. *Fenton Glass, the Second Twenty-five Years*. Marietta, Ohio: O-val Advertising Corp., 1980.

————. *Fenton Glass, the Third Twenty-five Years*. Marietta, Ohio: O-val Advertising Corp., 1989.

Newbound, Betty and Bill. *The Collector's Encyclopedia of Milk Glass, Identification and Values*. Paducah, Kentucky: Collector Books, 1995.

Catalogs

DeVilbiss Company. *DeVilbiss Perfume Atomizers*. Toledo, Ohio: The DeVilbiss Company, 1939 – 1955.

Randall, A. L. *Fenton for Flowers*. Chicago, Illinois: A. L. Randall Company, 1970 – 1980

Fenton Art Glass Company. Fenton General Catalogs and Supplements. Williamstown, West Virginia: Fenton Art Glass Company, 1940 – 1980.

Newsletters

Fenton Art Glass. *Glass Messenger*. Williamstown, West Virginia: Fenton Art Glass Company, 2000 – 2004.

Pacific Northwest Fenton Association. *The Fenton Nor'wester*. Tillamook, Oregon: P. N. W. F. A., 1992 – 2004.

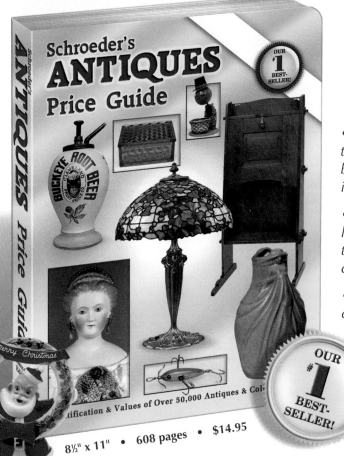